Sociology in Government

Published in cooperation with
the American Sociological Association
and
the Rural Sociological Society

Sociology in Government

A Bibliography of the Work of the
Division of Farm Population and Rural Life,
U.S. Department of Agriculture, 1919–1953

EDITED BY
Olaf F. Larson, Edward O. Moe,
and Julie N. Zimmerman

Westview Press
BOULDER • SAN FRANCISCO • LONDON

This Westview softcover edition is printed on acid-free paper and bound in library-quality, coated covers that carry the highest rating of the National Association of State Textbook Administrators, in consultation with the Association of American Publishers and the Book Manufacturers' Institute.

All rights reserved. No part of this publication may be reproduced or transmitted in any form or by any means, electronic or mechanical, including photocopy, recording, or any information storage and retrieval system, without permission in writing from the publisher.

Copyright © 1992 by Westview Press, Inc.

Published in 1992 in the United States of America by Westview Press, Inc., 5500 Central Avenue, Boulder, Colorado 80301-2847, and in the United Kingdom by Westview Press, 36 Lonsdale Road, Summertown, Oxford OX2 7EW

Library of Congress Cataloging-in-Publication Data
Sociology in government : a bibliography of the work of the
Division of Farm Population and Rural Life, U.S. Department of
Agriculture, 1919–1953 / edited by Olaf F. Larson, Edward O.
Moe, and Julie N. Zimmerman.
   p. cm.
   Includes index.
   ISBN 0-8133-8529-6
   1. Sociology, Rural—United States—Bibliography. 2. United
States—Rural conditions—Bibliography. 3. United States. Bureau
of Agricultural Economics. Division of Farm Population and Rural
Life—Bibliography. I. Moe, Edward O. II. Zimmerman, Julie N.
III. United States. Bureau of Agricultural Economics. Division of
Farm Population and Rural Life. IV. Title.
Z7164.S688L37   1992
[HT421]
016.30772′0973—dc20
                                                                92-2514
                                                                   CIP

Printed and bound in the United States of America

∞   The paper used in this publication meets the requirements of the American National Standard for Permanence of Paper for Printed Library Materials Z39.48-1984.

10   9   8   7   6   5   4   3   2   1

Dedicated to Charles Josiah Galpin (1864-1947), pioneer in rural sociology and Head of the Division of Farm Population and Rural Life, Bureau of Agricultural Economics, U.S. Department of Agriculture, from its establishment in 1919 until his retirement June 30, 1934; and to Carl Cleveland Taylor (1884-1975), Head of the Division 1935-1952, President of the Rural Sociological Society in 1939, and President of the American Sociological Association in 1946.

Contents

Foreword, William V. D'Antonio and Ronald C. Wimberley   vii
Acknowledgements   xi
Introduction   xiii

I. Bibliographies and reference lists   1
    A. 1919-1934
    B. 1935-1941
    C. 1942-1945
    D. 1946-1953

II. Books   3
    A. 1919-1934
    B. 1935-1941
    C. 1942-1945
    D. 1946-1953

III. Congressional testimony and reports   6
    A. 1935-1941
    B. 1942-1945
    C. 1946-1953

IV. Research publications   11
    A. 1919-1934
    B. 1935-1941
    C. 1942-1945
    D. 1946-1953

V. Restricted use reports and manuscripts   215
    A. 1919-1934
    B. 1935-1941
    C. 1942-1945
    D. 1946-1953

VI. Addresses (unpublished) 246
    A. 1919-1934
    B. 1935-1941
    C. 1942-1945
    D. 1946-1953

**VII. Publications issued by the Division
or cooperatively on periodic or occasional basis** 275

Addenda 279
Keyword index 283
    A. Substantive areas
    B. Ethnic-cultural groups studied
    C. Geographic locations of study

Foreword

The publication of *Sociology in Government: A Bibliography of the Work of the Division of Farm Population and Rural Life, U.S. Department of Agriculture, 1919-1953* is a cause for celebration.

First, much of it overlaps the tenure there of authors Olaf F. Larson and Edward O. Moe. They worked in the Division of Farm Population and Rural Life during the peak of the Division's activity during the 1930s and into the World War II years. They became personally and professionally acquainted with many of the authors and projects reported here. During this period, Larson was present at the organizational meeting of the Rural Sociological Society (RSS) in Chicago in 1937 and became a charter member of the Society. Both Larson (1957-1958) and Moe (1979-1980) have served as President of the RSS.

Second, publication of this document is the result of a joint effort of sociologists from the American Sociological Association (ASA) and the RSS. The volume allows us to reflect on the close relationship these two groups have enjoyed these many years. Charles J. Galpin and Carl C. Taylor, for example, were not just central figures in the development of the Division of Farm Population and Rural Life of the U.S. Department of Agriculture. They also were key early actors in the development of the ASA and the RSS. Indeed, Taylor was President of both the RSS and the ASA. Another example of the close relationship is provided by Dwight Sanderson, the first President of the RSS, who was also President of the ASA. And William H. Sewell, who served on the ASA Advisory Committee that recommended the publication of this Bibliography, served as President of both organizations. To extend the linkage a bit further, one of the authors of this Foreword (WVDA) was brought into sociology by Charles P. Loomis--also President of the ASA and RSS--who worked in the Division of Farm Population before going to chair the Department of Sociology at Michigan State University.

A third reason for celebration is that the Bibliography helps us recover a significant part of our history. A close look at the references should bring many surprises. Some will discover interesting research topics long overlooked in sociology. Others will find distinguished sociologists whose contributions while on the Division of Farm Population staff are little known. The range and quality of basic and applied research reported herein should impress all readers.

Many younger sociologists have no idea so much social research took place during this era. Nor is there proper appreciation for the role of sociologists in government in this earlier period. Knowing the roles sociologists played in the Division of Farm Population and Rural Life informs and enriches contemporary discussion of the uses of sociology.

A continuing reason for celebration is anticipation of a second part of this project. That will be an intellectual history of sociology and sociologists in the USDA from 1919 to 1953 and is being written by Olaf Larson and Edward Moe. The ASA and RSS anticipate co-sponsoring its publication as well.

We hope this Bibliography and the forthcoming intellectual history will become precedents for a series of similar studies on sociology in the several branches of government. It is important to future generations to know the vital contributions by sociologists in a wide range of government agencies including the Bureau of the Census, the Bureau of Labor Statistics, the National Institute on Aging, the National Institute on Child Health and Human Development, the National Institute of Mental Health, and the Research Branch in the War Department's Information and Education Division. Thus, we see this as the first in a series on contributions made by sociologists in government.

Finally, as we celebrate this happy occasion with a look into history, it is fitting to note that sociology is once again on the threshold of being called upon to contribute to the common weal in such areas as global change, world health, and development problems. ASA and RSS members are ready and eager to contribute. And we are gratefully reminded that such readiness to contribute goes back a long way.

William V. D'Antonio
Executive Officer (Retired)
American Sociological Association

Ronald C. Wimberley
North Carolina State University
President, Rural Sociological Society

Acknowledgements

This bibliography is the first major output of the project "Sociology in the U.S. Department of Agriculture: the Galpin-Taylor years, 1919-1953." This project is being conducted under a cooperative agreement between the Agriculture and Rural Economy Division, Economic Research Service, U.S. Department of Agriculture and the Department of Rural Sociology, New York State College of Agriculture and Life Sciences at Cornell University. We are grateful to both organizations for providing funds. Financial support has also been provided by the Cornell University Agricultural Experiment Station and by a grant from the budget for the Rural Sociological Society's 50th Anniversary Committee. The Farm Foundation awarded funds to support meetings of an Advisory Panel of former key members of the staff of the Division of Farm Population and Rural Life.

The American Sociological Association, the Rural Sociological Society, and the Cornell University Agricultural Experiment Station provided funds to assist in covering publication costs.

David L. Brown's interest and support, when he was Associate Director, Agriculture and Rural Economy Division, Economic Research Service, was crucial in the initiation of this project. His active support continued when, subsequently, he became Associate Director of the Cornell University Agricultural Experiment Station. John E. Lee, Jr., Administrator of the Economic Research Service, was instrumental in assuring that funds were made available to complete the project properly.

Eugene C. Erickson, as Chair, Department of Rural Sociology at Cornell, also had a major role in the initiation of the project and in providing resources essential for supporting the work. We gratefully acknowledge the encouragement of this endeavor by William V. D'Antonio,

Executive Officer, American Sociological Association which was given from an early stage.

The helpfulness, knowledge, and wisdom of the Advisory Panel has benefited our work greatly. The Panel members are Calvin L. Beale, Gladys K. Bowles, Louis J. Ducoff, Douglas Ensminger (deceased May 25, 1989), Paul J. Jehlik, and Conrad Taeuber. Ready access as needed to the collection of Division of Farm Population and Rural Life publications fortunately retained in the Economic Research Service was facilitated by Calvin Beale.

Other former staff members of the Division of Farm Population and Rural Life who contributed to the development of this bibliography by providing a list of their own publications or in other ways include Mary Montgomery Clawson, A. Lee Coleman, Donald G. Hay (deceased August 21, 1987), Helen Wheeler Johnson, Charles P. Loomis, Walter C. McKain, Jr., William H. Metzler, James E. Montgomery, Henry W. Riecken, Irwin T. Sanders, Jr., Edgar A. Schuler, T.G. Standing and Glenn L. Taggart. Also assisting were Mrs. May Alexander; Allen D. Edwards, at one time on the staff of the Social Research Section, Farm Security Administration; Mrs. Jane W. Hay; Anthony A. Hickey; John S. Holik; Mrs. Virginia Longmore; and Wayne Rasmussen and Vivian Wiser, both of the Agricultural and Rural History Section, Economic Research Service.

Two graduate students in Development Sociology, Cornell Department of Rural Sociology, assisted in compiling the bibliography. Michael Inskeep applied the Notebook II computer program to the needs of this project and, with J. Tadlock Cowan, did the initial work of entering citations.

The great resources of the Cornell University Libraries system and, especially, the help of the Albert R. Mann Library staff have been much appreciated.

We also gratefully acknowledge the comments of Eugene C. Erickson, William H. Sewell, and James J. Zuiches as members of the ad hoc publications review committee appointed by the Council of the American Sociological Association.

Olaf F. Larson
Edward O. Moe
Julie N. Zimmerman

Introduction

For a time the only unit in the federal government established to conduct sociological studies was that known for most of its 34-year life as the Division of Farm Population and Rural Life. This unit was located within the U.S. Department of Agriculture's Bureau of Agricultural Economics. Designated as Farm Life Studies when started in 1919 in what was then the Office of Farm Management and Farm Economics, the unit's name was indicative of its projected field of study. The name by which the Division has been best known was given in 1922 when the Bureau of Agricultural Economics replaced the Office of Farm Management and Farm Economics. From 1939 until 1947, "Welfare" replaced "Life" in the Division's title, a reflection of the research and planning role which the Department of Agriculture assigned to the Bureau of Agricultural Economics for a time starting near the end of the 1930s.

In 1953 the Bureau was abolished by order of then Secretary of Agriculture Ezra Benson in a reorganization of the USDA. This reorganization marked the end of the Division. Most of its by then reduced staff and program was placed in a new Farm Population and Rural Life Branch within the Division of Economics of the new Agricultural Marketing Service. A small part of the staff and program was assigned to the new Agricultural Research Service.

The Division and its work represents an important chapter in the development of the sociological enterprise in the United States and beyond. Not only did the Division make major pioneering and basic contributions to informed knowledge about rural society but it played a critical role in the development of methodological techniques. It helped create greater capacity for sociological inquiry in the total research system. This important chapter in the history of science has been at risk of being lost. This bibliography is one result of a project undertaken cooperatively by the Department of Rural Sociology at Cornell University and the Economic Research Service, U.S. Department of Agriculture to prevent that loss.

The bibliography identifies all publications prepared by the Division and its cooperators during 1919-1953 which we have been able to locate. All republications (e.g., of a journal article in a book) and revised editions within this period are shown with the citation for the original item to the extent that we were able to find such republications and revisions.

Sources Consulted to Identify Division's Publications

The major sources used to identify the publications of the Division and its cooperators were as follows: lists prepared by the Division covering parts of the 1919-1953 period; the collection of Division publications maintained in the Economic Research Service, USDA; journals in which Division staff members frequently published; and the compilers' personal files. Other sources included the Division's quarterly "Farm Population and Rural Life Activities," the *Dictionary Catalog of the National Agricultural Library, 1962-1965*; the U.S. Department of Agriculture's annual *Yearbook of Agriculture*; the proceedings of the conferences (usually annual) of the American Country Life Association; bibliographies of their work made available by some former members of the Division staff; correspondence with selected former staff members; and Carl C. Taylor's addresses and reprints deposited in the Cornell University Archives.

Two lists issued by the Division in mimeographed form, "Publications relating to farm population and rural life" (1935) and "Publications relating to farm population and rural life issued at the various state colleges of agriculture" (1936), together with a compilation for 1919 through June 1934 sent with a November 24, 1941 letter from Carl C. Taylor to Henry C. Taylor, were basic sources for the period when Dr. Galpin was Division head.

The January 1942-June 1944 period was covered in July 1, 1944 Division compilation "Publications and releases of the Division of Farm Population and Rural Welfare and its

Introduction xv

staff members between January 1942 and June 1944." The July 1944-June 1946 period was covered in a preliminary report, dated October 1, 1947, titled "Tentative supplement to publications and releases of the Division of Farm Population and Rural Welfare and its staff members between July 1944 and June 1946." The 1950-53 period was included in "Bibliography of the publications of the Farm Population and Rural Life branch 1950-59," compiled by Vera J. Banks and issued in 1960 by the Agricultural Marketing Service. Our searches of other sources yielded additions to these Division lists for specific time periods. What we have designated as "restricted use" items were included in some Division lists but not in others.

The following journals were searched for publications by Division staff members: *Agricultural Economics Research*, *American Journal of Sociology*, *American Sociological Review*, *Applied Anthropology* and its successor *Human Organization*, *Journal of Farm Economics*, *Land Policy Review*, *Rural America*, *Rural Sociology*, *Social Forces*, *Sociology and Social Research*, *Sociometry*, and *The Agricultural Situation*. The search utilized the cumulative index for a journal when such was available. Identification of the Division's professional staff during 1919-1953 and of the period of their employment preceded the search of journals because this allowed us to identify publications by the Division's staff. Journal articles by staff members rarely included their Division affiliation.

Our personal files and the collection of Division publications in the Economic Research Service were the principal means of identifying the "restricted use" and other fugitive literature items cited.

We are aware that the "restricted use" citations omit no fewer than 75 substantial reports that were originally prepared with the intent that after review they would be published for general use. We were unable, however to locate any record of surviving copies in the U.S. Archives or elsewhere. We believe that virtually all of the unpublished addresses of Charles J. Galpin and Carl C. Taylor are cited. It is possible that the record of the unpublished addresses of other members of the Division's staff, especially those located in regional offices, is less complete.

The citations are organized according to seven type-of-publication categories and four time periods.

Type-of-publication Categories

The seven categories used are (1) bibliographies and reference lists, (2) books, (3) Congressional testimony and reports, (4) research publications, (5) restricted use reports and manuscripts, (6) addresses (unpublished), and (7) publications issued by the Division or cooperatively on a periodic or occasional basis. A definition is in order for these categories.

Books includes all hard-cover publications. Soft-cover publications qualified for the book category only if they were booklike in length and organization and put out by a trade or university press.

Congressional testimony and reports includes testimony of Division staff members at hearings of committees of the U.S. Congress, statements submitted to such committees, and reports prepared for Congressional committees.

Research publications is a broad category. Included are all journal articles; research monographs not meeting the criteria for "book"; printed agricultural experiment station, U.S. Department of Agriculture and other bulletins; numbered mimeographed bulletins and reports; papers in proceedings; and miscellaneous research-related mimeographed reports not identified as "restricted."

Restricted use reports and manuscripts is the category covering items not available for general distribution. These items may be considered fugitive literature. All are in mimeographed, lithographed, or typed form. They were identified as for restricted use because they were labeled as "for administrative use" or "for review" or because there were other indications that at the time of issue they were clearly intended only for internal or limited distribution within the Division, the U.S. Department of Agriculture, or other agencies of the Federal government. These items are included so that the bibliography can achieve its goal of fully documenting the work of the Division. Moreover, if it had not been for special circumstances, such as the restraints

Introduction xvii

on normal publication activity imposed by World War II, many of the "restricted use" reports on research and the materials on methods used in the reported studies would have been issued in the customary outlets.

Addresses (unpublished) are addresses, including radio talks, which were not identified as having been subsequently published--e.g., as a journal article, in proceedings, as a USDA Extension Service bulletin, etc. Addresses given in a general citizen role rather than in a professional role were excluded.

Farm Population and Rural Life Activities, issued quarterly by the Division during 1927-1942, and annual and special reports on "Farm Population estimates" are examples of **periodicals** or publications put out by the Division on a periodic or occasional basis.

Time Periods

The citations are also organized according to the time of first publication or presentation, namely, 1919-34, 1935-41, 1942-45, and 1946-53. The Division's 34-year life history was characterized by marked fluctuations from time to time in the type and range of research activity and in staff and funding resources. These fluctuations were largely a consequence of changes in the economic, social, and political milieu in which the Division worked as a unit of the Federal government. The use of these four time periods is intended to facilitate analysis of the Division's work in relation to its changing milieu.

During the 1919-34 period, when Charles J. Galpin was Division head, sociology as a discipline was in its early stages of development. The Division's staff and budget resources were very limited, but Galpin used part of the meager budget to encourage rural sociological research through cooperative projects at numerous colleges and universities.

The Division's program during 1935-41, the early part of Carl C. Taylor's 17-year tenure as head, was shaped especially by the demands for information from the new agricultural agencies which had been created under President Franklin D. Roosevelt's administration during the Great Depression of the 1930s and to meet the information needs generated by agricultural planning, an activity assigned to the Bureau of Agricultural Economics by the Department of Agriculture. The Division's professional staff and funds expanded greatly during this period.

The nation's World War II needs dominated the Division's work during 1942-45, with post-war planning receiving attention during the latter part of the period. Substantial numbers of the professional staff were drawn off to military service and to war-time agencies and programs.

The post-war years, 1946-53, were marked by contraction and constraint of the Division's program. Part of this was associated with constraints and budgetary reductions imposed upon the Bureau of Agricultural Economics by Congress as a consequence of political opposition aroused by certain studies conducted by the Division and other units of the Bureau. This was also a time when the reconstruction of war-torn countries and the problems of less developed nations became of national concern. Accordingly, Division staff members were recruited for special assignments abroad or to serve with new agencies having international rehabilitation and development functions.

Keywords and Guide to Their Use

In order to provide more information, citations under the **research publications** heading have keywords. Three categories of keywords were devised. These are: (1) substantive areas; (2) ethnic or cultural groups which were the object of study or used as a variable in analysis; and (3) the geographic location of the study.

The following example of the keywords for Lowry Nelson's study of farm villages in Utah (entry 0253) illustrates how the three categories of keywords are entered:

Keywords: Community; social organization; religion; sociology of agriculture. Mormon. UT.

Introduction

Each category of keywords is separated by a period. When any category consists of more than one keyword, the keywords are separated by a semi-colon. While each citation under the **research publications** heading has at least one keyword from the substantive area category, the other two categories are keyworded only when they pertained. The keywords are indexed by citation entry number.

The keywords in the category **substantive area** are listed first. The order of the keywords entered represents a judgement as to the relative attention given the topic in the publication. The keyword entered first was ranked most important. In order to maintain consistency, keywords for those publications which were part of a series were entered in a similar manner. In those cases for which priority of keywords was not apparent, the keywords were listed from most inclusive to least inclusive. In these cases in particular, the grouping of keywords is important. For example, many of the farm wage rate studies disaggregated their data by sex. However, not all of them discussed the results of this disaggregation. For those publications which included such a discussion, the keywords population composition and women in agriculture are both entered. On the other hand, for those publications which simply disaggregated their data tables without any discussion, the keywords include population composition without any complementing keyword. Therefore, users interested in gender should also include in their search the keyword population composition.

In some cases, conventional usage of terminology in the literature changed over time. The terms "standard of living" and "level of living" provide an illustration. While the distinction between these two concepts was clarified over time, this was not the case during part of the period covered by the bibliography. Therefore, these keywords follow the terminology in the publication. However, if the terminology in the publication did not follow today's accepted definitions, when possible the appropriate term was also included in the keywords assigned.

In order to avoid excessively long keyword entries, more inclusive keywords were sometime selected. For example, while housing and income are separate keywords, if the discussion of housing and income fell under the rubric of level of living, then the keyword level of living was entered without also including housing or income in the keywords. Therefore, if a user is interested in housing, for example, they should also include in their search, the keyword level of living.

We sought to make the list of keywords for substantive areas as consistent as possible with established sociological practice. Accordingly, the foundation for the list was some 150 words taken or adapted from the subject index used in the *Rural Sociology 50-Year Index for 1936-85*. Additions were made as necessary to account for the more specialized areas of work conducted by the Division and its cooperators.

Keyword entries for **ethnic-cultural group** are listed second. When no ethnic or cultural group was indicated in a publication, this category of keywords was not entered. With the exception of blacks, the keywords follow the terminology used in the publication cited. Thus, in the index a user will find the keywords Spanish American, Indian-Mexican, Mexican nationals, and Mexican. The keyword blacks also includes studies referencing "colored," Negro, and non-white.

The last category of keywords indicates the **geographic location** of the study. For the United States, two-letter abbreviations used by the U.S. Postal Service were used for state names. Rather than force regional definitions, regional keywords follow the terminology used in the publication. For example, a user interested in the Midwest should watch for the keywords Great Plains and North Central as well as Midwest. Keywords for geographic locations outside the United States likewise follow the terminology used in the citation. When a publication was not geographic-specific, or referred to the United States as a whole, no keyword was entered for location.

Depositories for Publications Listed

The bibliographies, books, Congressional testimony, research publications, and publications issued by the Division on a periodic or occasional basis are, in general, readily accessible through university libraries. However, the fugitive literature, comprised primarily of restricted use reports and

Introduction xxi

manuscripts and unpublished addresses, may generally be found only in one of the following places: the National Agricultural Library; a special collection of Division publications which has been maintained in a unit of the USDA's Economic Research Service, currently named the Human Resources Branch of the Agriculture and Rural Economy Division; the National Archives, and the Cornell University Archives.

Items considered to be fugitive literature and for which a depository is known have the depository location shown within braces at the end of the citation. Abbreviations used for the depositories are as follows:

CU Archives, Cornell University Archives, Ithaca, New York.
NAL, National Agricultural Library, Washington, D.C.; without a number indicates Special Collections, at Beltsville, Maryland branch; with a volume number indicates the citation was found in the *Dictionary Catalog of the National Agricultural Library 1862-1965* which is a catalog for materials at the Beltsville, Maryland branch.
National Archives RG with number, Record Group number in National Archives, Washington, D.C.
usda with volume number, "Research publications of Division of Farm Population and Rural Life 1919-1953," bound volumes 1-56, located in Human Resources Branch, Agriculture and Rural Economy Division, Economic Research Service, U.S. Department of Agriculture, Washington, D.C.

The compilers have arranged to deposit their personal copies of the fugitive materials with the National Agricultural Library's Special Collections.

Abbreviations and Symbols Used in Citations and Keywords

Place of publication is indicated by the two-letter abbreviation used by the U.S. Postal Service for states. Other abbreviations and symbols used in the citations are as follows:

AES, Agricultural Experiment Station
BAE, Bureau of Agricultural Economics
DFPRL, Division of Farm Population and Rural Life
DFPRW, Division of Farm Population and Rural Welfare
FSA (used in some titles), Farm Security Administration
GPO, United States Government Printing Office
Mimeo, Mimeographed
RR (used in some titles), Rural Rehabilitation
USDA, United States Department of Agriculture
[ ], information inside brackets not available in publication cited but provided by compilers
[?], information inside brackets not available in publication and compilers not certain if entry made is correct, e.g., year of publication
*, citation not seen; keywords based on title, abstract, or a review.

An Assessment of the Division's Work

This bibliography cites all publications we have been able to locate and identify as products of the Division of Farm Population and Rural Life and its cooperators during the Division's existence, 1919-1953. Our intent is to follow with a monograph, provisionally titled *Sociology in the United States Department of Agriculture: The Galpin-Taylor Years 1919-1953*. The purpose is to analyze the Division's research and to assess the contributions made by the Division to substantive knowledge about rural life, to sociological concepts and theory, to research methods, to federal action programs, to the identification of issues of public concern, to the social science research system, and in other respects. It will include an analysis of research conducted on black populations and discuss the determinants of the Division's research priorities and programs.

Bibliography

I. Bibliographies and reference lists

A. 1919-1934
0001 Lacy, Mary G. (compiler).
1924. "A beginning of a bibliography of the literature of rural life." Mimeo. DC: USDA, BAE. [BAE Library with DFPRL cooperating]. Agricultural Economics Bibliography No. 3. Reprinted March 1925.

B. 1935-1941
0002 Colvin, Esther M., and Josiah C. Folsom (compilers), under the direction of Mary G. Lacy, Librarian, BAE.
1935. "Agricultural labor in the United States, 1915-1935: A selected list of references." Mimeo. DC: USDA, BAE. Agricultural Economics Bibliography No. 64.

0003 Colvin, Esther M., and Josiah C. Folsom (compilers), under the direction of Mary G. Lacy, Librarian, BAE.
1938. "Agricultural labor in the United States, 1936-1937: A selected list of references." Mimeo. DC: USDA, BAE. Agricultural Economics Bibliography No. 72.

0004 MacLeish, Kenneth, and Helen E. Hennefrund (compilers), under the direction of Mary G. Lacy, Librarian, BAE. Introduction by John H. Provinse.
1940. "Anthropology and agriculture: Selected references on agriculture in primitive cultures." Mimeo. DC: USDA, BAE. Agricultural Economics Bibliography No. 89.

C. 1942-1945
0005 Folsom, Josiah C. (compiler).
1944. "Social Security for farm people: A list of references." Dittoed. DC: USDA, BAE, DFPRW.

0006 McNeill, John M. (compiler). Introduction by Olaf F. Larson.
   1943. "Rehabilitation of low-income farmers: A list of references." Mimeo. DC: USDA Library. Library List No. 6.

0007 McNeill, John M., and Josiah C. Folsom (compilers), under the direction of Margaret T. Olcott, Librarian, BAE.
   1942. "Agricultural labor in the United States, 1938-June 1941: A selected list of references." Mimeo. DC: USDA, BAE. Agricultural Economics Bibliography No. 95.

0008 Moats, Ruby W., and John M. McNeill (compilers), in cooperation with Josiah C. Folsom.
   1943. "Agricultural labor in the United States, July 1941-February 1943: A list of references." Mimeo. DC: USDA, Library. USDA, BAE, [DFPRW] cooperating. Library List No. 4.

0009 USDA, BAE, DFPRW.
   1943. "Selected references for rural sociologists." Dittoed. DC: USDA, BAE, DFPRW.

0010 USDA, BAE, DFPRW.
   1944. "Publications and releases of the Division of Farm Population and Rural Welfare and its staff members between January 1942 and June 1944 (including those issued cooperatively with the state colleges of agriculture and other federal agencies)." Dittoed. DC: USDA, BAE, DFPRW.

D. 1946-1953

0011 Bernert, Eleanor H., and Gladys Bowles (compilers).
   1947. "Farm migration, 1940-45: An annotated bibliography." Mimeo. DC: USDA, Library. Library List No. 38.

0012 Folsom, Josiah C.
   1949. *Social Security and Related Insurance for Farm People: An Annotated Bibliography of Selected References.* DC: USDA, Library. Library List No. 50.

0013 Folsom, Josiah C. (compiler).
1953. *Migratory Agricultural Labor in the United States: An Annotated Bibliography of Selected References.* DC: USDA, Library. Library List 59.

0014 Johnston, Helen L., and Elsie S. Manny (compilers), under the general direction of Louis S. Reed and Wilson Longmore.
1953. *Rural Health: Annotated List of Selected References.* DC: USDA, Library. Library List No. 60.

0015 Watrous, Roberta C., and John M. McNeill (compilers).
1949. *Rural Community Organization: A List of References.* DC: USDA, Library. Library List No. 46.

II. Books

A. 1919-1934

0016 Fry, Luther C.
1925. *A Census Analysis of American Villages--Being a Study of the 1920 Census Data for 177 Villages Scattered over the United States.* New York: Institute of Social and Religious Research. U.S. Bureau of the Census and the USDA [BAE, DFPRL] cooperating.

0017 Galpin, Charles J.
1924. *Rural Social Problems.* New York: Century.

0018 Galpin, Charles J.
1925. *Empty Churches: The Rural-Urban Dilemma.* New York: Century.

0019 Galpin, Charles J., and Veda B. Larson (See also Turner).
1924. *Farm Population of Selected Counties: Composition, Characteristics, and Occupations in Detail for Eight Counties, Comprising Otsego County, N.Y., Dane County, Wis., New Madrid and Scott Counties, Mo., Cass County, N. Dak., Wake County, N.C., Ellis County, Tex., and King County, Wash..* DC:

0019 (continued).
Department of Commerce, Bureau of the Census. USDA, BAE, DFPRL cooperating. Reprinted in 1926 as pp. 319-536 in Leon E. Truesdell, *Farm Population of the United States: An Analysis of the 1920 Farm Population Figures, Especially in Comparison with a Study of the Main Economic Factors Affecting the Farm Population* (with Truesdell's analysis of the eight counties on pp. 135-176). Census Mongraphs VI. DC: Bureau of the Census.

0020 Hypes, James L.
1927. *Social Participation in a Rural New England Town.* New York: Columbia University, Teachers College, Bureau of Publications. Contributions to Education No. 258. USDA, [BAE], DFPRL cooperating. Also published as Columbia University Ph.D. thesis.

0021 Kirkpatrick, Ellis L.
1929. *The Farmer's Standard of Living.* New York: Century.

0022 Manny, Theodore B.
1930. *Rural Municipalities: A Sociological Study of Local Government in the United States.* New York: Century.

0023 Sorokin, Pitirim A., Carle C. Zimmerman, and Charles J. Galpin (editors).
1930-32. *A Systematic Source Book in Rural Sociology.* Minneapolis: University of Minnesota. Volume 1 published in 1930, Volume 2 in 1931, and Volume 3 in 1932.

B. 1935-1941

0024 Brunner, Edmund deS., and Irving Lorge.
1937. *Rural Trends in Depression Years: A Survey of Village-Centered Agricultural Communities, 1930-1936.* New York: Columbia University Press. USDA, BAR, DFPRL and the Columbia University Council for Research in the Social Sciences cooperating.

0025 Loomis, Charles P.
1940. *Fundamental Concepts of Sociology (Gemeinschaft und Gesellschaft), by Ferdinand Tonnies.* NY: American Book

0025 (continued).
Company. Supplementation, translation, and introduction by Loomis.

C. 1942-1945.
0026 Brunner, Edmund deS., Irwin T. Sanders, and Douglas Ensminger (editors).
1945. *Farmers of the World: The Development of Agricultural Extension.* NY: Columbia University Press.

0027 Raper, Arthur F.
1943. *Tenants of the Almighty.* New York: Macmillan.

D. 1946-1953
0028 Hagood, Margaret Jarman, Earl H. Bell, Douglas Ensminger, Michael R. Hanger, and Arthur F. Raper.
1946. *La Agricultura en los Estados Unidos.* DC: Union Panamericana, Oficina de Cooperacion Agricola.

0029 Hagood, Margaret J., and Daniel O. Price.
1952. *Statistics for Sociologists, Revised Edition.* New York: Henry Holt and Company.

0030 Larson, Olaf F.
1951. *Ten Years of Rural Rehabilitation in the United States: Summary of a Report.* An abridgement by Sri B. S. Mavinkurve from the full report by the same title (DC: USDA, BAE, [DFPRW], 1947). Bombay, India: Indian Society of Agricultural Economics.

0031 Lewis, Oscar.
1948. *On the Edge of the Black Waxy: A Cultural Survey of Bell County, Texas.* St. Louis, MO: Washington University Studies--New Series. Social and Philosophical Sciences No. 7.

0032 Taylor, Carl C.
1948. *Rural Life in Argentina.* Baton Rouge, LA: Louisiana State University Press.

0033 Taylor, Carl C.
1953. *The Farmer's Movement, 1620-1920.* New York: American Book Company.

0034 Taylor, Carl C., Arthur F. Raper, Douglas Ensminger, Margaret Jarman Hagood, T. Wilson Longmore, Walter C. McKain, Jr., Louis J. Ducoff, and Edgar A.Schuler.
1949. *Rural Life in the United States.* New York: Alfred A. Knopf.

III. Congressional testimony and reports

A. 1935-1941

0035 Folsom, Josiah C.
1940. "Strikes of agricultural laborers." Testimony May 10. U.S. Congress, Senate, Committee on Education and Labor. *Violations of Free Speech and Rights of Labor*: Hearings before a subcommittee, 76th Cong., 3rd Sess. Part 1--Supplementary Hearings: *National Farm Labor Problem.* 1941, pp. 171-177. DC: GPO.

0036 Folsom, J. C., E. J. Holcomb, and G. M. Murray.
1941. "Employment and earnings of cotton farm workers in southeast Missouri." Report to the Tolan Committee on the Cooperative Study of Farm Labor and Tenancy in Southeast Missouri. Part V: Analysis of Sub-Tenant and Wage Labor Records. Preliminary Report--Confidential. Statement prepared for the U.S. Congress, House, Select Committee Investigating National Defense Migration. Mimeo. Dated November 1940. DC: USDA, BAE, [DFPRW]. {usda 18}.

0037 Ham, William T.
1940. "Numbers, distribution, composition and employment status of the farm labor group in the United States." Testimony May 9-10. U.S. Congress, Senate, Committee on Education and Labor. *Violations of Free Speech and Rights of Labor*: Hearings before a subcommittee, 76th Cong., 3rd Sess. Part 1--*Supplementary Hearings: National Farm*

0037 *(continued)*.
Labor Problem. 1941, pp. 111-171. DC: GPO. Also under same title as undated mimeo. DC: USDA, BAE, [DFPRW]. {usda 13}.

0038 Hamilton, C. Horace.
1940. "The standard of living of farm laborers." Testimony May 13. U.S. Congress, Senate, Committee on Education and Labor. *Violations of Free Speech and Rights of Labor*: Hearings before a subcommittee, 76th Cong., 3rd Sess. Part 1--*Supplementary Hearings: National Farm Labor Problem*. 1941, pp. 201-231. DC: GPO. Also under same title as mimeo dated May 1940. DC: USDA, BAE, [DFPRW]. {usda 12}.

0039 Hay, Donald G.
1940. "Rural population migration in the Northern Great Plains." Testimony Sept. 16. U.S. Congress, House, Select Committee to Investigate the Interstate Migration of Destitute Citizens. Part 4, Lincoln Hearings pp. 1384-1397. House Report 367, 1941. Also under same title as mimeo. Lincoln NE: USDA, BAE, [DFPRW]. {usda 14}.

0040 Hay, Donald G.
1940. "Problems of farm workers in the wheat area." Testimony May 20. U.S. Congress, Senate, Committee on Education and Labor. *Violations of Free Speech and Rights of Labor*: Hearings before a subcommittee, 76th Cong., 3rd Sess. Part 2--*Supplementary Hearings, National Farm Labor Problem*. 1945, pp. 415-433. DC: GPO.

0041 Hay, Donald G.
1941. "Relationship of national defense activity to migration in Nebraska and the Dakotas." Testimony Nov. 25. U.S. Congress, House, Select Committee Investigating National Defense Migration, 77th Cong., 1st Sess. Part 22, Omaha Hearings, pp. 8598-8600. DC: GPO.

0042 Holcomb, Ernest J.
1940. "Income and earnings of farm laborers." Testimony

0042 (continued).
May 10 and 13. U.S. Congress, Senate, Committee on Education and Labor. *Violations of Free Speech and Rights of Labor*: Hearings before a subcommittee, 76th Cong., 3rd Sess. Part 1--*Supplementary Hearings: National Farm Labor Problem.* 1941, pp.177-201.DC: GPO. Also under same title as mimeo dated May 1940. DC: USDA, BAE, [DFPRW]. {usda 16}.

0043 Holcomb, Ernest J.
1940. "The sharecropper and wage laborer in cotton production." Testimony May 21. U.S. Congress, Senate, Committee on Education and Labor. *Violations of Free Speech and Rights of Labor*: Hearings before a subcommittee, 76th Cong., 3rd Sess. Part 2--*Supplementary Hearings: National Farm Labor Problem.* 1941, pp. 469-524. DC: GPO. Also under same title as mimeo dated May 1940. DC: USDA, BAE, [DFPRW]. {usda 12}.

0044 Holcomb, E[rnest] J.
1941. "Introduction." Report to the Tolan Committee on the Cooperative Study of Farm Labor and Tenancy in Southeast Missouri. Part I: Introduction. Preliminary Report--Confidential. Statement prepared for U.S. Congress, House, Select Committee Investigating National Defense Migration. Mimeo. DC: USDA, BAE, [DFPRW]. {usda 18}.

0045 Holcomb, E[rnest] J.
1941. "Farm organization." Report to the Tolan Committee on the Cooperative Study of Farm Labor and Tenancy in Southeast Missouri. Part III: Farm Organization. Preliminary Report--Confidential. Statement prepared for U.S. Congress, House, Select Committee Investigating National Defense Migration. Mimeo. DC: USDA, BAE, [DFPRW]. {usda 18}.

0046 Holcomb, Ernest J., G. McMurray, J. C. Folsom, and H. A. Turner.
1941. "Farm labor and tenancy in southeast Missouri." Tes

0046 (continued).
timony Nov. 26-27. U.S. Congress, House, Select Committee Investigating National Defense Migration, Part 23, pp. 9302-9347. DC: GPO.

0047 Holley, William C.
1940. "The farm labor situation in Texas." Testimony May 14. U.S. Congress, Senate, Committee on Education and Labor. *Violations of Free Speech and Rights of Labor*: Hearings before a subcommittee, 76th Cong., 3rd Sess. Part 1--*Supplementary Hearings: National Farm Labor Problem*. 1941, pp. 263-285, 316-318. DC: GPO. Also under same title as mimeo dated May 1940. DC: USDA, BAE, [DFPRW]. {usda 12}.

0048 Taeuber, Conrad.
1940. "Statement on farm population trends." Testimony May 8. U.S. Congress, Senate, Committee on Education and Labor. *Violations of Free Speech and Rights of Labor*: Hearings before a subcommittee, 76th Cong. 3rd Sess. Part 1--*Supplementary Hearings: National Farm Labor Problem*. 1941, pp. 89-110. DC: GPO. Also under same title as mimeo dated May 6, 1940. DC: USDA, BAE, [DFPRW]. {usda 12}.

0049 Taylor, Carl C.
1940. "Suggested programs for distressed farm families." Testimony May 24. U.S. Congress, Senate, Committee on Education and Labor. *Violations of Free Speech and Rights of Labor*: Hearings before a subcommittee, 76th Cong., 3rd Sess. Part 3--*Supplementary Hearings: National Farm Labor Problem*. 1941, pp. 720-728. DC: GPO. Also under same title as mimeo dated May 24, 1940. DC: USDA, BAE, [DFPRW]. {usda 12}.

0050 Taylor, Carl C.
1940. "A statement on rural problem areas." Testimony May 7. U.S. Congress, Senate, Committee on Education and Labor. *Violations of Free Speech and Rights of Labor*: Hearings before a subcommittee, 76th Cong., 3rd Sess.

0050 (continued).
Part 1--*Supplementary Hearings: National Farm Labor Problem*. 1941, pp. 35-63. DC: GPO. Also under same title as mimeo dated May 6, 1940. DC: USDA, BAE, [DFPRW]. {usda 16}.

0051 Taylor, Carl C., W. T. Ham, and E. J. Holcomb.
1940. "Data on opportunities for employment in agriculture, unemployment on farms, and the status of farm laborers and tenants." In mimeo dated April 23, for presentation by the Bureau of Agricultural Economics before the Temporary National Economic Committee. DC: USDA, BAE. {usda 14}.

0052 Taylor, Carl C.
1941. "Statement." Presented February 21 before the Temporary National Economic Committee. Mimeo. DC: USDA, BAE, [DFPRW]

B. 1942-1945
0053 Taeuber, Conrad.
1942. "Rural manpower and war production." Testimony Feb. 13. U.S. Congress, House, Select Committee Investigating National Defense Migration, 77th Cong., 2nd sess. *The Manpower of the Nation in War Production*--Book Two, Part 28. DC: GPO. Also under same title as mimeo dated Feb. 13, 1942. DC: USDA, BAE [DFPRL]. {usda 23}.

0054 Taeuber, Conrad.
1942. "Statement on farm population trends." Testimony. U.S. Congress, Senate, Committee on Education and Labor. *Investigation of Manpower Resources*: Hearings before a subcommittee, 77th Cong., 2nd sess. Part 1, pp.1-22. DC: GPO.

0055 Taylor, Carl C.
1944. "Extension of Social Security Programs to farm people." Pp. 36-37, Part 10 of Statements from the Department of Agriculture Interbureau Committee on Post-War Pro-

0055 (continued).
grams, Submitted to the House Special Committee on Economic Policy and Planning, August 23, 1944. Mimeo. DC: USDA. {usda 36}.

0056 Taylor, Carl C.
1944. "Statement." Testimony May 11. U.S. Congress, House, Special Committee on Post War Economic Policy and Planning, 78th Cong., 2nd sess. *The Problem of Unemployment and Reemployment after the War: Unemployment Compensation.* Part 3, pp. 684-694. DC: GPO. {usda 38}.

C. 1946-1953
0057 U.S. Congress, Senate, Committee on Education and Labor, Subcommittee on Wartime Health and Education.
1946. *The Experimental Health Program of the United States Department of Agriculture,* report prepared by T. Wilson Longmore under the leadership of Carl C. Taylor and Douglas Ensminger. Subcommittee Monograph 1, 79th Congress, 2nd Session. DC: GPO. {usda 47}.

0058 Goldschmidt, Walter R.
1946. *Small Business and the Community: A Study in Central Valley of California on Effects of Scale of Farm Operations [Comparative Study of Arvin and Dinuba, California.]* U.S. Congress, Senate Report of the Special Committee to Study Problems of American Small Business, 79th Congress, 2nd Session. DC: GPO. Senate committee print No. 13.

IV. Research Publications

A. 1919-1934
0059 Allred, C. E., and J. C. Fitch.
1928. *Effects of Industrial Development on Rural Life in Sullivan County, Tennessee.* Knoxville, TN: University of Tennessee. Record, Extension Series, Vol. 5, No. 3. Contri-

0059 (continued).
buted by University of Tennessee AES. USDA, BAE, DFPRL cooperating.

Keywords: Rural industries; rural life; evaluation. TN.

0060 Baumgartel, Walter H.
1923. *A Social Study of Ravalli County, Montana.* Bozeman: University of Montana AES Bulletin No. 160. USDA, Office of Farm Management and Farm Economics, Division of Farm Life Studies, cooperating.

Keywords: Social organization; community development. MT.

0061 Baumgartel, Walter H.
1925. *Centralized Management of a Large Corporate Estate Operated by Tenants in the Wheat Belt.* DC: USDA. Circular No. 351. Contributed by BAE, Division of LandEconomics [and DFPRL].

Keywords: Structure of agriculture; farm size; landlords; land tenure. ND.

0062 Baumgartel, Walter H., and Charles L. Stewart.
1924. "Farm tenants and owners on a corporate estate--A statistical analysis of the social and economic experience of tenants and owners on farms of the Amenia and Sharon Land Company, Cass County, North Dakota, 1893-1922: A preliminary report." Mimeo. DC: USDA, BAE, [DFPRL]. {NAL v.63}.

Keywords: Structure of agriculture; land tenure. ND.

0063 Beers, Howard W.
1933. *The Income, Savings, and Work of Boys and Girls on Farms in New York, 1930.* Ithaca, NY: Cornell University AES. Bulletin No. 560. USDA, BAE, [DFPRL] cooperating.

0063 (continued).
Keywords: Youth; income; social participation; farm family. NY.

0064 Benton, Alva H.
1924. *Cash and Share Renting of Farms.* Fargo, ND: North Dakota Agricultural College AES. Bulletin No. 171. USDA, BAE, DFPRL cooperating.

Keywords: Land tenure; landlords; structure of agriculture. ND.

0065 Berger, J. Wheeler.
1929. *Rural Community Halls in Montana.* Bozeman, MT: University of Montana AES. Bulletin No. 221. USDA, BAE, DFPRL cooperating.

Keywords: Community buildings and centers; community; community development. MT.

0066 Berger, J. Wheeler.
1929. *The County Library in Montana.* Bozeman, MT: University of Montana AES. Bulletin No. 219. USDA, BAE, DFPRL cooperating.

Keywords: Libraries; evaluation. MT.

0067 Berger, J. Wheeler.
1930. *The Rural Community Club in Montana.* [Bozeman, MT]: University of Montana AES. Bulletin No. 224. USDA, BAE, DFPRL cooperating.

Keywords: Community clubs/ organizations; community processes; social organization; rural life. MT.

0068 Burt, Henry J.
1929. *Contacts in a Rural Community.* Columbia, MO: University of Missouri, College of Agriculture AES. Research Bulletin No. 125. USDA, [BAE], DFPRL cooperating.

0068 (continued).
Keywords: Social psychology; community processes; social participation; villages. MO.

0069 Burt, Henry, J.
1933. *The Population of Missouri: A General Survey of Its Sources, Changes, and Present Composition.* Columbia, MO: University of Missouri, College of Agriculture AES. Research Bulletin No. 188. USDA, [BAE], DFPRL cooperating.

Keywords: Population; population composition; population trends. Blacks. MO.

0070 Clark, Edna, and E. L. Kirkpatrick.
1925. "Average quantities and costs of clothing purchased by farm families--Clothing purchased in one year by 1337 farm families of selected localities of Ohio, Kentucky, Missouri, and Kansas: A preliminary report." Mimeo. DC: USDA, BAE, [DFPRL]; USDA, Bureau of Home Economics; Ohio Wesleyan University; University of Kentucky; University of Missouri; Kansas State Agricultural College; and The Farmer's Wife, cooperating. {NAL v.63}.

Keywords: Level of living. OH; KY; MO; KS.

0071 Coen, B. F.
1927. *Successful Farm Families of Colorado.* [Fort Collins, CO]: Colorado Agricultural College. Colorado Agricultural Bulletin, Series 26, No. 3. USDA, BAE, DFPRL cooperating.

Keywords: Successes in rural life; farm family. CO.

0072 Dadisman, Andrew J.
1921. *French Creek as a Rural Community.* Morgantown, WV: West Virginia University, College of Agriculture AES. Bulletin No. 176. USDA, Office of Farm Management and Farm Economics cooperating.

0072 (continued).
Keywords: Community; community development; community processes; migration. WV.

0073 Dennis, W. V.
1931. *Organizations Affecting Farm Youth in Locust Township, Columbia County [Pennsylvania].* State College, PA: Pennsylvania State College, School of Agriculture and Experiment Station. Bulletin No. 265. USDA, BAE, DFPRL cooperating.

Keywords: Community clubs/ organizations; social participation; youth. PA.

0074 Dennis, W. V.
1933. *Social Activities of the Families in the Unionville District, Chester County, Pennsylvania.* State College, PA: Pennsylvania State College, School of Agriculture and Experiment Station. Bulletin No. 286. USDA, BAE, DFPRL cooperating.

Keywords: Social participation; community clubs/ organizations; youth. PA.

0075 Denune, Perry P.
1924. *Some Town-Country Relations in Union County, Ohio.* Columbus, OH: Ohio State University. Bulletin Sociology Series No. 1. Contributed by Ohio State University, Department of Sociology. USDA, [BAE, DFPRL] cooperating.

Keywords: *Social and economic areas (rural-urban relationships). OH.

0076 Denune, Perry P.
1927. *The Social and Economic Relations of the Farmers with the Towns of Pickaway County, Ohio.* Columbus, OH: Ohio State University. [University Studies], Bureau of Business Research Monograph No. 9. USDA, BAE, DFPRL cooperating.

0076 (continued).
Keywords: Social and economic areas (rural-urban relationships); towns; social organization. OH.

0077 Dickey, J. A., and E. C. Branson.
1922. *How Farm Tenants Live: A Social Economic Survey in Chatham County, North Carolina.* Chapel Hill, NC: University of North Carolina. Extension Bulletin, Vol. 2, No. 6.

Keywords: Land tenure; level of living. NC.

0078 Doggett, Allen B., Jr.
1923. *Three Negro Communities in Tidewater Virginia.* Hampton, VA: Hampton Normal and Agricultural Institute. Bulletin, Vol. 19, No. 4. Contributed by School of Agriculture. USDA, BAE, DFPRL cooperating.

Keywords: Community; community clubs/ organizations; leadership. Blacks. VA.

0079 Dorn, Harold F.
1931. *The Social and Economic Areas of Yates County, New York.* Ithaca, NY: Cornell University AES. Bulletin No. 529. [USDA, BAE, DFPRL cooperating]. Based on a February 1930 Cornell University M.S. Thesis.

Keywords: Social and economic areas (rural-urban relationships); villages; social organization; community. NY.

0080 Fry, C. Luther.
1924. *A Census Analysis of Middle Atlantic Villages.* Mimeo. New York, NY: Institute of Social and Religious Research. U.S. Bureau of the Census and the USDA, [BAE, DFPRL] cooperating. Reprinted in Luther C. Fry, *A Census Analysis of American Villages.* New York: Institute of Social and Religious Research, 1925.

Keywords: Population; population composition; villages. Blacks. Middle Atlantic.

0081 Fry, C. Luther.
1924. *A Census Analysis of Southern Villages.* Mimeo. New York, NY: Institute of Social and Religious Research. U.S. Bureau of the Census and the USDA, [BAE, DFPRL] cooperating. Reprinted in Luther C. Fry, *A Census Analysis of American Villages.* New York: Institute of Social and Religious Research, 1925.

Keywords: Population; population composition; villages. Blacks. South.

0082 Fry, C. Luther.
1924. *A Census Analysis of Middle Western Villages.* Mimeo. New York, NY: Institute of Social and Religious Research. U.S. Bureau of the Census and the USDA, [BAE, DFPRL] cooperating. Reprinted in Luther C. Fry, *A Census Analysis of American Villages.* New York: Institute of Social and Religious Research, 1925.

Keywords: Population composition; villages. Blacks. Midwest.

0083 Fry, C. Luther, and Gwendolyn S. Hughes.
1924. *A Census Analysis of Far Western Villages.* Mimeo. New York, NY: Institute of Social and Religious Research. U.S. Bureau of the Census and the USDA, [BAE, DFPRL] cooperating. Reprinted in Luther C. Fry, *A Census Analysis of American Villages.* New York: Institute of Social and Religious Research, 1925.

Keywords: Population composition; villages. Blacks. West.

0084 Galpin, Charles J.
1919. "The human side of farm economy." Paper delivered before a joint meeting of the American Country Life Association and the American Farm Economic Association on November 11, at Chicago, IL. *Journal of Farm Economics* 2(2): 101-109. Also published as pp. 82-92 in *Rural Health, Proceedings of the Second National Country Life Conference, Chicago, 1919.* DC: American Country Life Association, 1919.

0085 (continued).
Keywords: Research.

0085 Galpin, Charles, J.
1920. "Farm life studies and their relation to home economics work." Address before the Twelfth Annual Meeting of the American Home Economics Association in June, 1919 at Blue Ridge, NC. *Journal of Home Economics* 12(3): 159-61.

Keywords: Division of Farm Population and Rural Life.

0086 Galpin, Charles J.
1920. "The human side of farming." Address delivered at University of West Virginia, January 7. Published June 1948 in Galpin Memorial issue of *Rural Sociology* 13(2): 156-164.

Keywords: Rural life.

0087 Galpin, Charles J.
1920. "Signs of rural hope." Pp. 328-331 in *Proceedings of the 47th annual session National Conference of Social Work*, April 14-21, 1920, at New Orleans, LA. Chicago: University of Chicago Press for the National Conference of Social Work.

Keywords: Rural life.

0088 Galpin, Charles J.
1921. "Decrease in the United States rural population." Mimeo. DC: USDA, BAE, [DFPRL]. {NAL v.63}.

Keywords: *Population trends; rural.

0089 Galpin, Charles J.
1921. "Washington's home, Mt. Vernon, as a farm." Abstract of address given before the Country Planning Conference of the American Civic Association, Amherst, MA, October, 1920. *World Agriculture* 1(4): 65-86.

0089 (continued).
Keywords: Rural life.

0090 Galpin, Charles J.
1923. "Progress in the study of rural social problems." Pp. 89-95 in *Country Community Education, Proceedings of the 5th National Country Life Conference*. Teachers College, Columbia University, New York City, 1922. Chicago: Association Press for the American Country Life Association.

Keywords: Research; methodology.

0091 Galpin, Charles J.
1923. "Rural life in American art." Address delivered before the Fourteenth Annual Convention of the American Federation of Arts on November 9-11 at St. Louis, MO. *Social Forces* 2(1): 10-13. Also published as undated mimeo by the USDA, BAE, DFPRL in Washington, DC, and in May 1924 under the title "Art in the economy of the rural home" in the *Journal of Home Economics* 16(5): 235-240.

Keywords: Rural life.

0092 Galpin, Charles J.
1923. "The country life movement in the United States." *International Review of Agricultural Economics* (International Institute of Agriculture, Rome, Italy) 1(3): 295-315.

Keywords: Rural life.

0093 Galpin, Charles J.
1923. "Can the farm family afford modern institutions?" Address given at 6th National Country Life Conference, November 9, at St. Louis, MO. Published in *Journal of Rural Education* 3(4): 145-154, and as pp. 39-51 in *The Rural Home, Proceedings of the 6th National Country Life Conference*. Chicago: University of Chicago Press for the American Country Life Association, 1924.

0093 (continued).
Keywords: Community development.

0094 Galpin, Charles J.
1924. "The Division of Farm Population and Rural Life: An outline of its establishment, staff, cooperative policy, research problems, publications." Mimeo. DC: USDA, BAE, [DFPRL]. {NAL v.63}.

Keywords: Division of Farm Population and Rural Life.

0095 Galpin, Charles J.
1924. "Child crop." *Survey* 52(4): 224.

Keywords: Children; rural-urban population comparisons.

0096 Galpin, Charles J.
1924. "Democratizing farm and town." *Reformed Church Messenger* 93(41): 6.

Keywords: *Community processes.

0097 Galpin, Charles J.
1924. "Spending the dollar wisely in home and community: A plea for a larger place in agricultural teaching for consumption and the economics of consumption." Address at the Thirty-Eighth Annual Convention of the Association of Land-Grant Colleges on November 12 at New Willard Hotel, DC. Published in *Proceedings* [U.S. Office of Experiment Stations, Miscellaneous Bulletin], pp. 198-204. Burlington, VT: Free Press. Also published January 1925 under the title "Spending the dollar wisely" in *Rural America* 3(1): 3, 10.

Keywords: Level of living, rural life.

0098 Galpin, Charles J.
1925. "Rural sociology." In Walton C. John (editor), *Land-Grant College Education 1910-1920: Part 2, The Liberal Arts and Sciences, Including Miscellaneous Subjects and Activi-

0098 (continued).
ties. DC: U.S. Department of the Interior, Bureau of Education. Bulletin, 1924, No. 37.

Keywords: Rural life.

0099 Galpin, Charles J.
1926. "The challenge of the rural church." *Rural America* 4(3): 5, 7.

Keywords: Church; farm family; rural life.

0100 Galpin, Charles J.
1926. "Rural life." *American Journal of Sociology* 35(6): 1010-1016.

Keywords: Rural life; social change/trends.

0101 Galpin, Charles J.
1927. "Rural life progress in the United States, ten-year period, 1917-27." Address given at 10th National Country Life Conference, August 2, at East Lansing, MI. Shortened versions of the address published as "Rural progress 1917-27" in *Rural America* 5(7) 10-11; and as "Science in rural human relationships," pp. 18-21 in *A Decade of Rural Progress, Proceedings of the 10th and 11th National Country Life Conferences.* Chicago: University of Chicago Press for the American Country Life Association, 1928.

Keywords: Rural life; social change/trends.

0102 Galpin, Charles J.
1927. "Population flow from farms to cities declines." Pp. 591-592 in *Yearbook of Agriculture, 1926.* DC: GPO.

Keywords: Migration; farm population.

0103 Galpin, Charles J.
1927. "Rural progress as related to rural social forces." Pp 311-313 in Dwight Sanderson (ed.), *Farm Income and Farm Life: A Symposium on the Relation of the Social and*

0103 (continued).
Economic Factors in Rural Progress. Chicago: University of Chicago Press for the American Country Life Association.

Keywords: Rural life.

0104 Galpin, Charles J.
1927. "The human element in farm economy." Pp. 305-306 in Dwight Sanderson (ed.), *Farm Income and Farm Life: A Symposium on the Relation of the Social and Economic Factors in Rural Progress.* Chicago: University of Chicago Press for the American Country Life Association.

Keywords: Sociology of agriculture.

0105 Galpin, Charles J.
1927. "Analysis of migration of population to and from farms. Part 1. Study of 2,745 farm operators who have left farming for city, town or village. Part 2. Study of 1,167 persons who have left city, town or village for the farm." Mimeo. DC: USDA, BAE, [DFPRL]. {NAL v.53, v.63}.

Keywords: *Migration; farm population.

0106 Galpin, Charles J.
1928. "Population loss from farms ascribed to variety of reasons." Pp. 514-515 in *Yearbook of Agriculture, 1927.* DC: GPO.

Keywords: Migration; farm population; attitudes/opinions.

0107 Galpin, Charles J.
1928. "Population moving to farms includes many farm-bred men." Pp. 515-516 in *Yearbook of Agriculture, 1927.* DC: GPO.

Keywords: Migration; farm population; attitudes/opinions.

0108 Galpin, Charles J.
1928. "Losses in farm population." *Agricultural Situation* 12(4): 22-24.

Keywords: Farm population; farm population trends; migration.

0109 Galpin, Charles J.
1928. "Suggested uses of the bulletin 'Farm Population of Selected Counties' as laboratory statistics in college classes on rural sociology and rural economics." Mimeo. DC: USDA, BAE, [DFPRL]. {NAL v.53}.

Keywords: Uses of rural sociology research; farm population.

0110 Galpin, Charles J.
1929. "The standard of living of the farm population." Pp. 70-76 in National Bureau of Economic Research (Herbert Hoover, chairman), *Recent Economic Changes in the United States: Report of the Committee on Recent Economic Changes of the President's Conference on Unemployment, Including the Reports of a Special Staff of the National Bureau of Economic Research, Volume 1*. New York: McGraw-Hill.

Keywords: Standard of living.

0111 Galpin, Charles J.
1929. "Discriminations against rural people." *Rural America* 7(4): 5-6.

Keywords: Community; community development; attitudes/ opinions; social participation; rural life.

0112 Galpin, Charles J.
1929. "Farm living standards widely divergent on good and on poor U.S. farms." Pp. 284-286 in *Yearbook of Agriculture, 1928*. DC: GPO.

0112 (continued).
Keywords: Socioeconomic status-aggregate/area; income-low.

0113 Galpin, Charles J.
1929. "Standard of living may be improved by use of family budget." Pp. 555-557 in *Yearbook of Agriculture, 1928*. DC: GPO.

Keywords: Standard of living.

0114 Galpin, Charles J.
1929. "A high standard of living: Results of interviewing ten thousand 'back-to-the-landers'." Radio address published in *Rural America* 7(8):5-6 under title "Gentlemen preferring farms." Also published in *Hoard's Dairyman* 75(1):5,45 under original title and in *Bureau Farmer* (Illinois Agricultural Association Section) 5(3):16 under title "Read what men and women who have left the city for the country say about it."

Keywords: Attitudes/opinions; farm women; rural life.

0115 Galpin, Charles J.
1929. "Farm population reaches new low point." *Agricultural Situation* 13(4): 14-17.

Keywords: Farm population; farm population trends; migration.

0116 Galpin, Charles J.
1930. "The trend of farm population." *Rural America* 8(6): 5-6.

Keywords: Farm population trends; migration; farm-nonfarm population comparisons.

0117 Galpin, Charles J.
1930. "Part-time farming is common in alliance with rural

0117 (continued).
industries." Pp. 406-407 in *Yearbook of Agriculture, 1930*. DC: GPO.

Keywords: Part-time farming; rural industries.

0118 Galpin, Charles J.
1930. "Rural community often too small to support adequate institutions." Pp. 467-469 in *Yearbook of Agriculture, 1930*. DC: GPO.

Keywords: Community development; social organization.

0119 Galpin, Charles J.
1930. "My philosophy of rural life." Address before a meeting of the American Sociological Society [December 29, 1929] at DC. Also given August 1, before the Institute of Rural Affairs at Virginia Polytechnic Institute, Blacksburg, VA. *Rural America* 8(2): 13. Reprinted June 1948 in Galpin memorial issue of *Rural Sociology* 13(2): 164-170.

Keywords: Rural life.

0120 Galpin, Charles J.
1930. "The trend in farm population movements." *Agricultural Situation* 14(4): 6-9.

Keywords: Farm population; farm population trends; migration.

0121 Galpin, Charles J., and Florence N. Mather.
1930. "Vocational trends in a rural high school." (a supplementary report to Emily F. Hoag, USDA Bulletin No. 984). Mimeo. DC: USDA, BAE, [DFPRL]. {NAL v.63}.

Keywords: *Schools; education; social change/ trends.

0122 Galpin, Charles J.
1930. "My philosophy of rural recreation." Address before the Extension Section of the American Country Life

0122 (continued).
Association on October 7 at Madison, WI. Mimeo. DC: USDA, Extension Service, Office of Cooperative Extension Work in Agriculture and Home Economics. Extension Service Circular No. 135. USDA, BAE, [DFPRL] cooperating.

Keywords: Recreation; rural life.

0123 Galpin, Charles J.
1930. "Farm population associated with size of farms; with value of farm land and buildings; with mortgaged owner-operated farms; with location of farms on kind of roads--Based on the 1925 Census of Agriculture." Mimeo. DC: USDA, BAE, DFPRL.

Keywords: Farm population; graphic analysis.

0124 Galpin, Charles J.
1931. "Small-scale farming is widespread in U.S., census figures show." Pp. 479-481 in *Yearbook of Agriculture, 1931*. DC: GPO.

Keywords: Farm size.

0125 Galpin, Charles J.
1931. "Complete organization of the community." *Rural America* 9(5): 9.

Keywords: Community; social organization; community development; social participation; rural life.

0126 Galpin, Charles J.
1931. "Farm population starts growing." *Agricultural Situation* 15(3): 2-4.

Keywords: Farm population; farm population trends; migration.

0127 Galpin, Charles J.

0127 (continued).
1931. "Farm population." Pp. 209-220 in *A Graphic Summary of American Agriculture Based Largely on the Census,* compiled by O. E. Baker. USDA Miscellaneous Publication No. 105.

Keywords: Population; farm population; land tenure; graphic analysis. Blacks.

0128 Galpin, Charles J.
1932. "Farm population in decade 1920-1930 shows a considerable decrease." Pp. 495-497 in *Yearbook of Agriculture, 1932.* DC: GPO.

Keywords: Farm population; farm population trends.

0129 Galpin, Charles J.
1933. "Farm population reaches new high record." Radio address broadcast by Station WMAL and 49 other stations associated with the National Broadcasting Company on April 20 at DC. *Rural America* 11(6): 2. Extracts published in *Farm Population and Rural Life Activities* 7 (3): 11-12.

Keywords: Farm population estimates.

0130 Galpin, Charles, J.
1934. "When fortune favored the farmer." *Rural America* 12(8): 8-10; and pp. 24-32 in *National Planning and Rural Life, Proceedings of the 17th American Country Life Conference,* November 16-19, at DC. Chicago: University of Chicago Press for the American Country Life Association, 1935.

Keywords: Rural life.

0131 Galpin, Charles J.
1934. "Back-to-the-farm movement slowing up." Radio address broadcast by Station WMAL and other stations associated with the National Broadcasting Service on March 28 at DC. *Farm Population and Rural Life Activities* 8(2): 10-11.

0131 (continued).
Keywords: Farm population estimates; migration.

0132 Galpin, Charles J., B. L. Hummel, C. E. Lively, and C. C. Zimmerman.
1929. *Rural Sociological Adult Education in the United States*. New York: Social Science Research Council. A Social Science Research Monograph. Prepared under the direction of the Advisory Committee on Social and Economic Research in Agriculture--a committee of the Social Science Research Council.

Keywords: Sociology-rural sociology; uses of rural sociology research; extension.

0133 Galpin, Charles J., J. H. Kolb, Dwight Sanderson, and Carl C. Taylor.
1928. *Rural Sociological Research in the United States*. New York: Social Science Research Council. A Social Science Research Monograph. Prepared under the direction of the Advisory Committee on Social and Economic Research in Agriculture of the Social Science Research Council.

Keywords: Research.

0134 Galpin, Charles J., and T. B. Manny.
1932. "Farm population now increasing." *Agricultural Situation* 16(11): 2-5.

Keywords: Farm population; farm population trends; migration; rural nonfarm population.

0135 Galpin, Charles J., and T. B. Manny.
1933. "Farm population reaches new all-time peak." *Agricultural Situation* 17(5):2-5.

Keywords: Farm population; farm population trends; migration.

0136 Galpin, Charles J., and T. B. Manny.

0136 (continued).
1934. "Farm population increase less pronounced during 1933." *Agricultural Situation* 18(4): 2-6.

Keywords: Farm population; farm population trends; migration.

0137 Galpin, Charles J., and T. B. Manny.
1934. *Interstate Migrations among the Native White Population as Indicated by Differences between State of Birth and State of Residence: A Series of Maps Based on the Census 1870-1930.* DC: USDA, BAE, [DFPRL].

Keywords: Migration; graphic analysis.

0138 Garnett, William E.
1927. *Rural Organizations in Relation to Rural Life in Virginia--With Special Reference to Organizational Attitudes.* Blacksburg, VA: Virginia Polytechnic Institute, Virginia AES. Bulletin No. 256. USDA, BAE, [DFPRL] cooperating.

Keywords: Farm organizations; social psychology; attitudes/opinions. VA.

0139 Garnett, William E.
1930. *Young People's Organizations in Relation to Rural Life in Virginia--with Special Reference to 4-H Clubs.* Blacksburg, VA: Virginia Polytechnic Institute, Virginia AES. Bulletin No. 274. USDA, BAE, DFPRL cooperating.

Keywords: Youth; 4-H clubs; social participation. Blacks. VA.

0140 Garnett, William E., and Aja C. Seymour.
1932. *Membership Relations in Community Organizations: A Study of Factors Affecting Organizational Attitudes.* Blacksburg, VA: Virginia Polytechnic Institute, Virginia AES. Bulletin No. 287. USDA, BAE, [DFPRL] cooperating.

Keywords: Community clubs/organizations; attitudes/opinions. VA.

0141 Gee, Wilson.
1926. "Some of the best things in rural Virginia." Charlottesville, VA: University of Virginia. *Record, Extension Series*, Vol. 10 No. 9. [USDA, BAE, DFPRL cooperating].

Keywords: *Successes in rural life. VA.

0142 Gooden, Orville T.
1923. *Rural Life in Arkansas at Its Best.* Conway, AR: Hendrix College. Bulletin, Vol. 10, No. 3, Rural Series No. 1. USDA, BAE, DFPRL cooperating.

Keywords: *Successes in rural life. AR.

0143 Harris, T. L.
1931. *4-H Club Work in West Virginia.* Morgantown, WV: West Virginia University, College of Agriculture, AES. Bulletin No. 241. USDA, BAE, DFPRL cooperating.

Keywords: 4-H clubs; evaluation. WV.

0144 Harter, William L., and R. E. Stewart.
1930. *The Population of Iowa--Its Composition and Changes: A Brief Sociological Study of Iowa's Human Assets.* Ames, IA: Iowa State College of Agriculture and Mechanic Arts, AES. Bulletin No. 275. Contributed by Agricultural Economics Section. USDA, [BAE], DFPRL cooperating.

Keywords: Population; migration; population composition; socio-cultural groups; race. IA.

0145 Hawley, Edith.
1926. "Average quantity, cost and nutritive value of food consumed by farm families--Food consumed during one year by 1331 farm families of selected localities in Kansas, Kentucky, Missouri, and Ohio: A preliminary report." Mimeo. DC: USDA, Bureau of Home Economics; USDA, BAE, [DFPRL]; Ohio Wesleyan University; University of Missouri; University of Kentucky; Kansas State Agricultural College; and The Farmer's Wife, cooperating.

0145 (continued).
Keywords: Level of living. KS; KY; MO; OH.

0146 Hayes, Augustus W.
1922. *Some Factors in Town and Country Relationships.* New Orleans, LA: Tulane University of Louisiana, Department of Sociology. Research Bulletin. USDA, [BAE], DFPRL cooperating.

Keywords: Social and economic areas (rural-urban relationships). LA.

0147 Hayes, Augustus W.
1923. "Examples of community enterprises in Louisiana." Mimeo. New Orleans, LA: Tulane University of Louisiana. Research Bulletin No. 3. USDA, BAE, [DFPRL] cooperating. {NAL v.63}.

Keywords: *Community. LA.

0148 Hill, Randall C., E. L. Morgan, Mabel V. Campbell, and O. R. Johnson.
1930. *Social, Economic, and Homemaking Factors in Farm Living.* Columbia, MO: University of Missouri, College of Agriculture, AES. Research Bulletin No. 148. Contributed by University Departments of Rural Sociology, Home Economics, and Agricultural Economics. USDA, [BAE], DFPRL cooperating.

Keywords: Socioeconomic status-individual/family; level of living; farm family. MO.

0149 Hoag, Emily F. (see also Sawtelle).
1921. *The National Influence of a Single Farm Community: A Story of the Flow into National Life of Migration from the Farms.* DC: USDA. Department Bulletin No. 984. Contributed by Office of Farm Management and Farm Economics, [Division of Farm Life Studies].

Keywords: Migration; community. NY.

0150 Hoffer, C. R.
1926. "The development of rural sociology." *American Journal of Sociology* 32(1) (Part 1): 95-103. Also summarized as "The status of rural sociology in colleges and universities" for presentation at the December 27-30, 1927 annual meeting of the Rural Sociology Section of the American Sociological Society in DC.

Keywords: Sociology-rural sociology; research.

0151 Hoffer, C. R.
1928. *A Study of Town-Country Relationships.* East Lansing, MI: AES, Michigan State College of Agriculture and Applied Science. Special Bulletin No. 181. Contributed by Sociology Section. USDA, [BAE], DFPRL cooperating.

Keywords: Social and economic areas (rural-urban relationships); towns. MI.

0152 Hoffsommer, Harold C.
1934. *Relation of Cities and Larger Villages to Changes in Rural Trade and Social Areas in Wayne County, New York.* Ithaca, NY: Cornell University AES. Bulletin No. 582. USDA, BAE, DFPRL cooperating. Based in part on June 1929 Cornell University Ph.D thesis.

Keywords: Social and economic areas (rural-urban relationships); social organization; trade centers; towns; villages. NY.

0153 Kirkpatrick, Ellis L.
1923. *The Standard of Life in a Typical Section of Diversified Farming.* Ithaca, NY: Cornell University AES, Bulletin No. 423. USDA, BAE DFPRL, cooperating. Based in part on September 1922 Cornell University Ph.D thesis.

Keywords: Standard of living; farm family; land tenure. NY.

0154 Kirkpatrick, Ellis L.

0154 (continued).
1924. "Living conditions and the cost of living in farm homes of selected localities of Missouri: A preliminary report." Mimeo. DC: USDA, BAE [DFPRL]. University of Missouri, Agricultural Extension Service, cooperating. {NAL v.63}.

Keywords: Level of living. MO.

0155 Kirkpatrick, Ellis L.
1924. "Family living in farm homes." Substance of an address before graduate students at [Columbia University] Teachers College in July. *Teachers College Record* 26(4): 323-27.

Keywords: Level of living.

0156 Kirkpatrick, Ellis L.
1926. "Facts and factors with regard to the farmers' standard of living." Pp. 388-395 in *Proceedings of the 53rd annual session National Conference of Social Work*, May 26-June 2, at Cleveland, Ohio. Chicago: University of Chicago Press for the National Conference of Social Work.

Keywords: Level of living; farm family.

0157 Kirkpatrick, Ellis L.
1926. "The average quantities and values of fuel and other household supplies used by farm families--Fuel and other household supplies furnished by the farm and purchased in one year for family living purposes by 1,337 farm families of selected localities of Ohio, Kentucky, Missouri and Kansas: A preliminary report." Mimeo. DC: USDA, BAE, [DFPRL]; USDA, Bureau of Home Economics; Ohio Wesleyan University; University of Kentucky; University of Missouri; Kansas State Agricultural College; and The Farmer's Wife, cooperating.

Keywords: Level of living. OH; KY; MO; KS.

0158 Kirkpatrick, Ellis L.
1926. "Farmers' standards of living." Pp. 13-25 in Henry Israel and Benson Y. Landis (eds), *Handbook of Rural Social Resources*. Chicago, IL: University of Chicago Press.

Keywords: Standard of living.

0159 Kirkpatrick, Ellis L.
1926. "Average expenditures for household furnishings and equipment purchased by farm families--Household furnishings and equipment purchased in one year by 1,299 farm families of selected localities of Ohio, Kentucky, Missouri and Kansas: A preliminary report." Mimeo. DC: USDA, BAE, [DFPRL]; USDA, Bureau of Home Economics; Ohio Wesleyan University; University of Kentucky; University of Missouri; Kansas State Agricultural College; and The Farmer's Wife, cooperating. {NAL v.63}.

Keywords: Level of living. OH; KY; MO; KS.

0160 Kirkpatrick, Ellis L.
1926. *The Farmer's Standard of Living: A Socio-Economic Study of 2886 White Farm Families of Selected Localities in 11 States*. DC: USDA. Department Bulletin No. 1466.

Keywords: Standard of living; farm family. Northeast; South; Midwest.

0161 Kirkpatrick, Ellis L.
1926. "Housing conditions among 947 white farm families of Texas: A preliminary report." Mimeo. DC: USDA, BAE, [DFPRL]. Agricultural and Mechanical College of Texas cooperating. {NAL v.63}.

Keywords: Level of living. TX.

0162 Kirkpatrick, Ellis L.
1927. "Rural church in its relation to the farmer's standard of living." Address before the annual meeting of the International Association of Agricultural Missions on

0162 (continued).
December 2, 1926 at New York. *World Agriculture* 6(4): 457-458.

Keywords: Church; standard of living.

0163 Kirkpatrick, Ellis L.
1927. "Observations as a measure of the standard of living among farmers." *Journal of Home Economics* 19(8): 459-462.

Keywords: Standard of living; methodology-levels of living indicators/ scales.

0164 Kirkpatrick, Ellis L.
1927. "Attitudes and problems of farm youth." Mimeo. DC: USDA, Extension Service, [Office of Cooperative Extension Work], Circular 46.

Keywords: Youth; attitudes/ opinions; level of living. Blacks.

0165 Kirkpatrick, Ellis L.
1927. "Family living level on the farm." Pp. 351-53 in *Yearbook of Agriculture, 1926.* DC: GPO.

Keywords: Level of living; farm family.

0166 Kirkpatrick, Ellis L.
1927. "The effect of minimum and maximum economic status on the standard of life." Pp. 125-133 in Dwight Sanderson (ed.), *Farm Income and Farm Life: A Symposium on the Relation of the Social and Economic Factors in Rural Progress.* Chicago: University of Chicago Press for the American Country Life Association.

Keywords: Level of living; standard of living; socioeconomic status-individual/ family.

0167 Kirkpatrick, Ellis L.
1927. "The relation of types of farming to expenditure and culture." Pp. 210-213 in Dwight Sanderson (ed.), *Farm*

00167 (continued).
Income and Farm Life: A Symposium on the Relation of the Social and Economic Factors in Rural Progress. Chicago: University of Chicago Press for the American Country Life Association.

Keywords: Level of living; farm systems; sociology of agriculture.

0168 Kirkpatrick, Ellis L.
1927. "Joint cooperative studies on the economics and sociology of rural life." Paper read before the American Farm Economic Association and the Rural Sociology Section of the American Sociological Society on December 30, 1926 at St. Louis, MO. *American Journal of Sociology* 33(2): 222-230. Partially reprinted under the title "Joint cooperative studies in the field of rural life" *Journal of Farm Economics* 9(2): 210-215.

Keywords: Research.

0169 Kirkpatrick, Ellis L.
1927. "The relation of the standard of life to success in farming." Address given at 10th National Country Life Conference, August 1-4 at East Lansing, Michigan. Published in *Rural America* 5(October 1927): 28-31; and pp. 135-140 in *A Decade of Rural Progress, Proceedings of the 10th and 11th National Country Life Conference.* Chicago: University of Chicago Press for the American Country Life Association, 1928.

Keywords: Standard of living; level of living; rural life.

0170 Kirkpatrick, Ellis L.
1928. "Family living in farm homes at the bottom of agriculture." *Catholic Charities Review* 12(4): 123-125.

Keywords: *Farm family; income-low; level of living.

0171 Kirkpatrick, Ellis L.

0171 (continued).
1928. "Annual family living in selected farm homes of North Dakota: A preliminary report." Mimeo. DC: USDA, BAE, [DFPRL]. North Dakota Agricultural College cooperating. {NAL v.63}.

Keywords: Level of living. ND.

0172 Kirkpatrick, Ellis L., and Agnes Ellen Harris.
1924. "Living conditions and the cost of living in farm homes of selected areas of Alabama: A preliminary report." Mimeo. DC: USDA, BAE, [DFPRL]. Alabama Polytechnic Institute, Extension Service cooperating.

Keywords: Level of living. AL.

0173 Kirkpatrick, Ellis L., and B. L. Melvin.
1924. "Living conditions and the cost of living in farm homes of Delaware County, Ohio: A preliminary report." Mimeo. DC: USDA, BAE, [DFPRL]. {NAL v.63}.

Keywords: Level of living. OH.

0174 Kirkpatrick, Ellis L., and J. T. Sanders.
1924. "Cost of living in farm homes in several areas of Kentucky, Tennessee, and Texas: A preliminary report." Mimeo. DC: USDA, BAE, [DFPRL]. University of Kentucky, Kentucky AES, and the University of Tennessee AES cooperating. {NAL v.63}.

Keywords: Level of living. KY; TN; TX.

0175 Kirkpatrick, Ellis L., and George H. von Tungeln.
1924. "Cost of living in farm homes in several areas of Iowa: A preliminary report." Mimeo. DC: USDA, BAE, [DFPRL]. {NAL v.63}.

Keywords: Level of living. IA.

0176 Kirkpatrick, Ellis L., Walter Burr, and Ellen M. Batchelor.

0176 (continued).
1925. "Living conditions and family living in farm homes of selected localities of Kansas: A preliminary report." Mimeo. DC: USDA, BAE, [DFPRL]. Kansas State Agricultural College Agricultural Extension and Departments of Economics and Sociology cooperating. {NAL v.63}.
Keywords: Level of living. KS.

0177 Kirkpatrick, Ellis L., and Myrtle Brook.
1925. "Living conditions and family living in farm homes of selected localities of Alabama: A preliminary report." Mimeo. DC: USDA, BAE, [DFPRL]. Alabama College Department of Psychology and Sociology cooperating. {NAL v.63}.

Keywords: Level of living. AL.

0178 Kirkpatrick, Ellis L., and I. G. Davis.
1925. "Living conditions and family living in farm homes of Lebanon Town, New London County, Connecticut: A preliminary report." Mimeo. DC: USDA, BAE, [DFPRL]. Connecticut Agricultural College, Agricultural Extension Service cooperating. {NAL v.63}.

Keywords: Level of living. CT.

0179 Kirkpatrick, Ellis L., and J. A. Dickey.
1925. "Living conditions and family living in farm homes of Schoharie County, New York: A preliminary report." Mimeo. DC: USDA, BAE, [DFPRL]. New York State College of Agriculture at Cornell University, Department of Rural Social Organization cooperating. {NAL v.63}.

Keywords: Level of living. NY.

0180 Kirkpatrick, Ellis L., and Lonny I. Landrum.
1925. "Living conditions and family living in farm homes of selected localities of South Carolina: A preliminary report." Mimeo. DC: USDA, BAE, [DFPRL], and Winthrop College. Extension Service cooperating. {NAL v.63}.

0180 (continued).
Keywords: Level of living. SC.

0181 Kirkpatrick, Ellis L., and Lucile W. Reynolds.
1925. "Living conditions and family living in farm homes of selected localities of Massachusetts: A preliminary report." Mimeo. DC: USDA, BAE, [DFPRL], and Massachusetts Agricultural College. Agricultural Extension Service cooperating. {NAL v.63}.

Keywords: Level of living. MA.

0182 Kirkpatrick, Ellis L., and J. T. Sanders.
1925. "The cost of living among colored farm families of selected localities of Kentucky, Tennessee and Texas: A preliminary report." Mimeo. DC: USDA, BAE, [DFPRL]. University of Kentucky, Kentucky AES, and the University of Tennessee AES cooperating.

Keywords: Level of living. Blacks. KY; TN; TX.

0183 Kirkpatrick, Ellis L., and Agnes Ellen Harris.
1926. "Living conditions and family living in farm homes of Alabama: A preliminary report." Mimeo. DC: USDA, BAE, [DFPRL]. Alabama Polytechnic Institute, Extension Service cooperating.

Keywords: Level of living. AL.

0184 Kirkpatrick, Ellis L., and J. T. Sanders.
1926. *The Relation Between the Ability to Pay and the Standard of Living Among Farmers: A Socio-Economic Study of 861 White Farm Families of Kentucky, Tennessee, and Texas.* DC: USDA. Department Bulletin No. 1382.

Keywords: Standard of living. KY; TX; TN.

0185 Kirkpatrick, Ellis L., Agnes Ellen Harris, and Myrtle Brook.
1926. "Living conditions and family living in farm homes of Alabama: A preliminary report." Mimeo. DC: USDA,

0185 (continued).
BAE, [DFPRL]. Alabama Polytechnic Institute, Extension Service and Alabama College Department of Psychology and Sociology cooperating.

Keywords: Level of living. AL.

0186 Kirkpatrick, Ellis L., and Daisy D. Williamson.
1926. "Living conditions and family living in farm homes of Merrimack County, New Hampshire: A preliminary report." Mimeo. DC: USDA, BAE, [DFPRL], and the University of New Hampshire. Agricultural Extension Service cooperating. {NAL v.63}.

Keywords: Level of living. NH.

0187 Kirkpatrick, Ellis L., and A. T. Hoverstad.
1927. "Family living in 25 farm homes of Askov, Pine County, Minnesota, for the year ending December 31, 1925: A preliminary report." Mimeo. DC: USDA, BAE, [DFPRL]. University of Minnesota Department of Agriculture cooperating. {NAL v.63}.

Keywords: Level of living. MN.

0188 Kirkpatrick, Ellis L., and H. W. Hawthorne.
1928. "Family living among poorer farm people studied statistically." Pp. 293-295 in *Yearbook of Agriculture, 1927*. DC: GPO.

Keywords: Level of living; income-low. North Central.

0189 Kirkpatrick, Ellis L., and H. W. Hawthorn.
1928. "Sources and uses of income among 300 farm families of Vinton, Jackson, and Meigs Counties, Ohio, 1926: A preliminary report." Mimeo. DC: USDA, BAE, [DFPRL]. Ohio AES and Ohio State University cooperating.

Keywords: Level of living. OH.

0190 Kirkpatrick, Ellis L., J. H. Kolb, Creagh Inge, and A. F. Wileden.
1929. *Rural Organizations and the Farm Family: A Study of 282 Families in Twelve Selected Districts of Five Wisconsin Counties.* Madison, WI: University of Wisconsin AES. Research Bulletin No. 96. USDA, [BAE, DFPRL] cooperating.

Keywords: Community clubs/ organizations; social participation. WI.

0191 Kirkpatrick, Ellis L., P. E. McNall, and May L. Cowles. 1930. "Rural standards of living in Dunn County, Wisconsin." Madison, WI: University of Wisconsin, College of Agriculture. Stencil Bulletin No. 104. Contributed by University Departments of Rural Sociology, Home Economics, and Agricultural Economics. USDA, BAE, DFPRL, and Farm Management and Costs cooperating. {NAL v.71}.

Keywords: Standard of living. WI.

0192 Kirkpatrick, Ellis L., P. E. McNall, and May L. Cowles. 1930. "Rural standards of living in Walworth County, Wisconsin." Madison, WI: University of Wisconsin, College of Agriculture. Stencil Bulletin No. 105. Contributed by University Departments of Rural Sociology, Home Economics, and Agricultural Economics. USDA, BAE, DFPRL, and Farm Management and Costs cooperating.

Keywords: Standard of living. WI.

0193 Kirkpatrick, Ellis L., and Aileen Cripps.
1931. "Rural standards of living in Dane and Green Counties." Madison, WI: University of Wisconsin, College of Agriculture. Stencil Bulletin No. 106. Contributed by University Departments of Rural Sociology, Agricultural Economics, and Home Economics. USDA, BAE, [DFPRL, and Farm Management and Costs] cooperating.

Keywords: Standard of living. WI.

0194 Kirkpatrick, Ellis L., P. E. McNall, and May L. Cowles. 1931. "Rural standards of living in Portage, Langlade and Sawyer Counties, Wisconsin." Madison, WI: University of Wisconsin, College of Agriculture. Stencil Bulletin No. 108. Contributed by University Departments of Rural Sociology, Agricultural Economics, and Home Economics. USDA, BAE, DFPRL, and Farm Management and Costs cooperating.

Keywords: Standard of living. WI.

0195 Kirkpatrick, Ellis L., P. E. McNall, and May L. Cowles. 1933. *Farm Family Living in Wisconsin.* Madison, WI: University of Wisconsin AES. Research Bulletin No. 114. Contributed by University Departments of Rural Sociology, Agricultural Economics, and Home Economics. USDA, BAE, DFPRL, and Farm Management and Costs cooperating. Supplementary tables published separately in mimeo form.

Keywords: Farm family; income; standard of living; social participation. WI.

0196 Kirkpatrick, Ellis L., Rosalind Tough, and May L. Cowles. 1934. *The Life Cycle of the Farm Family--in Relation to its Standards of Living and Ability to Provide.* Madison, WI: University of Wisconsin AES. Research Bulletin No. 121. Contributed by University Departments of Rural Sociology and Home Economics. USDA, BAE, DFPRL and Farm Management and Costs cooperating.

Keywords: Farm family; family life cycle; standard of living. WI.

0197 Kolb, J. H. 1921. *Rural Primary Groups: A Study of Agricultural Neighborhoods.* Madison, WI: University of Wisconsin AES. Research Bulletin No. 51. USDA, Office of Farm Management and Farm Economics cooperating.

0197 (continued).
Keywords: Neighborhood; locality groups; social organization. WI.

0198 Kolb, J. H.
1923. *Service Relations of Town and Country: The Service Organization of Town and Country.* Madison, WI: University of Wisconsin AES. Research Bulletin No. 58. USDA, [BAE, DFPRL] cooperating.

Keywords: Social and economic areas (rural-urban relationships); towns; social organization. WI.

0199 Kolb, J. H.
1925. *Service Institutions for Town and Country.* Madison, WI: University of Wisconsin AES. Research Bulletin No. 66. USDA, [BAE, DFPRL] cooperating.

Keywords: Towns; social organization; community development; schools; libraries; hospitals. WI.

0200 Kolb, J. H.
1933. *Trends of Country Neighborhoods: A Restudy of Rural Primary Groups, 1921-1931.* Madison, WI: University of Wisconsin AES. Research Bulletin No. 120. USDA [BAE, DFPRL] cooperating.

Keywords: Neighborhood; locality groups; social organization; social change/trends. WI.

0201 Kolb, J. H., and C. J. Bornman.
1924. *Rural Religious Organization: A Study of the Origin and Development of Religious Groups.* Madison, WI: University of Wisconsin AES. Research Bulletin No. 60. USDA, [BAE, DFPRL] cooperating.

Keywords: Religion; social organization; socio-cultural groups; social change/trends. WI.

0202 Kolb, J. H., and R. A. Polson.

0202 (continued).
1933. *Trends in Town-Country Relations.* Madison, WI: University of Wisconsin AES. Research Bulletin No. 117. USDA, BAE, DFPRL, and the President's Committee for the Study of Recent Social Trends cooperating.

Keywords: Social and economic areas (rural-urban relationships); towns; social organization; social change/trends. WI.

0203 Kolb, J. H., and A. F. Wileden.
1927. *Special Interest Groups in Rural Society.* Madison, WI: University of Wisconsin AES. Research Bulletin No. 84. USDA, [BAE, DFPRL] cooperating.

Keywords: Voluntary associations; social organization. WI.

0204 Kolb, J. H. and A. F. Wileden.
1928. *Making Rural Organizations Effective.* Madison, WI: Unversity of Wisconsin AES. Bulletin No. 403. [USDA, BAE, DFPRL] cooperating.

Keywords: Community clubs/organizations; community development.

0205 Kumlien, W. F.
1927. *What Farmers Think of Farming.* Brookings, SD: South Dakota State College of Agriculture and Mechanic Arts AES. Bulletin No. 223. Contributed by College Department of Rural Sociology. USDA, BAE, DFPRL cooperating.

Keywords: Attitudes/opinions; rural life. SD.

0206 Kumlien, W. F.
1928. *Equalizing Library Opportunities in South Dakota.* Brookings, SD: South Dakota State College of Agriculture and Mechanic Arts AES. Bulletin No. 233. Contributed by College Department of Rural Sociology. USDA, BAE, DFPRL cooperating.

0206 (continued).
Keywords: Libraries. SD.

0207 Kumlien, W. F.
1930. *The High School Education of Farm Boys and Girls in South Dakota.* Brookings, SD: South Dakota State College of Agriculture and Mechanic Arts AES. Bulletin No. 250. Contributed by College Department of Rural Sociology. USDA, BAE, DFPRL cooperating for the first year of the study.

Keywords: Schools; education; children; rural family. SD.

0208 Kumlien, W. F.
1931. *Rural Health Situation in South Dakota.* Brookings, SD: South Dakota State College of Agriculture and Mechanic Arts AES. Bulletin No. 258. Contributed by College Department of Rural Sociology. USDA, BAE, DFPRL cooperating for the first year of the study.

Keywords: Health; health and medical care; farm family. SD.

0209 Landis, Paul H.
1932. *South Dakota Town-Country Trade Relations 1901-1931.* Brookings, SD: South Dakota State College of Agriculture and Mechanic Arts AES. Bulletin No. 274. Contributed by College Department of Rural Sociology. USDA, BAE, [DFPRL] cooperating.

Keywords: Trade centers; social and economic areas (rural-urban relationships); social change/trends. SD.

0210 Lively, C. E., and P. G. Beck.
1927. *The Rural Health Facilities of Ross County, Ohio.* Wooster, OH: Ohio AES. Bulletin No. 412. [USDA, BAE, DFPRL] cooperating.

Keywords: Health and medical care; social class. OH.

0211 Lott, Elmo H.
1932. *Rural Contributions to Urban Leadership in Montana.* Bozeman, MT: Montana State College AES. Bulletin No. 262. USDA, BAE, [DFPRL] cooperating.

Keywords: Leadership; population composition. MT.

0212 Manny, Theodore B.
1928. "What farmers say about marketing Eastern Shore potatoes and what farmers suggest for better marketing: A preliminary report." Mimeo. DC: USDA, BAE, [DFPRL]. Maryland AES and Virginia AES cooperating. {NAL v.63}.

Keywords: Marketing; cooperatives; attitudes/ opinions. MD; VA.

0213 Manny, Theodore B.
1929. "What farmers say about marketing." *Rural America* 7(6): 9-10.

Keywords: Marketing; attitudes/opinions; evaluation.

0214 Manny, Theodore B.
1929. "Cooperative marketing hampered by lapses into former practices." Pp. 220-221 in *Yearbook of Agriculture, 1928.* DC: GPO.

Keywords: Marketing; cooperatives.

0215 Manny, Theodore B.
1929. *Problems in Cooperation and Experiences of Farmers in Marketing Potatoes.* DC: USDA. Circular No. 87. Contributed by BAE, [DFPRL and Cooperative Marketing]. Maryland AES and Virginia AES cooperating.

Keywords: Marketing; cooperatives; social change/trends. MD, VA.

0216 Manny, Theodore B.
1929. "Attitudes toward rural government: A preliminary

0216 (continued).
report." Mimeo. DC: USDA, BAE, [DFPRL]. Hendrix College (Conway, AR) cooperating. {NAL v.63}.

Keywords: Local government; attitudes/ opinions.

0217 Manny, Theodore B.
1931. "Some problems of rural government." *Rural America* 9(2): 3-4.

Keywords: Local government; evaluation.

0218 Manny, Theodore B.
1931. "Cooperative spirit of farmer varies with schooling and habit." Pp. 154-156 in *Yearbook of Agriculture, 1931*. DC: GPO.

Keywords: Farm organizations; land tenure; social participation.

0219 Manny, Theodore B.
1931. *Farmers' Experiences and Opinions as Factors Influencing Their Cotton-Marketing Methods*. DC: USDA. Circular No. 144. Contributed by BAE, DFPRL. Division of Cooperative Marketing cooperating.

Keywords: Marketing; cooperatives; social change/trends; attitudes/opinions. AL, NC.

0220 Manny, Theodore B.
1931. "What kind of farmers will join cooperatives?". *School Life* 16(10): 188-9.

Keywords: Education; cooperatives; social psychology.

0221 Manny, Theodore B.
1931. "The new rural municipality: Dr. Galpin's ideas." *Rural America* 9 (October): 10-12; and pp. 18-25 in *Rural Government, Proceedings of the 14th American Country Life Conference*, August 17-20, at Ithaca, New York. Chicago:

0221 (continued).
University of Chicago Press for the American Country Life Association, 1932.

Keywords: Local government.

0222 Manny, Theodore B.
1932. "Government structure, powers and problems in the new rural municipality." Pp. 154-157 in *Rural Government, Proceedings of the 14th American Country Life Conference*, August, 17-20, 1931, at Ithaca, New York. Chicago: University of Chicago Press for the American Country Life Association.

Keywords: Local government.

0223 Manny, Theodore B.
1932. "The human factor from the viewpoint of social relations." Paper read before joint meeting of the Section on Rural Sociology of the American Sociological Society and the American Farm Economic Association on December 28, 1931 at DC. *Journal of Farm Economics* 14(1): 128-137.

Keywords: Level of living; social participation; farm population; population composition; migration.

0224 Manny, Theodore B.
1932. "The need for modernizing rural government." Address before the Seventeenth Annual New Jersey State Agricultural Convention on January 26 at Trenton, NJ. Pp. 42-52 in *Official Proceedings of the Seventeenth Annual State Agricultural Convention, State of New Jersey*. Trenton, NJ: Department of Agriculture. Circular No. 213.

Keywords: Local government. NJ.

0225 Manny, Theodore B.
1932. "Rural areas for rural government." Excerpts from an address before the Section on Rural Government of the

0225 (continued).
American Political Science Association on December 28, 1931 at DC. *National Municipal Review* 21(2): 481-483.

Keywords: Local government.

0226 Manny, Theodore B.
1932. *What Ohio Farmers Think of Farmer-Owned Business Organizations in That State.* DC: USDA. Circular No. 240. Contributed by [BAE, DFPRL]. Ohio State University and the Federal Farm Board cooperating.

Keywords: Marketing; cooperatives; attitudes/opinions. OH.

0227 Manny, Theodore B.
1933. *Farmer Opinions and Other Factors Influencing Cotton Production and Acreage Adjustments in the South.* DC: USDA. Circular No. 258.

Keywords: Agricultural production; extension; evaluation; attitudes/opinions. GA, MS, NC, SC, South.

0228 Manny, Theodore B., and R. C. Smith.
1931. "The Ohio Farm Bureau Federation from the farmers' viewpoint: A preliminary report." Mimeo. DC: USDA, BAE, [DFPRL]. The Federal Farm Board and Ohio State University [Department of Rural Economics] cooperating.

Keywords: Farm organizations; attitudes/ opinions; marketing; cooperatives. OH.

0229 Manny, Theodore B., and H. W. Gilbertson.
1932. *Fund-Raising Activities for Rural Groups: An Outline.* DC: USDA, [Extension Service], [Office of] Cooperative Extension Work in Agriculture and Home Economics. Miscellaneous Extension Publication No. 8. USDA, BAE, [DFPRL] cooperating.

Keywords: Community clubs/organizations; community development.

0230 Manny, Theodore B., and Wayne C. Nason.
1934. *Rural Factory Industries*. DC: USDA. Circular No. 312.

Keywords: Rural industries; social change/trends.

0231 Manny, Theodore B., Bushrod W. Allin, and Clifton J. Bradley.
1934. *Farm Taxes and Local Government in Crittenden and Livingston Counties, Kentucky*. Lexington, KY: University of Kentucky, Kentucky AES. Bulletin No. 355. USDA, BAE, [DFPRL] cooperating.

Keywords: Local government; evaluation. KY.

0232 Melvin, Bruce L.
1928. *Rural Population of New York, 1855 to 1925*. Ithaca, NY: Cornell University AES. Memoir No. 116.

Keywords: Population; rural; population trends. NY.

0233 Melvin, Bruce L.
1929. *Village Service Agencies, New York, 1925*. Ithaca, NY: Cornell University AES. Bulletin No. 493. USDA, BAE, DFPRL cooperating.

Keywords: Villages; social organization; social and economic areas (rural-urban relationships). NY.

0234 Morgan, E. L., and Owen Howells.
1925. *Rural Population Groups*. Columbia, MO: University of Missouri AES. Research Bulletin 74. USDA, BAE, [DFPRL] cooperating.

Keywords: Locality groups; neighborhood. Blacks. MO.

0235 Morgan, E. L., and Henry J. Burt.
1927. *Community Relations of Rural Young People*. Columbia, MO: University of Missouri, College of Agricul-

0235 (continued).
ture, AES. Research Bulletin No. 110. USDA, [BAE], DFPRL cooperating.

Keywords: Youth; attitudes/opinions; rural life.

0236 Nason, Wayne C.
1921. *Plans of Rural Community Buildings.* DC: USDA. Farmers' Bulletin No. 1173.

Keywords: Community buildings and centers; planning.

0237 Nason, Wayne C.
1921. *The Organization of Rural Community Buildings.* DC: USDA. Farmers' Bulletin No. 1192.

Keywords: Community buildings and centers; planning.

0238 Nason, Wayne C.
1922. *Uses of Rural Community Buildings.* DC: USDA. Farmers' Bulletin No. 1274.

Keywords: Community buildings and centers.

0239 Nason, Wayne C.
1923. *Rural Planning: The Social Aspects.* DC: USDA. Farmers' Bulletin No. 1325.

Keywords: Planning; community buildings and centers; community development.

0240 Nason, Wayne C.
1924. *Rural Planning: The Social Aspects of Recreation Places.* DC: USDA. Farmers' Bulletin No. 1388.

Keywords: Planning; recreation; community buildings and centers; community development.

0241 Nason, Wayne C.
1925. *Rural Planning: The Village.* DC: USDA. Farmers' Bulletin No. 1441. Excerpts published under title "Village

0241 (continued).
planning and replanning" in *American City* 33(1): 29-32. Revised in August 1935 and reissued under the same title and bulletin number.

Keywords: Planning; villages; community buildings and centers; community development.

0242 Nason, Wayne C.
1925. "Community building and the church." *Rural America* 3(8): 6, 8.

Keywords: Community buildings and centers; church; community development; community.

0243 Nason, Wayne C.
1926. *Rural Hospitals.* DC: USDA. Farmers' Bulletin No. 1485.

Keywords: Hospitals; planning-community services; community development.

0244 Nason, Wayne C.
1927. "Hospitals for agricultural communities." Pp. 439-442 in *Yearbook of Agriculture, 1926.* DC: GPO.

Keywords: Hospitals; health and medical care.

0245 Nason, Wayne C.
1927. "Recreation taught in pageants." Pp. 625-627 in *Yearbook of Agriculture, 1926.* DC: GPO.

Keywords: Recreation; community clubs/organizations.

0246 Nason, Wayne C.
1927. "Village planning contributing to better farm life." Pp. 752-756 in *Yearbook of Agriculture, 1926.* DC: GPO.

Keywords: Planning; villages.

0247 Nason, Wayne C.
1928. "Libraries for rural people springing up but more are needed." Pp. 424-426 in *Yearbook of Agriculture, 1927*. DC: GPO.

Keywords: Libraries.

0248 Nason, Wayne C.
1928. *Rural Libraries*. DC: USDA. Farmers' Bulletin No. 1559.

Keywords: Libraries; community development.

0249 Nason, Wayne C.
1930. *Rural Buildings for Business and Social Uses*. DC: USDA. Farmers' Bulletin No. 1622.

Keywords: Community buildings and centers; community development.

0250 Nason, Wayne C.
1931. *Rural Community Fire Departments*. DC: USDA. Farmers' Bulletin No. 1667.

Keywords: Fire protection services; planning-community services; community development.

0251 Nason, Wayne C.
1932. "Rural industries in Knott County, Kentucky: A preliminary report." Mimeo. DC: USDA, BAE, [DFPRL]. Kentucky AES cooperating.

Keywords: Rural industries. KY.

0252 Nason, Wayne C., and C. W. Thompson.
1920. *Rural Community Buildings in the United States*. DC: USDA. Department Bulletin No. 825.

Keywords: Community buildings and centers; community.

0253 Nelson, Lowry.

0253 (continued).
1925. *A Social Survey of Escalante, Utah.* Provo, UT: Brigham Young University Studies No. 1. Contributed by University Division of Research. USDA, BAE, [DFPRL] cooperating.

Keywords: Community; social organization; religion; sociology of agriculture. Mormon. UT.

0254 Nelson, Lowry.
1928. *The Utah Farm Village of Ephraim.* Provo, UT: Brigham Young University Studies No. 2. Contributed by University Division of Research. USDA, BAE, DFPRL cooperating.

Keywords: Community; social organization; religion; sociology of agriculture. Mormon. UT.

0255 Nelson, Lowry.
1933. *Some Social and Economic Features of American Fork, Utah.* Provo, UT: Brigham Young University Studies No. 4. Contributed by University Division of Research. USDA, BAE, DFPRL cooperating.

Keywords: Community; social organization; religion; sociology of agriculture. Mormon. UT.

0256 Nicholls, W. D., and E. L. Kirkpatrick.
1924. "Costs of living in farm homes, Mason County, Kentucky: A preliminary report." Mimeo. DC: USDA, BAE, [DFPRL]. {NAL v.63}.

Keywords: Level of living. KY.

0257 Oyler, Merton.
1930. *Cost of Living and Population Trends in Laurel County, Kentucky.* Lexington, KY: University of Kentucky, Kentucky AES. Bulletin No. 301. USDA, [BAE], DFPRL cooperating.

0257 (continued).
Keywords: Level of living; population composition. KY.

0258 Page, James Franklin.
1930. *Relation of Town and Country Interests in Garfield County, Oklahoma.* Stillwater, OK: Oklahoma Agriculture and Mechanical College AES. Bulletin No. 194. USDA, BAE, DFPRL cooperating.

Keywords: Social and economic areas (rural-urban relationships). OK.

0259 Paxson, Alfred Moore.
1934. *Relationships of Open-Country Families of Onondaga County, New York, to Socio-Economic Areas, Villages, and Cities.* Ithaca, NY: Cornell University AES. Bulletin No. 584. USDA, BAE, DFPRL cooperating. Based in part on September 1932 Cornell University Ph.D thesis.

Keywords: Social and economic areas (rural-urban relationships); social organization. NY.

0260 Price, H. Bruce, and C. R. Hoffer.
1928. *Services of Rural Trade Centers in Distribution of Farm Supplies.* University Farm, St. Paul, MN: University of Minnesota AES. Bulletin No. 249. USDA, BAE, [DFPRL] cooperating.

Keywords: Social and economic areas (rural-urban relationships); trade centers. MN.

0261 Rankin, J. O.
1922. *Reading Matter in Nebraska Farm Homes.* Lincoln, NB: University of Nebraska AES. Bulletin No. 180. USDA, Office of Farm Management and Farm Economics cooperating. Summary report issued in February 1924. Mimeo. DC: USDA, BAE, [DFPRL], University of Nebraska cooperating.

Keywords: Information sources-mass media; farm family. NE.

0262 Rankin, J. O.
1923. "A thousand Nebraska farm families and their homes in ten survey areas." Pp. 186-209 in *Proceedings of the 6th American Country Life Association Conference* on November 9-11 at St. Louis, MO. Also issued for conference as "A thousand Nebraska farm families and their homes in ten survey areas". Mimeo. DC: USDA, BAE, [DFPRL]. University of Nebraska cooperating.

Keywords: Rural life; farm family. NE.

0263 Rankin, J. O.
1923. *The Nebraska Farm Family: Some Land Tenure Phases*. Lincoln, NB: University of Nebraska AES. Bulletin No. 185. USDA, Office of Farm Management and Farm Economics cooperating.

Keywords: Structure of agriculture; land tenure; farm family; population composition. NE.

0264 Rankin, J. O.
1923. *Nebraska Farm Homes: A Comparison of Some Living Conditions of Owners, Part-Owners, and Tenants*. Lincoln, NE: University of Nebraska AES. Bulletin No. 191. USDA, BAE, [DFPRL] cooperating.

Keywords: Structure of agriculture; housing; land tenure; rural life. NE.

0265 Rankin, J. O.
1923. *Nebraska Farm Tenancy: Some Community Phases*. Lincoln, NE: University of Nebraska AES. Bulletin No. 196. USDA, BAE cooperating.

Keywords: Land tenure; community; social organization; social change/trends. NE.

0266 Rankin, J. O.
1924. *Landlords of Nebraska Farms*. Lincoln, NE: University of Nebraska AES. Bulletin No. 202. USDA, BAE,

0266 (continued).
[DFPRL] cooperating.

Keywords: Structure of agriculture; landlords. NE.

0267 Rankin, J. O.
1925. *Tenure and Farm Investment in Nebraska.* Lincoln, NE: University of Nebraska AES. Bulletin No. 205. USDA, BAE, [DFPRL] cooperating.

Keywords: Structure of agriculture; land tenure. NE.

0268 Rankin, J. O.
1926. *Steps to Nebraska Farm Ownership.* Lincoln, NE: University of Nebraska AES. Bulletin No. 210. USDA, BAE, [DFPRL] cooperating.

Keywords: Sociology of agriculture; agricultural ladder. NE.

0269 Rankin, J. O.
1927. *Cost of Feeding the Nebraska Farm Family: A Comparison of Costs and Standards of Food Consumption of Owners, Part-Owners, and Tenants.* Lincoln, NE: University of Nebraska AES. Bulletin No. 219. USDA, BAE, [DFPRL] cooperating.

Keywords: Level of living; farm family. NE.

0270 Rankin, J. O.
1931. *The Cost of Clothing the Nebraska Farm Family.* Lincoln, NE: University of Nebraska AES. Bulletin No. 248. [USDA, BAE, DFPRL cooperating].

Keywords: Level of living; farm family. NE.

0271 Rankin, J. O.
1931. *Housing and House Operation Costs on Nebraska Farms.* Lincoln, NE: University of Nebraska AES. Bulletin No. 264. USDA, BAE, [DFPRL] cooperating.

0271 (continued).
Keywords: Level of living; housing; structure of agriculture; farm family. NE.

0272 Rankin, J. O., and Eleanor H. Hinman.
1932. *A Summary of the Standard of Living in Nebraska Farm Homes.* Lincoln, NE: University of Nebraska AES. Bulletin No. 267. USDA, BAE, [DFPRL] cooperating.

Keywords: Standard of living; structure of agriculture. NE.

0273 Sanderson, Dwight.
1933. *Social and Economic Areas of Broome County, New York, 1928.* Ithaca, NY: Cornell University AES. Bulletin No. 559. USDA, BAE, DFPRL cooperating.

Keywords: Social and economic areas (rural-urban relationships); social organization. NY.

0274 Sanderson, Dwight.
1934. *Rural Social and Economic Areas in Central New York.* Ithaca, NY: Cornell University AES. Bulletin No. 614. USDA, BAE, DFPRL cooperating.

Keywords: Social and economic areas (rural-urban relationships); social organization. NY.

0275 Sanderson, Dwight, and Warren S. Thompson.
1923. *Social Areas of Otsego County.* Ithaca, NY: Cornell University AES. Bulletin No. 422. USDA, [BAE, DFPRL] cooperating.

Keywords: Locality groups; neighborhood; community. NY.

0276 Sanderson, Dwight, and Harold F. Dorn.
1934. "The rural neighborhoods of Otsego County, New York, 1931." Ithaca, NY: Cornell University AES, (Department of Rural Social Organization). Mimeograph Bulletin

0276 (continued).
No. 2. [USDA, BAE, DFPRL cooperating].

Keywords: Neighborhood; social organization. NY.

0277 Sawtelle, Emily H. (see also Hoag).
1924. "The advantages of farm life--a study by correspondence and interviews with eight thousand farm women: Digest of an unpublished manuscript." Mimeo. DC: USDA, BAE, [DFPRL]. {NAL v.63}.

Keywords: Farm women; attitudes/opinions; rural life.

0278 Smick, A. A., and F. R. Yoder.
1929. *A Study of Farm Migration in Selected Communities in the State of Washington.* Pullman, WA: State College of Washington AES. Bulletin No. 233. Contributed by College Division of Farm Management and Agricultural Economics. USDA, BAE, DFPRL cooperating.

Keywords: Migration; youth. WA.

0279 Sterling, Harvey W., and Fred R. Yoder.
1931. *Local Rural Leaders in Washington.* Pullman, WA: State College of Washington AES. Bulletin No. 257. Contributed by College Division of Farm Management and Agricultural Economics. USDA, BAE, DFPRL cooperating.

Keywords: Leadership; community clubs/organizations; farm organizations; attitudes/opinions. WA.

0280 Taylor, Carl C. and Carle C. Zimmerman (compilers and collators). Prepared under the direction of a committee appointed by the State Board of Agriculture consisting of representatives from the North Carolina State College of Agriculture and Engineering, and the University of North Carolina.
1922. *Economic and Social Conditions of North Carolina Farmers: Based on a Survey of 1000 North Carolina Farmers in Three Typical Counties of the State.* Raleigh, NC: North Carolina State College of Agriculture. USDA, BAE,

0280 (continued).
DFPRL cooperating.

Keywords: Socioeconomic status-aggregate/ area; land tenure. Blacks. NC.

0281 Taylor, Edward A.
1934. *The Relationship of the Open-Country Population of Genesee County, New York, to Villages and Cities.* Ithaca, NY: Cornell University AES. Bulletin No. 583. USDA, BAE, DFPRL cooperating. Based in part on September 1931 Cornell University Ph.D thesis.

Keywords: Social and economic areas (rural-urban relationships); social organization; trade centers; towns; villages. NY.

0282 Taylor, Edward A., and F. R. Yoder.
1926. *Rural Social Organization in Whitman County.* Pullman, WA: State College of Washington AES. Bulletin No. 203. Contributed by College Division of Farm Management and Agricultural Economics. USDA, BAE, DFPRL cooperating.

Keywords: Social organization; rural life. WA.

0283 Taylor, Edward A., and F. R. Yoder.
1927. *Rural Social Organization in Whatcom County.* Pullman, WA: State College of Washington AES. Bulletin No. 215. Contributed by College Division of Farm Management and Agricultural Economics. USDA, BAE, DFPRL cooperating.

Keywords: Social organization; rural life. WA.

0284 Taylor, Edward A. and F. R. Yoder.
1928. *Rural Social Organization of Clark County.* Pullman, WA: State College of Washington AES. Bulletin No. 225. Contributed by College Division of Farm Management and Agricultural Economics. USDA, BAE, DFPRL cooperating.

0284 (continued).
Keywords: Social organization; rural life. WA.

0285 Tetreau, E. D.
1930. "Farm family participation in lodges, grange, Farm Bureau, 4-H clubs, school and church." Columbus, OH: Ohio AES. Mimeograph Bulletin No. 29. USDA, BAE, DFPRL cooperating.

Keywords: *Social participation; voluntary associations; community clubs/organizations; farm organizations; 4-H clubs. OH.

0286 Tetreau, E. D.
1931. *Farm Equipment for Communication and Household Convenience as Found on 610 Ohio Farms, Madison and Union Counties, Ohio.* Columbus, OH: Ohio AES. AES Mimeograph Bulletin No. 30. USDA, BAE, DFPRL cooperating.

Keywords: *Level of living. OH.

0287 Thaden, J. F.
1926. *Standard of Living on Iowa Farms.* Ames, IA: Iowa State College of Agriculture and Mechanic Arts AES. Bulletin No. 238. Contributed by Rural Sociology Section. USDA, [BAE], DFPRL cooperating.

Keywords: Standard of living; farm family. IA.

0288 Turner, Veda Larson (see also Veda Larson).
1926. "Causes and conditions of retirement of 100 retired farmers living in Mt. Horeb, Wisconsin: A preliminary report." Mimeo. DC: USDA, BAE, [DFPRL]. {NAL v.63}.

Keywords: Retirement; aging; land tenure. WI.

0289 USDA, BAE.
1925. *Farm Population and Rural Life Socio-Economic Charts.* DC: USDA, BAE, [DFPRL]. {NAL v.63}.

0289 (continued).
Keywords: *Farm population; socioeconomic status-aggregate/ area; graphic analysis.

0290 USDA, BAE.
1930. "The Institute of Methods of Rural Sociological Research held at the Bureau of Agricultural Economics December 31, 1929-January 4, 1930: A summary report." Mimeo. DC: USDA, BAE, [DFPRL]. Agricultural Experiment Stations [Association of Land Grant Colleges and Universities] cooperating. {NAL v.63}.

Keywords: Methodology.

0291 USDA, BAE.
1930. "A supplement to the report of the Institute of Methods of Research in Rural Sociology. Part 1: Report of the Committee on the Case Study Method. Part 2: The case study method, by Dr. Ernest W. Burgess, University of Chicago." Mimeo. DC: USDA, BAE, [DFPRL]. {NAL v.63}.

Keywords: Methodology.

0292 Von Tungeln, George H., Ellis L. Kirkpatrick, C. R. Hoffer, and J. F. Thaden.
1923. *The Social Aspects of Rural Life and Farm Tenantry, Cedar County, Iowa.* Ames, IA: Iowa State College of Agriculture and Mechanic Arts AES. Bulletin No. 217. Contributed by Rural Sociology Section. USDA, BAE, DFPRL cooperating.

Keywords: Level of living; community; attitudes/ opinions. IA.

0293 Von Tungeln, George H., J. F. Thaden, and E. L. Kirkpatrick.
1926. *Cost of Living on Iowa Farms [Part 1]: An Economic and Sociological Study of 472 Farm Families and Farm Homes in Boone, Story, and Sac Counties, Iowa.* Ames, IA: Iowa State College of Agriculture and Mechanic Arts AES.

0293 (continued).
Bulletin No. 237. Contributed by Rural Sociology Section. USDA, BAE, DFPRL cooperating.

Keywords: Level of living. IA.

0294 Wakely, Ray E.
1931. *The Communities of Schuyler County, New York, 1927.* Ithaca, NY: Cornell University AES. Bulletin No. 524. [USDA, BAE, DFPRL cooperating]. Based on September 1928 Cornell University Ph.D. thesis.

Keywords: Community; social organization. NY.

0295 Wasson, C. R., and Dwight Sanderson.
1933. *Relation of Community Areas to Town Government in the State of New York.* Ithaca, NY: Cornell University AES. Bulletin No. 555. [USDA, BAE, DFPRL cooperating].

Keywords: Towns; local government; social and economic areas (rural-urban relationships). NY.

0296 Whittaker, Milo L.
1925. "Rural social agencies in northern Illinois." *Northern Illinois State Teachers College Quarterly* 2(2). De Kalb, IL: Northern Illinois State Teachers College.

Keywords: *Social agencies. IL.

0297 Whittaker, Milo L.
1929. "Rural community organization: A comparative study of two rural communities in northern Illinois." Mimeo. De Kalb, IL: Northern Illinois State Teachers College. USDA, BAE, [DFPRL] cooperating.

Keywords: *Community clubs/organizations. IL.

0298 Willson, E. A.
1928. *Social Organizations and Agencies in North Dakota.* Fargo, ND: North Dakota State College of Agriculture AES. Bulletin No. 221. USDA, [BAE, DFPRL] cooperating.

0298 (continued).
Keywords: Social agencies; community clubs/organizations. ND.

0299 Willson, E. A.
1931. *Rural Community Clubs in North Dakota: Factors Influencing their Success or Failure.* Fargo, ND: North Dakota Agricultural College AES. Bulletin No. 251. USDA, [BAE, DFPRL] cooperating.

Keywords: Community clubs/organizations. ND.

0300 Willson, E. A.
1933. *Incomes and Cost of Living of Farm Families in North Dakota, 1923-1931.* Fargo, ND: North Dakota Agricultural College AES. Bulletin No. 271. USDA, BAE, DFPRL cooperating.

Keywords: Level of living; farm family. ND.

0301 Yoder, Fred R.
1925. *Some Better Things in Farm Life in Washington.* Pullman, WA: State College of Washington AES. Bulletin No. 195. Contributed by Division of Farm Management and Agricultural Economics. USDA, BAE, DFPRL cooperating.

Keywords: Rural life. WA.

0302 Zimmerman, Carle C., and Carl C. Taylor.
1922. *Rural Organization: A Study of Primary Groups in Wake County, NC.* Raleigh, NC: North Carolina AES. Bulletin No. 245. Contributed by North Carolina State College, Department of Agricultural Economics. USDA [Office of Farm Management and Farm Economics, Division of Farm Life Studies] cooperating.

Keywords: Social organization; locality groups; community; trade centers. Blacks. NC.

0303 Zimmerman, Carle C., and John D. Black.
1926. *The Marketing Attitudes of Minnesota Farmers.* University Farm, St. Paul, MN: University of Minnesota AES. Technical Bulletin No. 45. Contributed by University Division of Agricultural Economics. USDA, [BAE], DFPRL cooperating.

Keywords: Attitudes/ opinions; marketing; cooperatives. MN.

B. 1935-1941
0304 Ainsworth, Harry F., Lynn Robertson, E. L. Hartman, O. E. Baker, and Nat T. Frame.
1941. "Rural youth, LaPorte County, Indiana." Mimeo. Lafayette, IN: Purdue University AES and Agricultural Extension Department, and USDA, BAE, [DFPRW] cooperating. {usda 19}.

Keywords: Youth. IN.

0305 Baker, Oliver E.
1935. "Commercial agriculture and the national welfare." Address before Agricultural Extension Conference on November 6, at East Lansing, MI. Undated mimeo. DC: USDA, BAE, [DFPRL]. {usda 4}.

Keywords: Population trends; structure of agriculture; social change/ trends.

0306 Baker, Oliver E.
1935. "Farming as a life work." Address before the Rural Youth Conference on April 27, at University of Illinois. Mimeo. DC: USDA, Extension Service, [Division of Cooperative Extension Work in Agriculture and Home Economics]. Circular 224. Revised under the title "Why I want my boy to be a farmer" for addresses at the Farmers' and Farm Women's Convention on August 4, 1938, at North Carolina State College of Agriculture and Engineering, Raleigh, NC and published February 1939 as Extension Service Circular 300.

0306 (continued).
   Keywords: Rural life.

0307 Baker, Oliver E.
   1935. "The church and the rural youth." Paper prepared for the 13th annual convention of the National Catholic Rural Life Conference at Rochester, NY. Pp. 7-29 in National Catholic Rural Life Conference, *Catholic Rural Life Objectives: A Series of Discussions on Some Elements of Major Importance in the Philosophy of Agrarianism*. St. Paul, MN: National Catholic Rural Life Conference. {usda 4}.

   Keywords: Youth; population trends; church.

0308 Baker, Oliver E.
   1935. "The Outlook for Rural Youth." Based on an address before the State Leaders' Conference, National 4-H Club Camp on June 13, at DC. Mimeo. DC: USDA, Extension Service, [Division of Cooperative Extension Work in Agriculture and Home Economics]. Circular No. 223.

   Keywords: Youth; migration; population; social change/ trends.

0309 Baker, Oliver E.
   1935. "The national welfare and rural urban migration in the U.S.A." A paper prepared for the Internationaler Kongress fur Bevolkerungswissenschaft on August 26-September 1, at Berlin, Germany. Mimeo. New York: Christian Rural Fellowship. Bulletin No. 4. {usda 4}.

   Keywords: Migration; social change/ trends.

0310 Baker. Oliver E.
   1936. "Rural and urban distribution of the population in the United States." *Annals of The American Academy of Political and Social Science*. 188: 264-79.

   Keywords: Farm population; farm population trends.

0311 Baker, Oliver E.
1936. "Rural and urban philosophies." *Rural America* 14(5): 6-8.

Keywords: Rural life.

0312 Baker, Oliver E.
1937. "I want my boy to be a farmer." *Rural America* 15 (7): 2.

Keywords: Rural life.

0313 Baker, Oliver E.
1937. "The effect of recent public policies on the future population prospect." *Rural Sociology* 2(2): 123-141.

Keywords: Population; fertility; migration; population trends.

0314 Baker, Oliver E.
1937. *A Graphic Summary of Physical Features and Land Utilization in the United States.* DC: USDA. Miscellaneous Publication No. 260.

Keywords: Graphic analysis; land use; social change/ trends.

0315 Baker, Oliver E.
1937. *A Graphic Summary of Farm Machinery, Facilities, Roads, and Expenditures (Based largely on the Census of 1930 and 1935).* DC: USDA. Miscellaneous Publication No. 264.

Keywords: Graphic analysis.

0316 Baker, Oliver E.
1937. *A Graphic Summary of the Number, Size, and Type of Farm, and Value of Products (Based largely on the Census of 1930 and 1935).* DC: USDA. Miscellaneous Publication No. 266.

0316 (continued).
Keywords: Graphic analysis; structure of agriculture; social change/ trends.

0317 Baker, Oliver E.
1937. "Significance of population trends to American agriculture." Address to the Population Association of America on October 30, 1936 at Princeton University, Princeton, NJ. *Milbank Memorial Fund Quarterly* 15(2): 121-134.

Keywords: Population trends.

0318 Baker, Oliver E.
1939. *A Graphic Summary of Farm Animals and Animal Products (Based largely on the Census of 1930 and 1935).* DC: USDA Micellaneous Publication No. 269.

Keywords: Graphic analysis; agricultural production; social change/ trends.

0319 Baker, Oliver E.
1939. "Population trends in relation to land use." Address before the Southern Regional Conference of Extension Directors, Supervisors, and Subject-Matter Specialists on February 7, at Texarkana, TX. Address also given on February 10 in Knoxville, TN. Mimeo. DC: USDA, Extension Service, ([Division of] Cooperative Extension Work in Agriculture and Home Economics). Circular No. 311.

Keywords: Population trends; population composition; graphic analysis.

0320 Baker, Oliver E.
1939. "Two trends of great agricultural significance." Address at the Farmers' and Farm Women's Convention on August 3, 1938, at North Carolina State College of Agriculture and Engineering, Raleigh, NC. Also given during September 1938 at four places in Illinois under the joint auspices of the Illinois Agricultural Extension Service and the Illinois Council of Churches. Mimeo. DC: USDA, Extension Service, ([Division of] Cooperative Extension

0320 (continued).
Work in Agriculture and Home Economics). Extension Service Circular No. 306.

Keywords: Structure of agriculture; population; social change/ trends.

0321 Baker, Oliver E.
1939. "The rural family and its significance to organized religion." Address before the 4th annual meeting of the Christian Rural Fellowship on December 2, 1938, at New York, NY. New York: Christian Rural Fellowship. Bulletin No. 43.

Keywords: Rural family; social change/ trends.

0322 Baker, Oliver E.
1940. "Round table on population problems." *American Economic Review, Supplement* 30(1): 386-393.

Keywords: Migration; farm population.

0323 Baker, Oliver E., and Theodore B. Manny.
[1935]. "Population trends and the national welfare: Facts and observations as to rural-urban migration and a declining birth-rate." Undated mimeo. [DC: USDA, BAE, DFPRL]. {usda 4}.

Keywords: Migration; population trends; social change/ trends; public policy.

0324 Baker, Oliver E., and A. B. Genung.
1938. *A Graphic Summary of Farm Crops (Based largely on the Census of 1930 and 1935).* DC: USDA Miscellaneous Publication No. 267.

Keywords: Graphic analysis; agricultural production.

0325 Baker, Oliver E., and Conrad Taeuber.
1940. "The rural people." Pp. 827-847 in *Yearbook of Agriculture, 1940.* DC: GPO. Reprinted in 1941 as Yearbook

0325 (continued).
Separate No. 1763.

Keywords: Population; population composition; population trends.

0326 Bankert, Zetta E. (preparer).
1936. "The farm family standard of living in Codington County, South Dakota." Typed. Brookings, SD: South Dakota State College, Rural Sociology Department. Standard of Living Studies, Bulletin 1. The W[orks] P[rogress] A[dministration], Social Research Division; South Dakota Works Progress Administration; USDA, [BAE], DFPRL; and South Dakota State College, Rural Sociology Department cooperating. {usda 5}.

Keywords: *Standard of living; farm family. SD.

0327 Bankert, Zetta E. (preparer).
1937. "Size of farm and relief status in South Dakota." Brookings, SD: South Dakota State College. Social Research Studies, Mimeo Circular No. 9. The W[orks]P[rogress] A[dministration], Social Research Division; South Dakota Works Progress Administration; USDA, [BAE], DFPRL; and South Dakota State College, Department of Rural Sociology cooperating. {usad 6}.

Keywords: Socioeconomic status-individual/ family; farm size. SD.

0328 Barton, Glen T., and J. G. McNeely.
1939. "Recent changes in farm labor organization in three Arkansas plantation counties: Preliminary report." Mimeo. Fayetteville, AR: University of Arkansas, College of Agriculture AES. College Department of Rural Economics and Sociology. USDA, Agricultural Adjustment Administration, Division of Program Planning, and BAE, DFPRW cooperating.

Keywords: Farm labor; farm systems; plantations. Blacks. AR.

0329 Beers, Howard W., Robin M. Williams, John S. Page, and Douglas Ensminger.
1941. *Community Land-Use Planning Committees: Organization, Leadership, and Attitudes, Garrard County, Kentucky, 1939.* Lexington, KY: University of Kentucky AES. Bulletin No. 417. USDA, BAE, [DFPRW] cooperating.

Keywords: Land-use planning; community; social participation; leadership; attitudes/ opinions. KY.

0330 Bell, Earl H.
1940. "About the people." *Land Policy Review* 3(6): 18.

Keywords: Rural life. Great Plains.

0331 Bell, Earl H.
1940. "A resurvey of Shell Rock community." *Farm Population and Rural Life Activities* 14(2): 1-17.

Keywords: Community; social change/ trends. IA.

0332 Clawson, Marion, Davis McEntire, and C. P. Heisig.
1940. "The migrants: V. 'Stump ranching'." *Land Policy Review* 3(3): 32-38.

Keywords: Migration; level of living.

0333 Coleman, [A] Lee.
1941. "Communities and administrative areas of Greene County, Georgia." A set of maps from Coleman's "Community organization and agricultural planning, Greene County, Georgia," 1942. DC: USDA, BAE, [DFPRW]. {usda 19}.

Keywords: Neighborhood; community; graphic analysis. Blacks. GA.

0334 Coleman, [A] Lee.
1941. "What is America? A study of alleged American traits." *Social Forces* 19(4): 492-499.

0334 (continued).
Keywords: Values.

0335 Cronin, Francis D.
1939. "Displaced families in the land utilization program." Paper read at the annual meeting of the Southwestern Sociological Society on April 7-8, at Dallas, TX. *Southwestern Social Science Quarterly* 20(1): 43-57.

Keywords: Resettlement; Land purchase programs.

0336 Cronin, Francis D., and Howard W. Beers (preparers), under the supervision of T. J. Woofter, Jr. (Works Progress Administration, Division of Social Research, Rural Research Section) and Carl C. Taylor ([USDA], BAE, DFPRL, and Social Research for the Resettlement Administration).
1937. *Areas of Intense Drought Distress, 1930-1936.* DC: Works Progress Administration. Research Bulletin, Series 5, No. 1.

Keywords: Drought; evaluation. Great Plains.

0337 Danhof, Ralph H.
1941. "Defense and decentralization." *Land Policy Review* 4(1): 3-10.

Keywords: Rural industries.

0338 Davidson, Dwight M., Jr., and B. L. Hummel.
1940. *Standards of Living in Six Virginia Counties.* DC: USDA, Farm Security Administration. Social Research Report No. 15. BAE, [DFPRW], Work Projects Administration, and Virginia Polytechnic Institute cooperating.

Keywords: Standard of living. Blacks. VA.

0339 Dodson, Linden S.
1937. *Living Conditions and Population Migration in Four Appalachian Counties.* DC: USDA, Farm Security Administration. Social Research Report No. 3. BAE, [DFPRL] cooperating.

0339 (continued).
Keywords: Farm population; population composition; level of living. Appalachia.

0340 Dodson, Linden S.
1939. *Social Relationships and Institutions in an Established Rurban Community, South Holland, Illinois.* DC: USDA, Farm Security Administration. Social Research Report No. 16. BAE, [DFPRL] cooperating.

Keywords: Social organization; community; schools; church. Dutch. IL.

0341 Dodson, Linden S., Douglas Ensminger, and Robert N. Woodworth.
1940. *Rural Community Organization in Washington and Frederick Counties, Maryland.* College Park, MD: University of Maryland AES. Bulletin No. 437. University of Maryland, Department of Sociology; USDA, BAE, [DFPRW]; and Washington and Frederick County Land Use Planning Committees cooperating.

Keywords: Locality groups; methodology-locality group identification/ classification. MD.

0342 Draper, C. R.
[1940]. "Levels of living in Maine." Undated mimeo. Orono, ME: Maine Agricultural Extension Service and USDA, BAE, [DFPRW] cooperating. {usda 16}.

Keywords: Level of living. ME.

0343 Draper, C. R.
1941. "A study of people and conditions in a low-income farming area of southern Lewis County, West Virginia." Mimeo. Upper Darby, PA: USDA, BAE, [DFPRW]. Lewis County Land Use Planning Committee cooperating. {usda 18}.

Keywords: Socioeconomic status-indvidual/ family. WV.

0344 Draper, C. R., E. J. Niederfrank, and W. C. McKain, Jr.
1940. "Recreation for farm people." *Land Policy Review* 3(4): 18-21.

Keywords: Recreation; land-use planning.

0345 Edwards, Allen D.
1939. *Influence of Drought and Depression on a Rural Community--A Case Study in Haskell County, Kansas.* DC: USDA, Farm Security Administration. Social Research Report No. 7. BAE, [DFPRL] cooperating.

Keywords: Drought; community. KS.

0346 Edwards, Allen D.
1939. "The sociology of drought." *Rural Sociology* 4(2): 150-161.

Keywords: Drought.

0347 Ensminger, Douglas.
1940. "The commmunity in county planning." *Land Policy Review* 3(2): 44-51.

Keywords: Community; planning.

0348 Ensminger, Douglas, and John S. Page.
1940. "A study of churches of Culpeper County, Virginia." Mimeo. DC: [USDA, BAE,DFPRW]. Culpeper Land Use Planning Committee cooperating. {usda 14}.

Keywords: Church. VA.

0349 Folsom, Josiah C.
1936. "Farm labor supply down--wages up." *Agricultural Situation* 20(8): 13-14.

Keywords: Farm wage rates; farm labor.

0350 Folsom, Josiah C.
1937. "Workmen's compensation acts and agricultural

0350 (continued).
labor." *Agricultural Situation* 21(4): 9-10.

Keywords: Social insurance; farm labor.

0351 Folsom, Josiah C.
1937. "Growing demand for farm labor." *Agricultural Situation* 21(2): 6-8.

Keywords: Farm labor.

0352 Folsom, Josiah C.
1938. "The discharged worker looks to the farm." *Agricultural Situation* 22(12): 11-12.

Keywords: Farm labor; social insurance.

0353 Folsom, Josiah C.
1939. "Farm labor conditions in Gloucester, Hunterdon, and Monmouth Counties, New Jersey, April-May, 1936." Mimeo. DC: USDA, BAE, [DFPRL].

Keywords: Farm labor; farm systems; sociology of agriculture. Blacks. NJ.

0354 Folsom, Josiah C.
1940. "The migrant farm laborer." *Agricultural Situation* 24(5): 12-13.

Keywords: Migrant farm workers.

0355 Folsom, Josiah C., and O. E. Baker.
1937. *A Graphic Summary of Farm Labor and Population (Based largely on the Census of 1930 and 1935).* DC: USDA. Miscellaneous Publication No. 265.

Keywords: Graphic analysis; farm labor; population.

0356 Foote, Conie C., and Donald G. Hay (compilers).
[1940]. "Rural housing facilities of selected Farm Security Administration borrowers in North Dakota, South Dakota,

0356 (continued).
Nebraska, and Kansas." Undated mimeo. [DC]: USDA. Farm Security Administration and Bureau of Agricultural Economics, [DFPRW] cooperating. {usda 14}.

Keywords: Housing; level of living; Farm Security Administration. ND; SD; NE; KS.

0357 Forsyth, F. Howard.
1941. "Measuring attitude toward rural and urban life." *Rural Sociology* 6(3): 234-241.

Keywords: Methodology; attitudes/ opinions. Blacks. MN; OK; AL.

0358 Frame, Nat T.
[1941?]. "Rural youth in southern Indiana: Questions for study, investigation, and discussion by older rural youth groups, community and county planning committees, ministerial associations, high school classes, and others." Mimeo. DC: USDA, BAE, [DFPRW]. {usda 19}.

Keywords: Youth. IN.

0359 Fuller, Varden.
1941. "Agricultural labor in relation to agricultural planning for national defense." Pp. 120-128 in *Proceedings of the 14th Annual Meeting of the Western Farm Economics Association* on June 25-27 at Salt Lake City, Utah.

Keywords: Farm labor; land-use planning.

0360 Fuller, Varden (preparer).
1941. "The California farm labor situation, October 1941." Prepared for the State and County Agricultural Planning Committees and Farm Labor Subcommittees of California. Mimeo. Berkeley, CA: USDA, BAE, [DFPRW]. {usda 19}.

Keywords: Farm labor. CA.

0361 Fuller, Varden, and Seymour J. Janow.

0361 (continued).
1940. "The migrants: IV. Jobs on farms in California." *Land Policy Review* 3(2): 34-43.

Keywords: Migration; income. CA.

0362 Fuller, Varden, and E. D. Tetreau.
1941. *Volume and Characteristics of Migration to Arizona, 1930-39*. Tucson, AZ: University of Arizona, Arizona AES. Bulletin No. 176. Arizona State Department of Education and USDA, BAE, [DFPRW] cooperating. Detailed statistical tables and description of methods published in "Statistical supplement to volume and characteristics of migration to Arizona, 1930-39". Undated mimeo. [DC]: USDA, BAE, [DFPRW]. Arizona AES, and Arizona State Department of Education cooperating.

Keywords: Migration. AZ.

0363 Galloway, Robert E.
[1940?]. "Reconnaissance survey of social problems of the rural population within Atlantic County [New Jersey]." Mimeo. New Brunswick, NJ: New Jersey State College of Agriculture, Extension Service, and AES. Atlantic County Board of Agriculture, and Atlantic County Extension Service cooperating. {usda 9}.

Keywords: Community development; agricultural agencies; youth. NJ.

0364 Gessner, Amy A.
1940. *Selective Factors in Migration from a New York Rural Community*. Ithaca, NY: Cornell University AES. Bulletin No. 736. USDA, BAE, [DFPRW] cooperating. A condensation of first part of a September 1939 Cornell University Ph.D. thesis.

Keywords: Migration; population composition. NY.

0365 Goodwin, Dorothy C. (compiler), under the direction of Paul H. Johnstone.

0365 (continued).
1940. "Appendix: A brief chronology of American agricultural history." Pp. 1184-1196 in *Farmers in a Changing World: Yearbook of Agriculture, 1940*. DC: GPO.

Keywords: Rural life; social change/ trends.

0366 Grigsby, S. Earl and Harold Hoffsommer.
1941. *Cotton Plantation Laborers: A Socio-Economic Study of Laborers on Cotton Plantations in Concordia Parish, Louisiana*. [Baton Rouge]: Louisiana State University and Agricultural and Mechanical College AES. Bulletin No. 328. Revision of S. Earl Grigsby's "The social and economic aspects of Negro farm labor on large cotton plantations, Concordia Parish, Louisiana." June 1937 Louisiana State University M.A. thesis.

Keywords: Farm labor; plantations. Blacks. LA.

0367 Grove, Ernest W.
1939. "Farm population, nonfarm population, and number of farms in the United States, 1910-39 (preliminary)." Section 1 of "Part V -- Population, Farms, and Farmers" in *Income Parity for Agriculture*. DC: USDA, BAE, Agricultural Adjustment Administration, and Bureau of Home Economics.

Keywords: Farm population; population.

0368 Halbert, Blanche.
1937. *Hospitals for Rural Communities*. DC: USDA. Farmers Bulletin No. 1792.

Keywords: Hospitals.

0369 Halbert, Blanche.
1938. *Community Buildings for Farm Families*. DC: USDA. Farmers Bulletin No. 1804.

Keywords: Community buildings and centers.

0370 Ham, William T.
1940. "The impact of industrial, labor, and agricultural control policies upon farm labor." *Rural Sociology* 5(1): 46-58.

Keywords: Public policy; farm labor.

0371 Ham, William T.
1941. "Who are the laborers on our farms?" *Land Policy Review* 4(11): 7-11.

Keywords: Land tenure; farm labor; structure of agriculture.

0372 Ham, William T.
1941. "The management of seasonal labor." *Land Policy Review* 4(9): 29-34.

Keywords: Farm labor; migrant farm workers.

0373 Ham, William T.
1941. "Farm labor in an era of change." Pp. 907-921 in *Farmers in a Changing World: The Yearbook of Agriculture, 1940*. DC: USDA. Reprinted as USDA Yearbook Separate No. 1767.

Keywords: Farm labor; socioeconomic status-aggregate/area; rural life; evaluation.

0374 Hamilton, C. Horace.
1937. "Texas farm population changes during 1936." Mimeo. College Station, TX: Texas AES. Progress Report 453. USDA, BAE, [DFPRL] cooperating.

Keywords: Farm population trends. TX.

0375 Hamilton, C. Horace.
1939. "Steel mules." *Land Policy Review* 2(2): 1-7.

Keywords: Mechanization.

0376 Hanger, M. R.
1940. "The population of Coos County, Oregon." Mimeo. DC: USDA, BAE, [DFPRW]. {usda 5}.

Keywords: Population. OR.

0377 Hay, Donald G., James P. Greenlaw, and Lawrence E. Boyle.
1940. *Problems of Rural Youth in Selected Areas of North Dakota*. Fargo: North Dakota Agricultural College, AES. Bulletin No. 293. Contributed by Department of Rural Sociology. USDA, BAE, [DFPRW] cooperating.

Keywords: Youth. ND.

0378 Hitt, Homer L.
1940. "A sampling technique for studying population changes in rural areas." *Social Forces* 19(2): 208-213.

Keywords: Methodology-population analysis.

0379 Hitt, Homer L., and Reed H. Bradford.
1940. "The relation of residential instability to fertility." *Rural Sociology* 4(1): 88-92.

Keywords: Migration; fertility. Blacks.

0380 Hoffsommer, Harold C.
1940. *The Sugar Cane Farm: A Social Study of Labor and Tenancy*. Baton Rouge, LA: Louisiana State University and Agricultural and Mechanical College AESs. Bulletin No. 320. USDA, Agricultural Adjustment Administration, Division of Program Planning, Tenure and Labor Relations Section cooperating.

Keywords: Plantations; farm labor; land tenure. Blacks. LA.

0381 Hoffsommer, Harold C., and Herbert Pryor.
1941. *Neighborhoods and Communities in Covington County, Mississippi*. DC: USDA, BAE, [DFPRW].

0381 (continued).
Keywords: Locality groups; neighborhood; community; methodology-locality group identification/ classification. Blacks. MS.

0382 Holcomb, Ernest J.
1939. "Wage laborers versus sharecroppers." *Agricultural Situation* 23(10): 13-15.

Keywords: Structure of agriculture; farm labor.

0383 Holcomb, Ernest J., and G. H. Aull.
1940. *Sharecroppers and Wage Laborers on Selected Farms in Two Counties in South Carolina.* Clemson, SC: Clemson Agricultural College, South Carolina AES. Bulletin No. 328. USDA, BAE cooperating.

Keywords: Land tenure; farm labor; income; social change/ trends. Blacks. SC.

0384 Holt, John B.
1937. *An Analysis of Methods and Criteria used in Selecting Families for Colonization Projects.* DC: USDA, Farm Security Administration. Social Research Report No. 1. BAE, [DFPRL] cooperating.

Keywords: Family selection for settlement projects.

0385 Holt, John B.
1940. "Holiness religion: Cultural shock and social reorganization." *American Sociological Review* 5(5): 740-747.

Keywords: Religion; social change/ trends; migration.

0386 Holt, John B.
1940. "Report of a reconnaissance survey of neighborhoods and communities of Caswell County, North Carolina, with recommendations." Mimeo. DC: USDA, BAE, [DFPRW]. Caswell County Land Use Planning Committee; and [USDA], BAE, [DFPRW] cooperating.

0386 (continued).
Keywords: Locality groups; neighborhood; community. NC.

0387 Holt, John B.
1941. *Rural Neighborhoods and Communities of Lee County, Alabama.* DC: USDA, BAE, [DFPRW].

Keywords: Locality goups; neighborhood; community. Blacks. AL.

0388 Janow, Seymour J., and Davis McEntire.
1940. "The migrants: VI. Migration to California." *Land Policy Review* 3(4): 24-36.

Keywords: Migration; occupations. CA.

0389 Janow, Seymour J.
1941. "Migration westward: Summary of a decade." *Land Policy Review* 4(10): 10-14.

Keywords: Migration.

0390 Jasny, Marie.
1937. "Discussion: Recent changes in German rural life." *Rural Sociology* 2(3): 278-285.

Keywords: Rural life. Germany.

0391 Jasny, Marie.
1938. *Family Selection on a Federal Reclamation Project--Tule Lake Division of the Klamath Irrigation Project, Oregon-California.* DC: USDA, Farm Security Administration. Social Research Report No. 5. BAE, [DFPRL] cooperating.

Keywords: Family selection for settlement projects; reclamation projects. CA; OR.

0392 Jehlik, Paul J.
1941. "Level of living on the Ropesville Project, Hockley

0392 (continued).
County, Texas." Mimeo. DC: USDA, BAE, [DFPRW]. {usda 18}

Keywords: Level of living; Farm Security Administration; resettlement. TX.

0393 Jehlik, Paul J., and Milton Rossoff.
1941. "John Doe and family on the farm ladder." *Land Policy Review* 4(12): 24-27.

Keywords: Farm tenant purchase program; evaluation.

0394 Johansen, John P.
1941. *One Hundred New Homesteads in the Red River Valley, North Dakota: A Study of the Resettlement and Rehabilitation of Farm Families*. Fargo, ND: North Dakota Agricultural College AES. Bulletin No. 204. Contributed by Department of Rural Sociology. Farm Security Administration cooperating.

Keywords: Resettlement; rural rehabilitation; Farm Security Administration. ND.

0395 Johnson, Helen W. (see also Wheeler).
1940. "Planning by the founding fathers." *Land Policy Review* 3(7): 36-37.

Keywords: Land-use planning; local government; social participation.

0396 Johnstone, Paul H. (preparer).
[1940]. "Culture and agriculture: cultural anthropology in relation to current agricultural problems." Report on a conference on cultural anthropology and the work of the USDA on May 17-19, 1939, at DC. Mimeo. [DC]: USDA, BAE. {usda 14}.

Keywords: Methodology; cultural anthropology.

0397 Johnstone, Paul H.

0397 (continued).
1940. "Grass roots and far horizons." *Land Policy Review* 3(8): 3-12.

Keywords: Rural life; social change/ trends.

0398 Johnstone, Paul H.
1940. "On the identification of the farmer." *Rural Sociology* 5(1): 32-45.

Keywords: Social change/ trends; sociology of agriculture.

0399 Johnstone, Paul H.
1940. "Old ideas versus new ideas in farm life." Pp. 111-170 in *Farmers in a Changing World: Yearbook of Agriculture, 1940*. DC: GPO.

Keywords: Rural life; culture of agriculture; social change/ trends.

0400 Kirkpatrick, E. L.
1938. *Analysis of 70,000 Rural Rehabilitation Families*. DC: USDA, Farm Security Administration, Social Research Report No. 9. BAE, [DFPRL], cooperating.

Keywords: Rural rehabilitation.

0401 Kollmorgen, Walter M.
1940. *The German-Swiss in Franklin County, Tennessee: A Study of the Significance of Cultural Considerations in Farming Enterprises*. DC: USDA, BAE, [DFPRW].

Keywords: Rural life. German-Swiss. TN.

0402 Kollmorgen, Walter M.
1941. "The German settlement in Cullman County, Alabama: An agricultural island in the Cotton Belt." Mimeo. DC: USDA, BAE, [DFPRW].

Keywords: Community. German. AL.

0403 Kraemer, Erich.
1937. *Tenure of New Agricultural Holdings in Several European Countries.* DC: USDA, Farm Security Administration. Social Research Report No. 2. BAE, [DFPRL] cooperating.

Keywords: Land tenure. Europe.

0404 Kumlien, W. F., Charles P. Loomis, Zetta E. Bankert, Edmund deS. Brunner, and Robert L. McNamara.
1938. *The Standard of Living of Farm and Village Families in Six South Dakota Counties, 1935.* Brookings, SD: South Dakota State College of Agriculture and Mechanic Arts AES. Bulletin No. 320. Works Progress Administration, Social Research Division; USDA, Farm Security Administration, Social Research Section; and [USDA], BAE, [DFPRL] cooperating. Also identified as Social Research Report No. 12; DC: USDA, Farm Security Administration, and BAE, [DFPRL], cooperating.

Keywords: Standard of living; farm family; villages. SD.

0405 Kumlien, W. F., Robert L. McNamara, and Zetta E. Bankert.
1938. *Rural Population Mobility in South Dakota (1928-1935).* Brookings, SD: South Dakota State College of Agriculture and Mechanic Arts AES. Bulletin No. 315. Contributed by Department of Rural Sociology. Works Progress Administration, Division of Social Research, and USDA, [BAE, DFPRL] cooperating.

Keywords: Migration; socioeconomic status-individual/family; population trends. SD.

0406 Landis, Paul H.
1940. "Farm population changes during 1939 in Washington State and in the United States." Mimeo. State College of Washington, Washington AES, Division of Rural Sociology, and USDA, BAE, DFPRW cooperating. {usda 15}.

0406 (continued).
Keywords: Farm population trends. WA.

0407 Landis, Paul H., and Carl F. Reuss.
1937. "Washington farm population increases in 1936." Mimeo. Pullman, WA: State College of Washington, Washington AES. Contributed by AES Division of Farm Management and Agricultural Economics. USDA, BAE, DFPRL cooperating. {usda 5}.

Keywords: Farm population trends. WA.

0408 Larson, Olaf F.
1939. "Cultural patterns in relation to economic welfare." Pp. 108-119 in *Proceedings of the 12th annual meeting of the Western Farm Economics Association* June 14-16 at University of California, Berkeley.

Keywords: Social change/ trends.

0409 Larson, Olaf F.
1940. "The people of Dolores County, Colorado: Preliminary report." Mimeo. Amarillo, TX: USDA, BAE, [DFPRW]. Colorado AES cooperating.

Keywords: Population.

0410 Larson, Olaf F.
1940. "Farm population mobility in the Southern Great Plains." *Social Forces* 18(4): 514-520.

Keywords: Farm population; migration. Southern Great Plains.

0411 Leonard, Olen E.
1938. "The enumerator and the farm operator place a value on the farm dwelling." *Rural Sociology* 3(4): 446-447.

Keywords: Methodology.

0412 Leonard, Olen E., and Charles P. Loomis.

0412 (continued).
1939. "A study of mobility and levels of living among Negro sharecropper and wage-laborer families of the Arkansas River valleys." DC: USDA, BAE, [DFPRW]. *Farm Population and Rural Life Activities* 13(2): 1-11. Reprinted as pp. 227-237 in Charles P. Loomis, *Studies of Rural Social Organization in the United States, Latin America and Germany.* East Lansing, MI: State College Book Store, 1945.

Keywords: Land tenure; farm labor; migration; level of living; income-low. Blacks. AR.

0413 Leonard, Olen E., and C. P. Loomis.
1941. *Culture of a Contemporary Rural Community: El Cerrito, New Mexico.* [DC]: USDA, BAE, [DFPRW]. Rural Life Series No. 1.

Keywords: Community; rural life. Spanish American. NM.

0414 Link, Irene (preparer), under the supervision of T. J. Woofter (Works Progress Administration, Division of Social Research, Rural Research Section) and Carl C. Taylor ([USDA], BAE, DFPRL, and Social Research for the Resettlement Administration).
1937. *Relief and Rehabilitation in the Drought Area.* DC: Works Progress Administration, Division of Social Research. Series 5, No. 3.

Keywords: Drought.

0415 Lively, C. E., and Conrad Taeuber.
1939. *Rural Migration in the United States.* DC: Works Progress Administration, Division of Research. Research Monograph No. 19.

Keywords: Migration; farm population; population; rural; population composition; population trends. Blacks.

0416 Longmore, T. Wilson.
1940. "The people of Kit Carson County, Colorado."

0416 (continued).
Mimeo. DC: USDA, BAE, [DFPRW]. Colorado AES cooperating.

Keywords: Population. CO.

0417 Longmore, T. Wilson, Milton Rossoff, T. G. Standing, and Merton Otto (preparers), and T. G. Standing (editor), in consultation with Douglas Ensminger (DFPRW), Roger Stewart (BAE) and Randall C. Hill (Kansas State College).
1940. "Kansas rural communities: A study of Nemaha County." Mimeo. Amarillo, TX: USDA, BAE, [DFPRW]. Kansas AES cooperating.

Keywords: Methodology-locality group identification/classification; locality group; community. Amish. KS.

0418 Loomis, Charles P.
1935. "The group method in rural studies, based on German techniques." *Sociology and Social Research* 20(2): 127-135. Reprinted as pp. 173-177 in Charles P. Loomis, *Studies of Rural Social Organization in the United States, Latin America and Germany.* East Lansing, MI: State College Book Store, 1945.

Keywords: Methodology; community.

0419 Loomis, Charles P.
1935. "The modern settlement movement in Germany: I, Rural; II, Suburban." DC: USDA, BAE, DFPRL. Social Science Research Council cooperating. Part I reprinted as pp. 3-40 in Charles P. Loomis, *Studies of Rural Social Organization in the United States, Latin America and Germany.* East Lansing, MI: State College BookStore, 1945.

Keywords: Resettlement; social organization; population. Germany.

0420 Loomis, Charles P.
1935. "Some attempts to change rural life. I. German. II. Russian." Mimeo. DC: USDA, BAE, DFPRL.

0420 (continued).
Keywords: Sociology of agriculture; farm systems; public policy. Germany; Russia.

0421 Loomis, Charles P.
1936. "The study of the life cycle of families." Contains the substance of a paper prepared for the 12th Congres de l'Institut International de Sociologie on August 25-29, 1935, at Brussels, Belgium. *Rural Sociology* 1(2): 180-199. Reprinted as pp. 190-199 in Charles P. Loomis, *Studies of Rural Social Organization in the United States, Latin America and Germany.* East Lansing, MI: State College Book Store, 1945.

Keywords: Family life cycle; farm family. NC.

0422 Loomis, Charles P.
1937. "Byproduct of a questionaire." *Agricultural Situation* 21(5): 26.

Keywords: Attitudes/ opinions; social change/ trends.

0423 Loomis, Charles P.
1937. "The human ecology of the Great Plains area." Address before the 25th Annual Meeting of the Oklahoma Academy of Science on December 4, 1936, at Oklahoma Agricultural and Mechanical College, Stillwater, OK. *Proceedings of the Oklahoma Academy of Science* 17: 14-28.

Keywords: Drought; soil conservation; migration. Great Plains.

0424 Loomis, Charles P.
1938. "The development of planned rural communities." *Rural Sociology* 3(4): 385-409.

Keywords: Resettlement; community development. Indian-Mexican; Dutch.

0425 Loomis, Charles P.
1939. "Plans and the man." *Land Policy Review* 2(5): 30-34.

0425 (continued).
Keywords: Planning; uses of rural sociology research; Division of Farm Population and Rural Life.

0426 Loomis, Charles P.
1939. "Educational status and its relationship to reading and other activities." *Social Forces* 18(1): 56-59. Reprinted as pp. 238-240 in Charles P. Loomis, *Studies of Rural Social Organization in the United States, Latin America and Germany*. East Lansing, MI: State College Book Store, 1945.

Keywords: Information sources-mass media; education; land tenure; level of living.

0427 Loomis, Charles P.
1939. "Informal social participation in the planned rural communities." *Sociometry* 2(4): 1-37.

Keywords: Social participation; informal groups; community; resettlement.

0428 Loomis, Charles P.
1940. "Rebuilding American community life." Address before the American Sociological Society on December 27, 1939, at Philadelphia. *American Sociological Review* 5(3): 311-324. Reprinted as pp. 144-150 in Charles P. Loomis, *Studies of Rural Social Organization in the United States, Latin America and Germany*. East Lansing, MI: State College Book Store, 1945.

Keywords: Community; subsistence homesteads.

0429 Loomis, Charles P.
1940. *Social Relationships and Institutions in Seven New Rural Communities*. DC: USDA, Farm Security Administration. Social Research Report No. 18. BAE, [DFPRW] cooperating. Reprinted as pp. 41-124 in Charles P. Loomis, *Studies of Rural Social Organization in the United States, Latin America and Germany*. East Lansing, MI: State College Book Store, 1945.

0429 (continued).
Keywords: Resettlement; social participation; community.

0430 Loomis, Charles P.
1941. "Informal groupings in a Spanish-American village." *Sociometry* 4(1): 36-51.

Keywords: Community; social participation; informal groups. Spanish-American. NM.

0431 Loomis, Charles P., and C. Horace Hamilton.
1936. "Family life cycle analysis." *Social Forces* 15(2): 225-231. Reprinted as "The cross-section vs. the historical method in family life cycle analysis," pp. 200-204 in Charles P. Loomis, *Studies in Rural Social Organization in the United States, Latin America and Germany*. East Lansing, MI: State College Book Store, 1945.

Keywords: Methodology; family life cycle.

0432 Loomis, Charles P., E. deS. Brunner, and D. M. Davidson, Jr.
1938. "What the farmer is thinking about." *Rural Sociology* 3(1): 84-88. Reprinted as pp. 187-189 in Charles P. Loomis, *Studies in Rural Social Organization in the United States, Latin America and Germany*. East Lansing, MI: State College Book Store, 1945.

Keywords: Atttitudes/ opinions; depression.

0433 Loomis, Charles P., and O. E. Leonard.
1938. *Standards of Living in an Indian-Mexican Village and on a Reclamation Project*. DC: USDA, Farm Security Administration. Social Research Report No. 14. BAE, [DFPRL] cooperating. Reprinted as "A study of Tortugas, an Indian-Mexican village," pp. 205-226 in Charles P. Loomis, *Studies of Rural Social Organizationin the United States, Latin America and Germany*. East Lansing, MI: State College Book Store, 1945.

0433 (continued).
Keywords: Standard of living; reclamation projects; irrigation. Indian Mexican. NM; CA; OR.

0434 Loomis, Charles P., and L[inden] S. Dodson.
1938. *Standards of Living in Four Southern Appalachian Mountain Counties.* DC: USDA, Farm Security Administration. Social Research Report No. 10. BAE, [DFPRL] cooperating.

Keywords: Standard of living. Appalachia.

0435 Loomis, Charles P., and Dwight M. Davidson, Jr.
1938. *Standards of Living of the Residents of Seven Rural Resettlement Communities.* DC: USDA, Farm Security Administration. Social Research Report No. 11. BAE, [DFPRL] cooperating.

Keywords: Standard of living; resettlement; population composition. Blacks.

0436 Loomis, Charles P., Joseph L. Lister, and Dwight M. Davidson, Jr.
1938. *Standards of Living in the Great Lakes Cut-over Area.* DC: USDA, Farm Security Administration. Social Research Report No. 13. BAE, [DFPRL] cooperating.

Keywords: Standard of living. MN; MI; WI.

0437 Loomis, Charles P., and D[wight] M. Davidson, Jr.
1939. "Measurement of the dissolution of in-groups in the integration of a rural resettlement project." *Sociometry* 2(2): 84-94.

Keywords: Methodology-sociometric; community development; resettlement.

0438 Loomis, Charles P., and Dwight M. Davidson, Jr.
1939. "Social agencies in the planned rural communities." *Sociometry* 2(3): 24-42.

0438 (continued).
Keywords: Social agencies; resettlement.

0439 Loomis, Charles P., and Dwight [M.] Davidson, Jr.
1939. "Sociometrics and the study of new rural communities." *Sociometry* 2(1): 56-76.

Keywords: Methodology-sociometric; community; resettlement.

0440 Loomis, Charles P., Douglas Ensminger, and Jane Wooley.
1941. "Neighborhoods and communities in county planning." *Rural Sociology* 6(4): 339-341.

Keywords: Division of Farm Population and Rural Life; research; locality groups; neighborhood; community.

0441 Mangus, A. R., with the assistance of Robert L. McNamara and Lois E. Meeker.
1941. "The rural youth of Ross County, Ohio: Part 1--Their education and training." Columbus, OH: Ohio State University and Ohio AES. Department of Rural Economics and Rural Sociology, Mimeograph Bulletin No. 140. USDA, BAE, [DFPRW], and Ohio Agricultural Extension Service cooperating.

Keywords: Youth. OH

0442 Mangus, A. R. (preparer), with the assistance of Robert L. McNamara and Lois Meeker.
1941. "The rural youth of Ross County, Ohio: Part 2--Their home, family, and community life." Columbus, OH: Ohio State University and Ohio AES, Department of Rural Economics and Rural Sociology. Mimeograph Bulletin No. 141. USDA, BAE, [DFPRW], and the Ohio Agricultural Extension Service cooperating.

Keywords: Youth. OH.

0443 Manny, Theodore B.
1935. "Population distribution and changes." Pp. 120-136 in *Economic and Social Problems and Conditions of the Southern Appalachians*. Bureau of Agricultural Economics, Bureau of Home Economics, and Forest Service. DC: USDA. Miscellaneous Publication No. 205. Office of Education, U.S. Department of the Interior, and Agricultural Experiment Stations of Tennesee, Virginia, West Virginia, and Kentucky cooperating.

Keywords: Population; farm population; rural nonfarm population. Appalachia.

0444 Manny, Theodore B.
1935. "The conditions of rural life." *American Journal of Sociology* 40(6): 720-728.

Keywords: Level of living; social change/ trends.

0445 Manny, Theodore B.
1935. "The government of Upper Freehold Township." Pp. 11-30 in New Jersey Department of Agriculture, *Upper Freehold Township: A Survey of the Life, Resources and Government of a New Jersey Rural Township, with a Program for Improvement*. Trenton, NJ: New Jersey Department of Agriculture. {usda 4}.

Keywords: Local government. NJ.

0446 Manny, Theodore B.
1935. "School finances in Upper Freehold Township." Pp. 31-34 in New Jersey Department of Agriculture, *Upper Freehold Township: A Survey of the Life, Resources and Government of a New Jersey Rural Township, with a Program for Improvement*. Trenton, NJ: New Jesery Department of Agriculture. {usda 4}.

Keywords: Schools. NJ.

0447 Manny, Theodore B.
1935. "Some economic and social conditions reported by

0447 (continued).
farm families in Upper Freehold Township." Pp. 35-56 in New Jersey Department of Agriculture, *Upper Freehold Township: A Survey of the Life, Resources and Government of a New Jersey Rural Township, with a Program for Improvement.* Trenton, NJ: New Jersey Department of Agriculture. {usda 4}.

Keywords: Level of living; farm family. NJ.

0448 Manny, Theodore B.
1935. "Farm population, January 1, 1935." *Agricultural Situation* 19(5): 2-5.

Keywords: Farm population; farm population trends; migration.

0449 Manny, Theodore B.
1936. "The Division of Farm Population anf Rural Life, U. S. Department of Agriculture." *Rural America* 14(2): 12-13.

Keywords: Division of Farm Population and Rural Life.

0450 Mathews, M. Taylor, David R. Jenkins, and Raymond F. Sletto.
1942. *Attitudes of Edgefield County Farmers Toward Farm Practices and Rural Programs.* South Carolina AES of Clemson Agricultural College, South Carolina AES. Bulletin No. 339. USDA, BAE, [DFPRW] cooperating.

Keywords: Attitudes/ opinions. SC.

0451 [citation deleted].

0452 McEntire, Davis.
1941. "Migration and resettlement in the far western states." *Journal of Farm Economics* 23(2): 478-482.

Keywords: Migration; resettlement. CA; AZ; OR; WA; ID.

0453 McEntire, Davis, and N. L. Whetten.
1939. "The Migrants: I. Recent migration to the Pacific coast." *Land Policy Review* 2(5): 7-17.

Keywords: Migration. Pacific Coast.

0454 McKain, Walter C., Jr.
1939. "The concept of plane of living and the construction of a plane of living index." *Rural Sociology* 4(3): 337-343.

Keywords: Methodology-levels of living indicators/ scales. VT.

0455 McNamara, Robert L.
1941. "Farmers study their communities in Hand County, South Dakota." DC: USDA, BAE, [DFPRW]; Hand County Land Use Planning Committee; and South Dakota AES, Rural Sociology Department cooperating. {usda 19}.

Keywords: Social organization; locality groups. SD.

0456 McNamara, Robert L., and A. R. Mangus.
1941. "The rural youth of Ross County, Ohio: Part 3-- Their employment and occupations." Columbus, OH: Ohio State University and Ohio AES. Mimeograph Bulletin No. 142. The USDA, BAE, [DFPRW], and Ohio Agricultural Extension Service cooperating.

Keywords: Youth. OH.

0457 Meldrum, Gilbert, and Ruth Sherburne.
1941. *Rural Youth in Massachusetts*. Amherst, MA: Massachusetts State College, Massachusetts AES. Bulletin No. 386.

Keywords: Youth. MA.

0458 Miner, Horace.
1939. "Culture and agriculture." Pp. 48-56 in *Standards of Value for Program Planning and Building: Proceedings of*

0458 (continued).
School for Washington Staff of BAE, October 17-20. Mimeo. DC: USDA, BAE.

Keywords: Rural life.

0459 Nichols, Ralph R.
1941. "Locating neighborhoods and communities in Red River Parish, Louisiana." Mimeo. Baton Rouge, LA: Louisiana State University. USDA, BAE, [DFPRW], and Louisiana State Extension Service cooperating. {usda 18}.

Keywords: Locality groups; community; neighborhood; methodology-locality group identification/ classification. Blacks. LA.

0460 Nichols, Ralph R.
1941. "Short cuts in community delineation procedure." Dittoed. [DC]: [USDA], BAE, [DFPRW]. {usda 20}.

Keywords: Methodology-locality group identification/ classification.

0461 Nichols, Ralph R., and John S. Page.
1941. "Community and neighborhood areas, Lincoln County, Oklahoma." Mimeo. DC: USDA, BAE, [DFPRW]. Oklahoma Joint Land-Grant Colege--BAE Committee cooperating. {usda 18}.

Keywords: Locality groups; community; neighborhood; methodology-locality group identification/ classification. OK.

0462 Niederfrank, E. J., and C. R. Draper.
1940. *Use of Recreation Sites Developed on Federal Submarginal Land-Purchase Areas in Maine.* Orono, ME: University of Maine, College of Agriculture, [AES]. Bulletin No. 280. USDA, BAE, [DFPRW] cooperating.

Keywords: Recreation; land purchase programs. ME.

0463 Page, John S., and Paul T. Sant (preparers).
1941. "Identification of neighborhoods and communities: Roane County, Tennessee." Mimeo. Knoxville, TN: University of Tennessee, Agricultural Extension Service; USDA, BAE, [DFPRW], and University of Tennessee AES cooperating. {usda 18}.

Keywords: Locality groups; community; neighborhood. Blacks. TN.

0464 Parmelee, Maurice, and Olen E. Leonard.
1939. "A social and cultural survey in the tobacco region of southern Maryland." *Farm Population and Rural Life Activities* 13(1): 1-17.

Keywords: Soil conservation; attitudes/ opinions. MD.

0465 Provinse, John H., and Carl C. Taylor.
1940. "Sociological considerations in a national policy for agriculture." Pp. 109-117 in *Proceedings of the 13th annual meeting of the Western Farm Economics Association* at Pullman, WA. Also published as an undated mimeo. [DC]: USDA, BAE, [DFPRW].

Keywords: Public policy; uses of rural sociology research.

0466 Reuss, Carl F., and Lloyd H. Fisher.
1941. *The Adjustment of New Settlers in the Yakima Valley, Washington*. Pullman, WA: State College of Washington AES. Bulletin No. 397. Division of Rural Sociology and the USDA, BAE, [DFPRW] cooperating. Also published as *New Settlers in Yakima Valley, Washington*. Washington, DC: USDA, BAE, DFPRW, Migration and Settlement on the Pacific Coast, Report No. 8. Washington AES, cooperating, 1941.

Keywords: Migration; resettlement. WA.

0467 Robertson, Lynn, H. F. Ainsworth, W. V. Rush, O. E. Baker, and Nathaniel T. Frame.
1940. "Rural youth: Blackford County, Indiana." Mimeo.

0467 (continued).
Lafayette, IN: Purdue University AES, and USDA, BAE, [DFPRW]. {usda 14}.

Keywords: Youth. IN.

0468 Robertson, Lynn, with the assistance of Harry F. Ainsworth, Nat T. Frame, O. E. Baker, and Warren O'Hara.
[1941?]. "Facts collected by Older Rural Youth of Hancock County [Indiana]." Mimeo. Purdue University, AES and Agricultural Extension Department, and the USDA, BAE, [DFPRW] cooperating. {usda 19}.

Keywords: Youth. IN.

0469 Roskelley, R. W., and Olaf F. Larson.
1939. *Educational Foundations for Rural Rehabilitation.* Fort Collins, CO: Colorado State College, Colorado Experiment Station. Bulletin No. 457. Experiment Station, Cooperative Plan of Rural Research, and Federal Work Projects Administration, Rural Section cooperating.

Keywords: Education; rural rehabilitation. CO.

0470 Rural Sociological Society of America and the BAE (prepared by a committee).
1938. "The field of research in rural sociology." Mimeo. DC: USDA, BAE, [DFPRL].

Keywords: Research.

0471 Sanders, Irwin T., and Douglas Ensminger.
1940. *Alabama Rural Communities: A Study of Chilton County.* Montevevallo, AL: Alabama College. Bulletin No. 136 (Vol 33, No. 1A). USDA, BAE, [DFPRW] cooperating.

Keywords: Community; social organization; methodology-locality groups identification/ classification. Blacks. AL.

0472 Schuler, Edgar A.
1938. *Social Status and Farm Tenure--Attitudes and Social*

0472 (continued).
Conditions of Corn Belt and Cotton Belt Farmers. DC: USDA, Farm Security Administration. Social Research Report No. 4. BAE, [DFPRL] cooperating.

Keywords: Land tenure; race; agricultural ladder; migration; level of living; standard of living; attitudes/ opinions. Blacks.

0473 Schuler, Edgar A.
1938. "The present social status of American farm tenants." Paper presented before the American Sociological Association, Section on Rural Sociology, December 1937 at Atlantic City, NJ. *Rural Sociology* 3(1): 20-33.

Keywords: Social status; land tenure. Blacks.

0474 Shafer, Karl.
1937. *A Basis for Social Planning in Coffee County, Alabama.* DC: USDA, Farm Security Administration. Social Research Report No. 6. BAE, [DFPRL] cooperating.

Keywords: Population composition; population trends; community clubs/ organizations; planning; community buildings and centers. Blacks. AL.

0475 [citation deleted].

0476 Taeuber, Conrad.
1936. "Farm population was virtually stationary last year." *Agricultural Situation* 20(11): 3-6.

Keywords: Farm population; farm population trends; migration.

0477 Taeuber, Conrad.
1936. "The farm population of the Great Plains." *Agricultural Situation* 20(9): 13-17.

Keywords: Farm population; farm population trends; migration. Great Plains.

0478 Taeuber, Conrad.
1936. "A registration system as a source of data concerning internal migration." *Rural Sociology* 1(4): 441-451.

Keywords: Migration; population composition. Germany.

0479 Taeuber, Conrad.
1937. "Population adjustments in the Great Plains." *Agricultural Situation* 21(9): 21-22.

Keywords: Farm population; farm population trends; migration. Great Plains.

0480 Taeuber, Conrad.
1937. "Farm population decreases during 1936." *Agricultural Situation* 21(7): 17-18.

Keywords: Farm population; farm population trends; migration.

0481 Taeuber, Conrad.
1937. "Aesthetics and decimals." *Rural Sociology* 2(3): 334.

Keywords: Methodology.

0482 Taeuber, Conrad.
1938. "Changes in farm population." *Agricultural Situation* 22(6): 11-12.

Keywords: Farm population; farm population trends; mechanization.

0483 Taeuber, Conrad.
1938. "The movement to Southern farms, 1930-35." *Rural Sociology* 3(1): 69-76.

Keywords: Migration; population trends. Blacks. South.

0484 Taeuber, Conrad.
1939. "Farm population--near record." *Agricultural Situation* 23(6): 17-18.

0484 (continued).
Keywords: Farm population; farm population trends; mechanization.

0485 Taeuber, Conrad.
1939. "Rural-urban migration in an industrialized nation." Pp. 84-89 in *Proceedings of the National Conference on Planning* held on May 15-17 at Boston, MA. Chicago, IL: American Society of Planning Officials.

Keywords: Migration.

0486 Taeuber, Conrad.
1939. "Agriculture and current population trends." Paper presented at Symposium on Population Growth on November 18, 1938. *Proceedings of the American Philosophical Society* 80(4): 477-89.

Keywords: Population trends. Blacks.

0487 Taeuber, Conrad.
1940. "Our changing farm population." *Agricultural Situation* 24(8): 17-19.

Keywords: Farm population; farm population trends; migration.

0488 Taeuber, Conrad.
1940. "Migration and rural population adjustment." *Rural Sociology* 5(4): 399-410.

Keywords: Migration; farm population trends.

0489 Taeuber, Conrad.
1941. "Changes in the farm population." *Agricultural Situation* 25(4): 16-19.

Keywords: Farm population; farm population trends; population composition.

0490 Taeuber, Conrad.

0490 (continued).
1941. "Analysis shows marked changes in Nebraska population." *Nebraska Education Bulletin* 6(1): 3.

Keywords: Population trends. NE.

0491 Taeuber, Conrad.
1941. "Rural-urban migration." *Agricultural History* 15(3): 151-160.

Keywords: Migration.

0492 Taeuber, Conrad, and Charles S. Hoffman.
1937. "Recent migration from the drought areas." *Land Policy Circular*, September: 16-20.

Keywords: Migration; drought.

0493 Taeuber, Conrad, and Carl C. Taylor (preparers), under the supervision of T. J. Woofter (Works Progress Administration, Division of Social Research, Rural Research Section) and Carl C. Taylor (BAE, DFPRL, and Social Research for the Resettlement Administration).
1937. *The People of the Drought States*. DC: Works Progress Administration, Division of Social Research, Series 5. No. 2.

Keywords: Population; population trends; migration; drought. Great Plains.

0494 Taeuber, Conrad, and Irene B. Taeuber.
1938. "Measures of changes in fertility in Germany." *Journal of the American Statistical Association* 33(204): 709-712.

Keywords: Fertility; population trends. Germany.

0495 Taeuber, Conrad, and Irene B. Taeuber.
1938. "Short distance interstate migrations." *Social Forces* 16(4): 503-506.

0495 (continued).
Keywords: Migration. Blacks.

0496 Taeuber, Conrad, and Irene B. Taeuber.
1940. "Negro rural fertility ratios in the Mississippi Delta." *Southwestern Social Science Quarterly* 21(3): 210-220.

Keywords: Fertility. Blacks. MS.

0497 Taeuber, Conrad, and Irene B. [Taeuber].
1940. "German fertility trends, 1933-39." *American Journal of Sociology* 46(2): 150-164.

Keywords: Fertility; population trends. Germany.

0498 Taeuber, Conrad, and Rachel Rowe [see also Swiger].
1941. *Five Hundred Families Rehabilitate Themselves: Summarized from Annual Reports of Twenty-two Farm Security Administration Farm and Home Supervisors.* DC: USDA, BAE, [DFPRW], and Farm Security Administration cooperating.

Keywords: Rural rehabilitation; Farm Security Administration; evaluation.

0499 Taylor, Carl C.
1935. "What kind of rural life can we look forward to in the United States?" (Presidential address.) Pp. 5-18 in *Country Life Programs, Proceedings of the 18th American Country Life Conference*, September 19-22, at Columbus, OH. Chicago: University of Chicago Press for the American Country Life Association.

Keywords: Rural life.

0500 Taylor, Carl C.
1937. "Population changes in southern states." *Agricultural Situation* 21(4): 17-18.

Keywords: Population; population composition; population trends. South.

0501 Taylor, Carl C.
1937. "Opportunities in the field of rural sociology." *Rural America* 15(4): 13-14.

Keywords: Sociology-rural sociology.

0502 Taylor, Carl C.
1937. "What shall we conserve in rural life?" Pp. 46-51 in *The People and the Land, Proceedings of the 20th American Country Life Conference*, October 14-16, at Manhattan, KS. Chicago: University of Chicago Press for the American Country Life Association. A condensed version of this address was published under the same title in *Rural America* 15 (December 1937): 7-8.

Keywords: Rural life.

0503 Taylor, Carl C.
1937. "Attaining a national policy and program of conservation." Pp. 18-33 in *Education for Democracy, Proceedings of the 19th American Country Life Conference,* August 10-13, 1936, at Kalamazoo, MI. Chicago: Chicago University Press for the American Country Life Association. Same address given August 10, 1936 before the National Rural Forum, Teachers College, Columbia University, NY. A condensed version of this address was published under the same title in *Rural America* 14 (December 1963): 3-7.

Keywords: Public policy.

0504 Taylor, Carl C.
1937. "The sociology of family life." *Journal of Home Economics* 29(8): 512-516.

Keywords: Sociology-rural sociology; rural family.

0505 Taylor, Carl C.
1937. "Sociology on the spot." *Rural Sociology* 2(4): 373-381.

Keywords: Sociology-rural sociology.

0506 Taylor, Carl C.
1938. "Resettlement." Pp. 253-256 in "The remedies: Policies for private lands," by George S. Wehrwein, Clarence I. Henderson, Philip M. Glick, Carl C. Taylor, Francis R. Kenny, and Marshall Harris, pp. 241-264 in *Soils and Men: Yearbook of Agriculture, 1938*. DC: GPO. Article also distributed as Yearbook Separate No. 1619.

Keywords: Resettlement; evaluation.

0507 Taylor, Carl C.
1938. "The social elements in land planning." *Plan Age* 4(6): 149-155.

Keywords: Land-use planning.

0508 Taylor, Carl C.
1938. "Constructive measures for dealing with the South's population problems." *Rural Sociology* 3(3): 239-257.

Keywords: Public policy; population. South.

0509 Taylor, Carl C.
1938. "The human aspects of land-use planning." *Land Policy Review* 1(3): 6-10.

Keywords: Land-use planning.

0510 Taylor, Carl C.
1939. "The interdependence of rural and urban women." Pp. 154-159 in *Disadvantaged People in Rural Life, Proceedings of the 21st American Country Life Conference*, November 2-4, 1938, at Lexington, KY. Chicago: Chicago University Press for the National Country Life Association. Condensed version of this address was published under the same title in *Rural America* 17(March 1939): 3-4.

Keywords: Women; social participation.

0511 Taylor, Carl C.
1939. "The work of the Division of Farm Population and

0511 (continued).
Rural Life of the Bureau of Agricultural Economics, U. S. Department of Agriculture." *Rural Sociology* 4(2): 221-228.

Keywords: Division of Farm Population and Rural Life.

0512 Taylor, Carl C.
1939. "Prospective development of cultural patterns in rural America and their possible influence on population trends." Paper presented at Symposium on Population Growth, November 18, 1938. *Proceedings of the American Philosophical Society* 80(4): 569-85.

Keywords: Rural life; population trends.

0513 Taylor, Carl C.
1940. "Social theory and social action." (Presidential address before the Rural Sociological Society, Philadelphia, PA, December 27, 1939) *Rural Sociology* 5(1):17-31.

Keywords: Theory; uses of rural sociology research.

0514 Taylor, Carl C.
1940. "Recruiting personnel for government service." *Rural Sociology* 5(4): 460-462.

Keywords: Sociology-rural sociology.

0515 Taylor, Carl C.
1940. "The contribution of sociology to agriculture." Pp. 1042-1055 in *Farmers in a Changing World: Yearbook of Agriculture, 1940*. DC: GPO. Reprinted in 1941 as USDA Yearbook Separate No. 1774.

Keywords: Uses of rural sociology research.

0516 Taylor, Carl C.
1941. "Social science and social action in agriculture." *Social Forces* 20(2): 154-159.

0516 (continued).
Keywords: Division of Farm Population and Rural Life; uses of rural sociology research.

0517 Taylor, Carl C.
1941. "Discussion of Dr. Charles P. Loomis' paper on informal groupings in a Spanish-American village." *Sociometry* 4(1): 52-55.

Keywords: Methodology; uses of rural sociology research.

0518 Taylor, Carl C., and Conrad Taeuber.
1937. "Social factors associated with farm tenancy." *Agricultural Situation* 21(2): 2-6.

Keywords: Land tenure; standard of living; level of living.

0519 Taylor, Carl C., Bushrod W. Allin, and O. E. Baker.
1938. "Public purposes in soil use." Pp. 47-59 in *Soils and Men: Yearbook of Agriculture, 1938*. DC: GPO. Also published as Yearbook Separate No. 1608.

Keywords: Soil conservation; migration; resettlement.

0520 Taylor, Carl C., and Charles P. Loomis.
1938. "The American rural culture of the future: What the rural sociologists and agricultural economists think it should and will be." *Farm Population and Rural Life Activities* 12(4): 1-14. Reprinted pp. 178-186 in Charles P. Loomis, *Studies of Rural Social Organization in the United States, Latin America and Germany*. East Lansing, MI: State College Book Store, 1945.

Keywords: Attitudes/ opinions; rural life.

0521 Taylor, Carl C., and Conrad Taeuber.
1938. "Constructive rural farm population policies." *Milbank Memorial Fund Quarterly* 16(3): 233-252.

Keywords: Farm population; population trends; public policy.

0522 Taylor, Carl C., Helen W. Wheeler [see also Johnson], and E[llis] L. Kirkpatrick.
1938. *Disadvantaged Classes in American Agriculture.* DC: USDA, Farm Security Administration. Social Research Report No. 8. BAE, [DFPRL] cooperating.

Keywords: Structure of agriculture; income-low; land tenure; farm labor; level of living. Blacks.

0523 Taylor, Carl C., and Helen W. Wheeler (see also Johnson).
1938. "Disadvantaged classes in agriculture." *Agricultural Situation* 22(11): 17-18.

Keywords: Income-low.

0524 Taylor, Carl C., and Conrad Taeuber.
1939. "Wanted: population adjustment, too." *Land Policy Review* 2(2): 20-26.

Keywords: Population; land-use planning.

0525 University of Missouri, College of Agriculture.
[1937]. "Proceedings of the First Mid-western Conference on Rural Population Research, April 23-24, 1937." Sponsored by the University of Missouri, College of Agriculture, and the USDA, BAE, DFPRL. Undated mimeo. Columbia, MO: University of Missouri, College of Agriculture AES. {usda 7}.

Keywords: Methodology-population analysis.

0526 [USDA, BAE, DFPRW].
[1940?]. "Significant social facts for county and community planning committees to know about their county." Undated mimeo. [DC: USDA, BAE, DFPRW.] {usda 17}.

Keywords: Planning.

0527 USDA, BAE, [DFPRW].
1940. *Communities and Neighborhoods in Land Use Planning.*

0527 (continued).
DC: GPO. County Planning Series No. 6. USDA, BAE, and USDA, Extension Service cooperating.

Keywords: Methodology-locality group identification/classification; land-use planning.

0528 USDA, BAE, [DFPRW].
1941. "Agricultural census analyses--Changes in land in farms by size of farm." Analyses done for selected states, 1930-1940. Mimeo. DC: USDA, BAE, [DFPRW]. Work Projects Administration cooperating. {usda 20}.

Keywords: Farm size; structure of agriculture.

0529 USDA, BAE, DFPRW.
1940. "Service and research in community organization." Undated mimeo. DC: USDA,BAE, [DFPRW]. {usda 17}.

Keywords: Division of Farm Population and Rural Life.

0530 USDA, BAE, DFPRW.
1941. "Farm labor reconnaissance surveys." *Farm Population and Rural Life Activities* 15(2): 1-7.

Keywords: Farm labor; methodology.

0531 USDA, Farm Security Administration, and BAE.
1941. "An analysis of farm and home plans and record books on 170 FSA farms in the cotton area of FSA Region XII in Texas, 1940." Mimeo. Amarillo, TX: USDA, Farm Security Administration. BAE, Division of Farm Management and Costs, and DFPRW cooperating.

Keywords: Farm Security Administration; rural rehabilitation; evaluation. TX.

0532 Vasey, Tom, and Josiah C. Folsom.
1937. *Survey of Agricultural Labor Conditions in Karnes County, Texas.* DC: USDA, Farm Security Administration. BAE, [DFPRL] cooperating.

0532 (continued).
Keywords: Farm labor. Blacks; Mexicans. TX.

0533 Vasey, Tom, and Josiah C. Folsom.
1937. *Survey of Agricultural Labor Conditions in Livingston County, Illinois.* DC: USDA, Farm Security Administration. BAE, [DFPRL] cooperating.

Keywords: Farm labor. IL.

0534 Vasey, Tom, and Josiah C. Folsom.
1937. *Survey of Agricultural Labor Conditions in Fentress County, Tennessee.* DC: USDA, Farm Security Administration. BAE, [DFPRL] cooperating.

Keywords: Farm labor. TN.

0535 Vasey, Tom, and Josiah C. Folsom.
1937. *Survey of Agricultural Labor Conditions in Archuleta County, Colorado.* DC: USDA, Farm Security Administration. BAE, [DFPRL] cooperating.

Keywords: Farm labor. Mexicans. CO.

0536 Vasey, Tom, and Josiah C. Folsom.
1937. *Survey of Agricultural Labor Conditions in Hamilton County, Iowa.* DC: USDA, Farm Security Administration. BAE, [DFPRL] cooperating.

Keywords: Farm labor. IA.

0537 Vasey, Tom, and Josiah C. Folsom.
1937. *Survey of Agricultural Labor Conditions in Pawnee County, Kansas.* DC: USDA, Farm Security Administration. BAE, [DFPRL] cooperating.

Keywords: Farm labor. KS.

0538 Vasey, Tom, and Josiah C. Folsom.
1937. *Survey of Agricultural Labor Conditions in Todd County, Kentucky.* DC: USDA, Farm Security Administra-

0538 (continued).
tion. BAE, [DFPRL] cooperating.

Keywords: Farm labor. Blacks. KY.

0539 Vasey, Tom, and Josiah C. Folsom.
1937. *Survey of Agricultural Labor Conditions in Concordia Parish, Louisiana.* DC: USDA, Farm Security Administration. BAE, [DFPRL] cooperating.

Keywords: Farm labor. Blacks. LA.

0540 Vasey, Tom, and Josiah C. Folsom.
1937. *Survey of Agricultural Labor Conditions in Lac Qui Parle County, Minnesota.* DC: USDA, Farm Security Administration. BAE, [DFPRL] cooperating.

Keywords: Farm labor. MN.

0541 Vasey, Tom, and Josiah C. Folsom.
1937. *Survey of Agricultural Labor Conditions in Wayne County, Pennsylvania.* DC: USDA, Farm Security Administration. BAE, [DFPRL] cooperating.

Keywords: Farm labor. PA.

0542 Vasey, Tom, and Josiah C. Folsom.
1937. *Survey of Agricultural Labor Conditions in Placer County, California.* DC: USDA, Farm Security Administration. BAE, [DFPRL] cooperating.

Keywords: Farm labor. Orientals. CA.

0543 Voelker, Stanley W., and T. Wilson Longmore.
1939. "Assessment of dry-farming and grazing lands in Weld County, Colorado." Lincoln, NE: USDA, BAE.

Keywords: *Land-use planning. CO.

0544 Wilkening, Eugene A., and Cecil L. Gregory.
1941. *Planning for Family Relocation (Preliminary Report on*

0544 (continued).
Procedures Followed and Results Obtained in Evacuation of the Basin of the Wappapello Dam, Wayne County, Missouri). Columbia, MO: University of Missouri, College of Agriculture AES. Bulletin No. 427. Missouri AES, Rural Sociology Department, and USDA, BAE, [DFPRW] cooperating.

Keywords: Family relocation. MO.

0545 Yoder, Fred R., and A. A. Smick.
1935. *Migration of Farm Population and Flow of Farm Wealth.* Pullman, WA: State College of Washington AES. Bulletin No. 315. Contributed by College Department of Sociology and Division of Farm Management and Agricultural Economics. USDA, BAE, DFPRL cooperating.

Keywords: Migration; population trends; wealth. WA.

0546 Young, Kimball.
1939. "The relation of the administrator to the farmer and the expert." Pp. 93-103 in *Standards of Value for Program Planning and Building: Proceedings of School for Washington Staff of BAE,* October 17-20, 1939. Mimeo. DC: USDA, BAE.

Keywords: Planning; rural life.

C. 1942-1945

0547 Alexander, Frank D.
1944. "A mountain school in the life of a community." *Mountain Life and Work* 20(4): 3-8.

Keywords: Schools; community; social organization. GA.

0548 Alexander, Frank D.
1944. "Some effects of two years of war on a rural community." Condensation of a paper read before the Eighth

0548 (continued).
Annual Meeting of the Southern Sociological Society on March 31, at Atlanta, GA. *Social Forces* 23(2): 196-201.

Keywords: World War II-impacts on rural areas; population; community; social agencies; rural family. GA.

0549 Alexander, Frank D.
1945. "A rural community in time of war: The Valley community in Rabun County, Georgia." Mimeo. Atlanta, GA: USDA, BAE, [DFPRW]. {usda 41}.

Keywords: World War II-impacts on rural areas; community. Blacks. GA.

0550 Alexander, Frank D.
1945. "Constructive measures for Southern rural communities." *Social Forces* 24(2): 181-185.

Keywords: Community; rural life. Blacks. South.

0551 Almack, Ronald B., and Ruth McCammon.
1943. "Report on the Share the Meat Campaign in Missouri." Mimeo. Milwaukee, WI: USDA, BAE, [DFPRW]. {usda 27}.

Keywords: World War II-mobilization of local areas. MO.

0552 Almack, Ronald B., and Cannon C. Hearne.
1944. *Suggestions for Securing Effective Participation of Rural People in Educational Programs*. Columbia, MO: University of Missouri, College of Agriculture, Agricultural Extension Service. Manual 35. University of Missouri College of Agriculture and USDA, BAE, [DFPRW] cooperating.

Keywords: Extension.

0553 Anderson, Anton H.
[1943]. "The rural neighborhood has gone to war." Mimeo. Lincoln, NE: USDA, BAE, [DFPRW]. {usda 33}.

0553 (continued).
Keywords: World War II-mobilization of local areas; methodology-locality group identification/ classification. Northern Great Plains.

0554 Anderson, Anton H.
1943. "The neighborhood leader in time of war." Mimeo. Lincoln, NE: USDA, BAE, [DFPRW]. {usda 27}.

Keywords: World War II-mobilization of local areas; leadership; neighborhood.

0555 Anderson, Anton H.
1943. "Farmers in Buffalo County, Nebraska, mobilize for war." Mimeo. Lincoln, NE: USDA, BAE, [DFPRW]. {usda 29}.

Keywords: World War II-mobilization of local areas; leadership; methodology-local leader identification. NE.

0556 Anderson, Anton H.
1943. "Government payments to agriculture in Boone County, Nebraska, 1936-39." Mimeo. Lincoln, NE: USDA, BAE, [DFPRW]. {usda 32}.

Keywords: Public policy; Agricultural Adjustment Administration; Farm Security Administration; farm size; land tenure; land use. NE.

0557 Anderson, Anton H.
1943. "Neighborhood leadership organization in three sample counties in Kansas." Dittoed. Lincoln, NE: USDA, BAE, [DFPRW], and Kansas State Extension Service cooperating.

Keywords: *Leadership-neighborhood. KS.

0558 Anderson, Anton H.
1943. "The neighborhood group approach in the war effort." Mimeo. Lincoln, NE: USDA, BAE, [DFPRW]. {usda 27}.

0558 (continued).
Keywords: World War II-mobilization of local areas; neighborhood.

0559 Anderson, Anton H.
1944. "Experience with organization for wartime programs (Adams, Boulder, Elbert, El Paso, Logan and Washington Counties, Colorado)." Dittoed. Lincoln, NE: USDA, BAE, [DFPRW].

Keywords: *World War II-mobilization of local areas. CO.

0560 Anderson, Anton H.
1944. "Neighborhood leader system in selected counties in Kansas (Greenwood, Hamilton, and Pawnee)." Dittoed. Lincoln, NE: USDA, BAE, [DFPRW].

Keywords: *Leadership-neighborhood. KS.

0561 Anderson, Anton H.
1944. "Reconnaissance mail survey, Neighborhood Action Groups, FSA Region VII." Dittoed. Lincoln, NE: USDA, BAE, [DFPRW].

Keywords: *Neighborhood discussion/ action groups (RR-FSA).

0562 Anderson, Anton H.
1944. "Rural community leadership: A vital part of the home front." Mimeo. Lincoln, NE: USDA, BAE, [DFPRW]. {usda 37}.

Keywords: Leadership; World War II.

0563 Anderson, Anton H.
1944. "Rural communities and neighborhoods in the Northern Great Plains." Mimeo. Lincoln, NE: USDA, BAE, [DFPRW]. {usda 37}.

Keywords: Locality groups; methodology-locality group identification/ classification; community; neighborhood.

0563 (continued).
Northern Great Plains.

0564 Anderson, Anton H.
1945. *Hamilton County Medical Aid Association, Hamilton County, Nebraska.* DC: USDA, Farm Security Administration, Health Services Division, and BAE, [DFPRW]. Rural Health Report No. 4.

Keywords: Experimental health programs (USDA); Farm Security Administration. NE.

0565 Anderson, Anton H.
1945. "The rural community and the war: A study of Ryder, North Dakota." Mimeo. Lincoln, NE: USDA, BAE, [DFPRW]. {usda 41}.

Keywords: World War II-impacts on rural areas; community. ND.

0566 Anderson, Anton H.
1945. "Significance of rural communities in the Northern Great Plains." Mimeo. Lincoln, NE: USDA, BAE, [DFPRW]. {usda 39}.

Keywords: Rural life; locality groups. Northern Great Plains.

0567 Anderson, Anton H., and Melvin H. Dreifels.
1942. "Survey of communities in Franklin County, Nebraska." Mimeo. DC: USDA, BAE, [DFPRW], and Franklin County Land Use Planning cooperating.

Keywords: *Community. NE.

0568 Anderson, Anton H., and Olen E. Leonard.
1942. "Local leadership in Elbert County, Colorado." Dittoed. Albuquerque, NM: USDA, BAE, [DFPRW], and Colorado State Extension Service, cooperating.

Keywords: *Leadership-neighborhood. CO.

0569 Atchley, F. M., E. F. Rebman, and D. L. Gibson.
1944. "Rural youth in Branch County, Michigan." Mimeo. East Lansing, MI: Michigan State College AES. F.M. 340. Sections of Farm Management and Sociology, and USDA, BAE, [DFPRW] cooperating.

Keywords: Youth; structure of agriculture. MI.

0570 Baker, O. E., H. L. Greiner, John Muehlbeier, James Greenlaw, and Pauline M. Reynolds.
1942. "Facts about rural youth in Ward County, North Dakota." Mimeo. Fargo, ND: North Dakota Agricultural College AES and Extension Service, USDA, BAE, [DFPRW] cooperating.

Keywords: Youth; attitudes\ opinions; migration. ND.

0571 Barton, Glen T.
1942. "Rural manpower and total war." *Land Policy Review* 5(2): 11-13.

Keywords: World War II-mobilization of local areas; farm labor.

0572 Beers, Howard W.
1943. "Farm population changes in eastern Kentucky, 1940-42 (progress report)." Lexington, KY: [University of Kentucky], Kentucky AES, and [USDA, BAE], DFPRW, cooperating.

Keywords: *Farm population; farm population trends. KY.

0573 Bell, Earl H.
1942. "Living with nature." *Land Policy Review* 5(6): 30-33.

Keywords: Culture of agriculture; social change/ trends.

0574 Bell, Earl H.
1942. "The Shell Rock Community in war, Butler County,

0574 (continued).
Iowa." Dittoed. [DC]: USDA, BAE, [DFPRW]. {usda 21}.

Keywords: World War II-impacts on rural areas; community. IA.

0575 Bell, Earl H.
1942. *Culture of a Contemporary Rural Community: Sublette, Kansas.* [DC]: USDA, BAE, [DFPRW]. Rural Life Studies No. 2.

Keywords: Community; rural life. KS.

0576 Bell, Earl H.
1944. "Settler selection." Dittoed. DC: USDA, BAE, [DFPRW].

Keywords: *Family selection for settlement projects.

0577 Bell, Earl, F. A. Wells, Clifford Davis, Clay Cochran, and Dan Boyd.
1942. "A local war program on agricultural labor." *Land Policy Review* 5(4): 25-32.

Keywords: World War II-mobilization of local areas; farm labor; public policy.

0578 Bell, Earl H., and Orlin Scoville.
1945. *Part-Time Farming.* DC: USDA. Farmers' Bulletin No. 1966. Slightly revised and reissued July 1948 with same authors and title.

Keywords: Part-time farming.

0579 Bernert, Eleanor H.
1944. "Volume and composition of net migration from the rural-farm population, 1930-40, for the United States, major geographic divisions and states." Mimeo. [DC]: USDA, BAE, [DFPRW].

Keywords: Migration; farm population trends; population

0579 (continued).
composition. Blacks.

0580 Bernert, Eleanor H.
1944. "County variation in net migration from the rural-farm population, 1930-40." Mimeo. DC: USDA, BAE, [DFPRW].

Keywords: Migration; farm population trends.

0581 Bradshaw, Nettie P. (compiler).
1944. "County classifications by size of largest city, United States, April 1940." Dittoed. DC: USDA, BAE, [DFPRW]. {usda 38}.

Keywords: Population; methodology-population analysis.

0582 Bradshaw, Nettie P., under the general direction of a committee of the USDA, BAE (Conrad Taeuber, chair).
1943. *A Graphic Summary of Farm Crops (Based largely on the Census of 1940)*. DC: USDA. Miscellaneous Publication No. 512.

Keywords: Graphic analysis; agricultural production.

0583 Bradshaw, Nettie P., under the general direction of a committee of the USDA, BAE (Conrad Taeuber, chair).
1943. *A Graphic Summary of Farm Animals and Animal Products (Based largely on the Census of 1940)*. DC: USDA. Miscellaneous Publication No. 530.

Keywords: Graphic analysis; agricultural production.

0584 Brady, Dorothy S., and Margaret J. Hagood.
1943. "Income of farm families." *Agricultural Situation* 27(8): 9-11.

Keywords: Income; farm family.

0585 Brooks, E. M., L. J. Ducoff, C. A. Gibbons, and Wylie D. Goodsell.

0585 (continued).
1943. "Farm wage rates, farm employment, and related data." Mimeo. DC: USDA, BAE.

Keywords: Farm wage rates; labor force; income.

0586 Coleman, A. Lee.
1942. "Community organization and agricultural planning, Greene County, Georgia." Mimeo. Atlanta, GA: USDA, BAE, [DFPRW].

Keywords: *Community; social organization; planning. Blacks. GA.

0587 Cooper, M. R., W. C. Holley, H. W. Hawthorne, and R. S. Washburn.
1943. "Labor requirements for crops and livestock." Mimeo. DC: USDA, BAE, [Division of Farm Management and Costs].

Keywords: Labor requirements for agriculture.

0588 Cottam, Howard R., with the assistance of E. L. Kirkpatrick, Arnold Green, Jane Woolley, and Miriam Sadagursky.
1944. *Effectiveness of Campaigns in Minimizing Consumer Food Waste: A Report of Experiments Conducted in Elmira, New York, and New Kensington, Pennsylvania, 1943.* [DC]: War Food Administration, Office of Distribution. USDA, BAE, [DFPRW], and the Nutrition Committees of Elmira, NY, and New Kensington, PA cooperating.

Keywords: Evaluation; adoption-diffusion; World War II-mobilization of local areas. NY; PA.

0589 Cullum, Robert M., Josiah C. Folsom, and Donald G. Hay.
1942. "Men and machines in the North Dakota harvest." Mimeo. DC: USDA, BAE, [DFPRW], and Farm Security Administration cooperating. Statistical supplement issued separately.

0589 (continued).
Keywords: Farm labor. ND.

0590 Dahlke, H. Otto.
1945. *A Rural Community in Time of War--Shelley, Idaho.* Berkeley, CA: USDA, BAE, [DFPRW]. {usda 41}.

Keywords: World War II-impacts on rural areas; community. ID.

0591 Danhof, Ralph H.
1942. "Jersey Homesteads." Pp. 136-161 in Russell Lord and Paul H. Johnstone (eds.), *A Place on Earth: A Critical Appraisal of Subsistence Homesteads.* DC: USDA, BAE.

Keywords: Subsistence homesteads; cooperatives; evaluation. NJ.

0592 Davidson, Dwight M., Jr.
1942. "Longview Homesteads." Pp. 162-169 in Russell Lord and Paul H. Johnstone (eds.), *A Place on Earth: A Critical Appraisal of Subsistence Homesteads.* DC: USDA, BAE.

Keywords: Subsistence homesteads; evaluation; farm women. WA.

0593 Davidson, Dwight M., and Olen E. Leonard.
1942. "Cumberland Homesteads." Pp. 82-96 in Russell Lord and Paul H. Johnstone (eds.), *A Place on Earth: A Critical Appraisal of Subsistence Homesteads.* DC: USDA, BAE.

Keywords: Subsistence homesteads; cooperatives; evaluation. TN.

0594 Dodson, Linden S., and Jane Woolley.
1943. *Community Organization in Charles County, Maryland.* College Park, MD: University of Maryland AES; University of Maryland, Department of Sociology; USDA, BAE, [DFPRW]; and Charles County Agricultural

0594 (continued).
Planning Committee cooperating. Bulletin No. A-21.

Keywords: Community; social organization. MD.

0595 Downing, James C., and Robert E. Galloway.
1942. "Farm resources and farming systems needed to meet living needs of farm families in five type-of-farming areas: Part II--Lower Piedmont of Georgia and South Carolina." Mimeo. Atlanta, GA: USDA, BAE.

Keywords: Level of living; farm systems; planning. GA; SC.

0596 Ducoff, Louis J.
1943. "Farm employment in 1943." *Agricultural Situation* 27(5): 11-14.

Keywords: Farm labor.

0597 Ducoff, Louis J.
1943. "Farm wage rates." *Agricultural Situation* 27(9): 9-13.

Keywords: Farm wage rates. Blacks.

0598 Ducoff, Louis J.
1944. "Do larger farms pay higher wages?" *Agricultural Situation* 28(10): 17-20.

Keywords: Farm wage rates; farm size.

0599 Ducoff, Louis J. (prepared in consultation with a committee of the BAE under the project leadership of Carl C. Taylor.).
1945. *Wages of Agricultural Labor in the United States.* DC: USDA. Technical Bulletin No. 895.

Keywords: Farm wage rates.

0600 Ducoff, Louis J., and Margaret Jarman Hagood.
1943. "Changes in composition of agricultural employ-

0600 (continued).
ment, January to July, 1942 and 1943." Mimeo. DC: USDA, BAE, [DFPRW]. {usda 30}.

Keywords: Farm labor; labor force; World War II-impacts on rural areas.

0601 Ducoff, Louis J., Margaret J. Hagood, and Conrad Taeuber.
1943. "Effects of the war on the agricultural working force and on the rural-farm population." *Social Forces* 21(4): 406-412.

Keywords: World War II-impacts on rural areas; labor force; farm population.

0602 Ducoff, Louis J., and Margaret Jarman Hagood.
1944. "The farm working force of 1943." Mimeo. DC: USDA, BAE, [DFPRW]. [BAE, Special Surveys Division, cooperating.]

Keywords: Farm labor.

0603 Ducoff, Louis J., and Margaret Jarman Hagood.
1944. "Differentials in productivity and in farm income of agricultural workers by size of enterprise and by regions." Mimeo. DC: USDA, BAE, [DFPRW].

Keywords: Farm labor; agricultural production; income; farm size.

0604 Ducoff, Louis J., and Gertrude Bancroft.
1945. "Experiment in the measurement of unpaid family labor in agriculture." Paper presented at 104th Annual Meeting of the American Statistical Association on December 28, 1944, at DC. *Journal of the American Statistical Association* 40(230): 205-213.

Keywords: Methodology-labor force analysis.

0605 Ducoff, Louis J., and Gladys K. Bowles.

0605 (continued).
1945. "Wages and wage rates of seasonal farm workers in special crop areas of Louisiana, April-May, 1945." Mimeo. DC: USDA, BAE. Surveys of Wages and Wage Rates in Agriculture, Report No. 3.

Keywords: Farm wage rates. Blacks. LA.

0606 Ducoff, Louis J., and Margaret Jarman Hagood.
1945. "Full employment in agriculture." *Agricultural Situation* 29(10): 11-14.

Keywords: Farm labor; public policy.

0607 Ducoff, Louis J., and Hagood, Margaret J.
1945. "Wages and wage rates of seasonal farm workers in special crop areas of Florida, February-March. 1945." Mimeo. DC: USDA, BAE. Surveys of Wages and Wage Rates in Agriculture, Report No. 1.

Keywords: Farm wage rates. Blacks. FL.

0608 Ducoff, Louis J., and Hagood, Margaret J.
1945. "Wages and wage rates of hired farm workers, United States and major regions, March 18-24, 1945." Mimeo. DC: USDA, BAE. Surveys of Wages and Wage Rates in Agriculture, Report No. 4.

Keywords: Farm wage rates. Blacks.

0609 Ellickson, John C., and John M. Brewster.
1942. "Manpower and the American farm plant." *Land Policy Review* 5(5): 17-22.

Keywords: Farm labor.

0610 Ensminger, Douglas.
1942. "Rural community mobilization in the war effort." *Land Policy Review* 5(4):36-37.

Keywords: World War II-mobilization of local areas.

0611 Ensminger, Douglas.
1943. "The impacts of the war on the rural community." *Social Forces* 22(1): 76-79.

Keywords: World War II-impacts on rural areas.

0612 Ensminger, Douglas.
1945. "What is the community made of?" *Extension Service Review* 16(11): 168.

Keywords: Community; social organization.

0613 Ensminger, Douglas.
1945. "Social organization for extension education." DC: USDA, Extension Service.

Keywords: *Social organization; extension.

0614 Ensminger, Douglas (Chairman, Conference Over-all Committee).
1945. *Conference Report on the Contribution of Extension Methods and Techniques Toward the Rehabilitation of War-Torn Countries, Washington, D.C., September 19-22, 1944.* DC: USDA, Extension Service, and Office of Foreign Agricultural Relations.

Keywords: Extension; post-war II planning.

0615 Ensminger, Douglas, Ronald B. Almack, Olen E. Leonard, and Walter C. McKain, Jr.
1943. "Organizing for face-to-face nutrition education." Mimeo. [DC]: USDA, BAE, Food Distribution Administration, Nutrition and Food Conservation Branch. {usda 28}.

Keywords: World War II-mobilization of local areas.

0616 Ensminger, Douglas, and Irwin T. Sanders.
1945. "What extension is." Pp. 1-7 in Edmund deS. Brunner, Irwin T. Sanders, and Douglas Ensminger. *Farmers of the World: The Development of Agricultural*

0616 (continued).
Extension. NY: Columbia University Press.

Keywords: Extension.

0617 Eselun, Mary P. B.
1943. "A study of the methods of mobilizing rural people for war emergencies, Sutter County, California." Mimeo. [Berkeley, CA]: USDA, BAE, [DFPRW].

Keywords: World War II-mobilization of local areas. CA.

0618 Fisher, Lloyd H.
1943. "What is a minimum adequate farm income?" *Journal of Farm Economics* 25(3):662-670.

Keywords: Planning-Columbia River Basin; level of living.

0619 [Folsom, Josiah C.]
1945. "Social Security for farmers and farm workers." DC: USDA, Office of Information. {usda 42}.

Keywords: Social Security.

0620 Folsom, Josiah C., and R. M. Cullum.
1942. "Manpower in the big wheat harvest." *Agricultural Situation* 26(6): 20-21.

Keywords: Farm labor.

0621 Foote, Nelson, W. A. Anderson, and Walter C. McKain, Jr.
1944. "Families displaced in a federal sub-marginal land purchase program." Ithaca, NY: Cornell University, Department of Rural Sociology. Mimeograph Bulletin No. 11. [USDA, BAE, DFPRW cooperating.]

Keywords: Land purchase programs; evaluation; attitudes/ opinions. NY.

0622 Forster, G. W., C. Horace Hamilton, R. E. L. Greene, and Selz C. Mayo.
1943. *Farm Manpower Situation in North Carolina, 1943.* Raleigh, NC: North Carolina State College of Agriculture and Engineering AES. Bulletin No. 340. North Carolina Department of Agriculture [and USDA, BAE, DFPRW] cooperating.

Keywords: Farm labor. NC.

0623 Forsyth, F. Howard.
1944. "The use of road turnings in community research." *Rural Sociology* 9(4): 384-385.

Keywords: Methodology-locality group identification/classification.

0624 Frame, Nat T.
1945. "Rushmore: Village centered community in the Cornbelt in wartime." Mimeo. Milwaukee, WI: USDA, BAE, [DFPRW]. {usda 43}.

Keywords: World War II-impacts on rural areas; community. MN.

0625 Frame, Nat T., and Warren Schmidt, assisted by Fred R. Keeler.
1942. "Whither rural youth." Mimeo. Columbus, OH: Ohio State University, Agricultural Extension Service, and USDA, BAE, [DFPRW] cooperating.

Keywords: Youth. OH.

0626 Fuller, Varden.
1942. "A year on the farm labor front." *Land Policy Review* 5(7): 14-19.

Keywords: Farm labor.

0627 Fuller, Varden.
1943. "Should farm wages be regulated?" Pp. 107-113 in

0627 (continued).
Proceedings of the 16th Annual Meeting of the Western Farm Economics Association on June 25-26 at University of California, Berkeley, CA.

Keywords: Farm wage rates.

0628 Goldschmidt, Walter R.
1942. "Mobilizing rural people for war emergencies." Dittoed. Berkeley, CA: USDA, BAE, [DFPRW].

Keywords: *World War II-mobilization of local areas.

0629 Goldschmidt, Walter R.
1943. "Some evidence on the future pattern of rural settlement." *Rural Sociology* 8(4): 387-395.

Keywords: Land division/ settlement patterns. ID; WA; OR.

0630 Goldschmidt, Walter R.
1943. "A study of the methods of mobilizing rural people for war emergencies, Tulare County, California." Mimeo. Berkeley, CA: USDA, BAE, [DFPRW].

Keywords: World War II-mobilization of local areas. CA.

0631 Goldschmidt, Walter R.
1944. "Large farms or small: The social side." Pp. 216-227 in *Agriculture in Transition from War to Peace, Proceedings of the 17th Annual Conference of the Western Farm Economics Association* on June 27-29 at Los Gatos, CA. Also published under the same author and title as undated mimeo. [DC: USDA, BAE, DFPRW].

Keywords: Sociology of agriculture; structure of agriculture; farm size.

0632 Goldschmidt, Walter R.
1944. "Class denominationalism in rural California churches." Prepared for the Regional Land Tenure

0632 (continued).
Conference arranged by the Farm Foundation for the Department of Town and Country Work, Home Missions Council, and Federal Council of Churches on February 10, 1943, at Berkeley, CA. *American Journal of Sociology* 49(4): 348-355.

Keywords: Church; social class; social organization. CA.

0633 Goldschmidt, Walter R., and John S. Page.
1942. "A study of the methods of mobilizing rural people for war emergencies, San Joaquin County." Preliminary. Dittoed. Berkeley, CA: USDA, BAE, [DFPRW]. {usda 23}.

Keywords: World War II-mobilization of local areas; evaluation. CA.

0634 Goldschmidt, Walter R., and John S. Page.
1943. "A study of the methods of mobilizing rural people for war emergencies, Kern County, California." Mimeo. Berkeley, CA: USDA, BAE, [DFPRW].

Keywords: World War II-mobilization of local areas. CA.

0635 Gordon, William R., and Gilbert S. Meldrum.
1942. *Land, People, and Farming in a Rurban Zone.* [Providence, RI]: Rhode Island AES. Bulletin No. 285. USDA, BAE, [DFPRW] cooperating.

Keywords: Rural life. RI.

0636 Greiner, Harold L.
1942. "Rural school problems in Ward County, North Dakota." Mimeo. Lincoln NE: USDA, BAE, [DFPRW]; Ward County Land Use Planning Committee; and North Dakota AES, Rural Sociology Department cooperating.

Keywords: Schools; social organization; land-use planning. ND.

0637 Hagood, Margaret J.

0637 (continued).
1943. "Rural level of living indexes." *Rural Sociology* 8(3): 292-293.

Keywords: Methodology-levels of living indicators/scales.

0638 Hagood, Margaret J.
1943. "Statistical methods for delineation of regions applied to data on agriculture and population." *Social Forces* 21(3): 287-297.

Keywords: Methodology-regional analysis.

0639 Hagood, Margaret J.
1943. "Development of a 1940 rural-farm level of living index for counties." *Rural Sociology* 8(2): 171-180.

Keywords: Methodology-levels of living indicators/scales.

0640 Hagood, Margaret J.
1943. "Rural level of living indexes for counties of the United States, 1940." Mimeo. DC: USDA, BAE, [DFPRW].

Keywords: Levels of living indicators.

0641 Hagood, Margaret J., and Louis J. Ducoff.
1944. "What level of living indexes measure." Presented at the 38th Annual Meeting of the American Sociological Society on December 5, 1943, at New York. *American Sociological Review* 9(1): 78-84.

Keywords: Methodology-levels of living indicators/scales.

0642 Hagood, Margaret J., and Eleanor H. Bernert.
1945. "Component indexes as a basis for stratification in sampling." *Journal of the American Statistical Association* 40(231): 330-341.

0642 (continued).
Keywords: Methodology-regional analysis.

0643 Hainsworth, Reginald G., Oliver E. Baker, and Albert P. Brodell.
1942. *Seedtime and Harvest Today.* DC: USDA. Miscellaneous Publication No. 485.

Keywords: Agricultural production; mechanization.

0644 Ham, William T.
1942. "To fix or not to fix farm wage rates." *Land Policy Review* 5(7): 35-39.

Keywords: Farm wage rates. Great Britain.

0645 Ham, William T.
1943. "Farm labor and 1943 goals." *Agricultural Situation* 27(1): 12-15.

Keywords: Farm labor.

0646 Ham, William T.
1944. "Stabilization of farm wages." *Agricultural Situation* 28(1): 18-21.

Keywords: Farm wage rates.

0647 Ham, William T.
1945. "Wage stabilization in agriculture." *Journal of Farm Economics* 27(1): 104-120.

Keywords: Farm wage rates.

0648 Hamilton, C. Horace.
1944. "Farm population changes in North Carolina during 1943." Mimeo. Raleigh, NC: North Carolina State College of Agriculture and Engineering, North Carolina AES. Progress Report No. RS-2. USDA, BAE, [DFPRW] cooperating.

0648 (continued).
Keywords: Farm population; farm population trends. Blacks. NC.

0649 Hay, Donald G. (contributor).
1942. "Adjusting agriculture in the Northern Great Plains for war and post-war needs." Mimeo. Lincoln, NE: USDA, BAE.

Keywords: *Agricultural production; World War II. Northern Great Plains.

0650 Hay, Donald G.
1944. "Recent population changes in the Northern Great Plains, 1940 to 1944." Mimeo. Lincoln, NE: USDA, BAE, [DFPRW]. {usda 37}.

Keywords: Population trends; World War II-impacts on rural areas. Northern Great Plains.

0651 Hay, Donald G.
1944. "Social security for farm people in the Great Plains." Mimeo. Lincoln, NE: USDA, BAE, [DFPRW].

Keywords: *Social security; public policy. Great Plains.

0652 Hay, Donald G.
1944. "Replacement opportunities in agriculture and replacement rates in the Northern Great Plains." Mimeo. Lincoln, NE: USDA, BAE, [DFPRW].

Keywords: *Replacement rates. Northern Great Plains.

0653 Hay, Donald G., et al.
1943. "The dairy labor situation in the Kansas City milkshed, November, 1942." Mimeo. DC: USDA, BAE.

Keywords: *Farm labor.

0654 Hitt, Homer L.

0654 (continued).
1942. "A comparative analysis of the people on new ground farms, plantations, and old family farms in the upper Mississippi Delta of Louisiana." *Rural Sociology* 7(4): 404-414.

Keywords: Population; population composition; level of living; plantations; resettlement; social change/ trends. Blacks. LA.

0655 Hitt, Homer L.
1943. *Recent Migration into and within the Upper Mississippi Delta of Louisiana.* Baton Rouge, LA: State University and Agricultural and Mechanical College AES. Louisiana Bulletin 364. USDA, BAE, [DFPRL] cooperating.

Keywords: Migration; population composition; land tenure; level of living. Blacks. LA.

0656 Holcomb, Ernest J.
1942. "Wartime wage rates." *Land Policy Review* 5(5): 33-37.

Keywords: Farm wage rates; World War II.

0657 Holt, John B.
1944. "Measurement of similarity in social profiles having few components." *Social Forces* 22(3): 297-302.

Keywords: Methodology.

0658 Jehlik, Paul J., and Olaf F. Larson.
1943. *Movement from Farms: A Report on New Off-farm Work by FSA Family Heads and Migration from Farms by FSA and Other Low-income Families, 1942.* Cincinnati, OH: USDA, FSA, Program and Reports Division. 1942 Family Progress Report, Release No. 2. [BAE, DFPRW cooperating.]

Keywords: Farm Security Administration; migration.

0659 Jehlik, Paul J., and Olaf F. Larson.
1943. *Obstacles to Increased War-food Production by Low-income Farmers: A Summary of Reports made by FSA County Supervisors.* Cincinnati, OH: USDA, FSA, Program and Reports Division. 1942 Family Progress Report, Release No. 3. [BAE, DFPRW cooperating.]

Keywords: Farm Security Administration; agricultural production; World War II; income-low.

0660 Johansen, Sigurd, and Milton Rossoff.
1942. *Community Planning in Eddy County, New Mexico.* State College, NM: New Mexico College of Agriculture and Mechanic Arts AES. Bulletin No. 297. [USDA, BAE, DFPRW, cooperating.]

Keywords: Community development; planning. Spanish American. NM.

0661 Johnstone, Paul H.
1942. "What has been learned." Pp. 177-184 in Russell Lord and Paul H. Johnstone (eds.), *A Place on Earth: A Critical Appraisal of Subsistence Homesteads.* DC: USDA, BAE.

Keywords: Subsistence homesteads; evaluation.

0662 Johnstone, Paul H., and Dorothy C. Goodwin.
1942. Part I. Pp. 1-55 in Russell Lord and Paul H. Johnstone (eds.), *A Place on Earth: A Critical Appraisal of Subsistence Homesteads.* (Part I includes Ch. 1, "Introduction"; Ch. 2, "Background"; Ch. 3, "The back-to-the-land movement"; Ch.4, "The drive for legislation"; and Ch. 5, "The administration of the subsistence-homestead program.") DC: USDA, BAE.

Keywords: Subsistence homesteads.

0663 Johnstone, Paul H., and Bernard R. Bell.
1942. "Appendix." Pp. 185-198 in Russell Lord and Paul

0663 (continued).
H. Johnstone (eds.), *A Place on Earth: A Critical Appraisal of Subsistence Homesteads.* DC: USDA, BAE.

Keywords: Subsistence homesteads; evaluation.

0664 Keepper, W. E., Walter C. McKain, and M. S. Parsons.
1942. *Pennsylvania Farm Adjustments to the Wartime Labor Situation.* State College, PA: Pennsylvania State College, School of Agriculture AES. Journal Series, Paper No. 1146. Pennsylvania AES and USDA, BAE, [DFPRW] cooperating.

Keywords: Farm labor; World War II-impacts on rural areas. PA.

0665 Kirkpatrick, E. L.
1945. "Rural youth and democratic building." *Land Policy Review* 8(1): 27-31.

Keywords: Youth; community development.

0666 Kollmorgen, Walter M.
1942. *Culture of a Contemporary Rural Community: The Old Order Amish of Lancaster County, Pennsylvania.* [DC]: USDA, BAE, [DFPRW]. Rural Life Studies No.4.

Keywords: Community; rural life. Amish. PA.

0667 Kollmorgen, Walter M.
1942. "The Subsistence homesteads near Birmingham." Pp. 65-82 in Russell Lord and Paul H. Johnstone (eds.), *A Place on Earth: A Critical Appraisal of Subsistence Homesteads.* DC: USDA, BAE.

Keywords: Subsistence homesteads; cooperatives; evaluation. AL.

0668 Kollmorgen, Walter M.
1943. "The agricultural stability of the Old Order Amish and Old Order Mennonites of Lancaster County, Penn

0668 (continued).
sylvania." *American Journal of Sociology* 49(3): 233-241.

Keywords: Social-cultural groups; religion; social organization. German; Amish; Mennonites. PA.

0669 Kollmorgen, Walter R.
1943. "Agricultural-cultural islands in the South--Part II." *Economic Geography* 19(2): 109-117.

Keywords: Social-cultural groups; culture of agriculture; farm systems; migration. Blacks. South.

0670 Lantis, Margaret, M. R. Hanger, and Philip W. Woods, under the general direction of Douglas Ensminger.
1945. *The Farm Security Administration Dental Program of Randolf County, Georgia.* DC: USDA, Farm Security Adminstration, Health Services Division, and BAE, [DFPRL]. Rural Health Report No. 8. Also published in condensed form with the same authors and title. DC: GPO.

Keywords: Experimental health programs (USDA); Farm Security Administration. Blacks.

0671 Larson, Olaf F.
1943. "Wartime migration and the manpower reserve on farms in Eastern Kentucky." *Rural Sociology* 8(2):148-161.

Keywords: World War II-impacts on rural areas; migration; farm population trends; population composition; labor force. KY.

0672 Larson, Olaf F., and James C. Downing.
1943. "Manpower for war work: Eastern Kentucky." Mimeo. DC: USDA, BAE.

Keywords: Labor force; World War II-impacts on rural areas; income-low; farm population trends; sociology of agriculture. KY.

0673 Leonard, Olen E.
1942. "Neighborhood leadership organization in El Paso County." Dittoed. Albuquerque, NM: USDA, BAE, [DFPRW].

Keywords: *Leadership-neighborhood. NM.

0674 Leonard, Olen E.
1942. "Study of neighborhood leadership system in Emery and Utah Counties, Utah." Dittoed. Albuquerque: USDA, BAE, [DFPRW]. Utah State Extension Service cooperating.

Keywords: *Leadership-neighborhood.

0675 Leonard, Olen E.
1942. "El Monte," pp. 97-106, and "Phoenix Homesteads," pp.170-176, in Russell Lord and Paul H. Johnstone (eds.), *A Place on Earth: A Critical Appraisal of Subsistence Homesteads*. DC: USDA, BAE.

Keywords: Subsistence homesteads; evaluation. CA; AR.

0676 Leonard, Olen E.
1944. "Some efforts of rural sociology in the present war." *Rural Sociology* 9(2): 142-151.

Keywords: Uses of rural sociology research; leadership-neighborhood. Spanish Americans; Mormons. NM; UT.

0677 Leonard, Olen E.
1944. "Rural community adjustments to recent population shifts in selected areas of the Southeast." *Social Forces* 23(1): 41-46.

Keywords: Population trends; migration; social change/trends; community. Blacks. Southeast.

Lindstrom, D. E.
"Wartime movement of rural youth (a study of ₁ County, Illinois)." Mimeo. Urbana, IL: Univer-

0678 (continued).
sity of Illinois AES, Department of Agricultural Economics. USDA, BAE, [DFPRW]; University of Illinois, Extension Service in Agriculture and Home Economics; and Randolph County Farm Adviser cooperating.

Keywords: Youth; migration; World War II-impacts on rural areas. IL.

0679 Lindstrom, D. E., E. G. Mosbacher, R. B. McKenzie, O. E. Baker, N. T. Frame, and E. C. Secor, assisted by L. L. Colvis and G. T. Hudson.
1942. "Rural youth in wartime Illinois: Randolph County." Urbana, IL: University of Illinois AES. USDA, BAE, [DFPRW] cooperating.

Keywords: Youth. IL.

0680 Longmore, T. Wilson.
1943. "Neighborhood discussion groups in relation to the FSA program in Desha County, Arkansas, 1942." Mimeo. Little Rock: USDA, BAE, [DFPRW].

Keywords: Neighborhood discussion/ action groups (RR-FSA). Blacks. AR.

0681 Longmore, T. Wilson.
1943. "Neighborhood discussion groups among low-income farm families in Texas." Mimeo. Little Rock, AR: USDA, BAE, [DFPRW]. {usda 27}.

Keywords: Neighborhood discussion/ action groups (RR-FSA); income-low. TX.

0682 Longmore, T. Wilson.
1943. "Neighborhood discussion groups among low-income farm families in Oklahoma." Mimeo. Little Rock, AR: USDA, BAE, DFPRW. {usda 27}.

Keywords: Neighborhood discussion/ action groups (RR-FSA); income-low. OK.

0683 Longmore, T. Wilson.
1945. "Watson, Arkansas: Effect of war in a Mississippi Delta community." Mimeo. Little Rock, AR: USDA, BAE, [DFPRW]. (usda 39).

Keywords: World War II-impacts on rural areas; community. Blacks. AR.

0684 Longmore, T. Wilson, and Homer L. Hitt.
1943. "A demographic analysis of first and second generation Mexican population of the United States: 1930." *Southwestern Social Science Quarterly* 24(2): 138-149.

Keywords: Population; population composition; socioeconomic status-individual/ family; women. Mexicans.

0685 Longmore, T. Wilson, and T. G. Standing.
1944. "Developing local leadership in agriculture's war effort." *Rural Sociology* 9(1): 44-49.

Keywords: Leadership-neighborhood; rural life; World War II.

0686 Longmore, T. Wilson, and Theo L. Vaughan.
1944. *Taos County Cooperative Health Association, 1942-43, Taos County, New Mexico.* DC: USDA, Farm Security Administration, Health Services Division, and BAE, [DFPRW]. Rural Health Report No. 1.

Keywords: *Experimental health programs (USDA); Farm Security Adminstration. Spanish Americans. NM.

0687 Longmore, T. Wilson, and Theo L. Vaughan.
1945. *Cass County Rural Health Service, Cass County, Texas, 1942-44.* DC: USDA, Farm Security Administration, Health Services Division, and BAE, [DFPRW]. Rural Health Report No. 3.

Keywords: Experimental health programs (USDA); Farm Security Administration; health and medical care; evaluation. Blacks. TX.

0688 Loomis, Charles P.
1942. "Wartime migration from the rural Spanish speaking villages of New Mexico." *Rural Sociology* 7(4): 384-395.

Keywords: World War II-impacts on rural areas; migration. Spanish Americans. NM.

0689 Loomis, Charles P.
1942. "Wartime impacts upon the schools." *Applied Anthropology* 2(1): 29-32.

Keywords: World War II-impacts on rural areas; schools.

0690 Loomis, Charles P.
1942. "Applied anthropology in Latin America." *Applied Anthropology* 2(1): 37-39.

Keywords: Cultural anthropology; rural development-less developed countries. Latin America.

0691 Loomis, Charles P.
1943. "Extension work at Tingo Maria, Peru." *Applied Anthropology* 3(1): 18-34. A shorter version also published in *Agriculture in the Americas* 4 (February 1944): 23-26. Reprinted as pp. 245-264 in Charles P. Loomis, *Studies of Rural Social Organization in the United States, Latin America and Germany*. East Lansing, MI: State College Book Store, 1945.

Keywords: Extension; rural development-less developed countries. Peru.

0692 Loomis, Charles P.
1943. "Ethnic cleavages in the Southwest as reflected in two high schools." *Sociometry* 6(1): 7-25. Reprinted as pp. 339-349 in Charles P. Loomis, *Studies of Rural Social Organization in the United States, Latin America and Germany*. East Lansing, MI: State College Book Store, 1945.

0692 (continued).
Keywords: Children; race relations. Spanish Americans. NM.

0693 Loomis, Charles P.
1943. "De charro a cowboy." *Defensa* 3(21).

Keywords: *Rural life. Latin America.

0694 Loomis, Charles P.
1943. "Deporte del caballo--el 'cowboy' tomo del charro mexicano su destreza y habilidad." *Mexico* 10(141).

Keywords: *Rural life. Latin America.

0695 Loomis, Charles P.
1943. "Applied anthropology in Latin America." *Applied Anthropology* 2(2): 33-35.

Keywords: Cultural anthropology; rural development-less developed countries. Latin America.

0696 Loomis, Charles P.
1943. "Applied anthropology in Latin America: Developing a permanent and stable supply of needed agricultural materials." *Applied Anthropology* 2(4): 15-17.

Keywords: World War II; agricultural production. Latin America.

0697 Loomis, Charles P.
1944. "Extension work for Latin America." *Applied Anthropology* 3(4): 27-40.

Keywords: Extension; culture of agriculture. Latin America.

0698 Loomis, Charles P.
1944. "Visiting patterns and miscegenation at Oxapampa, Peru." *Rural Sociology* 9(1): 68.

0698 (continued).
Keywords: Methodology-sociometric; community; race. German. Peru.

0699 Loomis, Charles P.
1945. "Extension work in Latin America." Pp. 117-137, in Edmund deS. Brunner et al. (eds.), *Farmers of the World: The Development of Agricultural Extension.* NY: Columbia University Press.

Keywords: Extension. Latin America.

0700 Loomis, Charles P.
1945. "A cooperative health association in Spanish speaking villages or the organization of the Taos County Cooperative Health Association." *American Sociological Review* 10(2): 149-157.

Keywords: Experimental health programs (USDA); Farm Security Administration; health and medical care; evaluation. Spanish Americans. NM.

0701 Loomis, Charles P., and Douglas Ensminger.
1942. "Governmental administration and informal local groups." *Applied Anthropology* 1(2): 41-62. Reprinted as pp. 151-172 in Charles P. Loomis, *Studies of Rural Social Organization in the United States, Latin America, and Germany.* East Lansing, MI: State College Book Store, 1945.

Keywords: Agricultural agencies; evaluation. Blacks. GA.

0702 Loomis, Charles P., and Nellie H. Loomis.
1942. "Skilled Spanish-American war-industry workers from New Mexico." *Applied Anthropology* 2(1): 33-36.

Keywords: World War II; labor force. Spanish Americans. NM.

0703 Loomis, Charles P., and Glen Grisham.
1943. "The New Mexican experiment in village rehabili-

0703 (continued).
tation." *Applied Anthropology* 2(3): 12-37. Reprinted as pp. 366-388 in Charles P. Loomis, *Studies of Rural Social Organization in the United States, Latin America and Germany*. East Lansing, MI: State College Book Store, 1945.

Keywords: Rural rehabilitation; evaluation. Spanish Americans. NM.

0704 Loomis, Charles P., and Jesse Taylor Reed.
1944. "The Taos County project of New Mexico--an experiment in local cooperation among bureaus, private agencies, and rural people." *Applied Anthropology* 3(3): 21-33.

Keywords: Rural rehabilitation; agricultural agencies. Spanish Americans. NM.

0705 Lord, Russell, and Paul H. Johnstone (editors).
1942. *A Place on Earth: A Critical Appraisal of Subsistence Homesteads*. DC: USDA, BAE, [DFPRW].

Keywords: Subsistence homesteads; evaluation.

0706 Losey, J. Edwin, with the assistance of Lynn Robertson and Irma Windleblack.
1944. "Wartime adjustments of Indiana rural youth--Tentative summary for Leadership Training School for Indiana rural youth." Dittoed. Lafayette, IN: Purdue University, Department of Agricultural Extension.

Keywords: Youth; World War II-impacts on rural areas; migration. IN.

0707 Lyall, Lawrence B.
1942. "Rural school problems in Hand County, South Dakota." Mimeo. Lincoln, NE: USDA, BAE, [DFPRW]. Hand County Agricultural Planning Committee; and South Dakota AES, Rural Sociology Department cooperating.

0707 (continued).
Keywords: Schools. SD.

0708 Lyall, Lawrence B.
1945. "The rural community and the war: A study of Beaver Crossing, Nebraska." Mimeo. Lincoln, NE: USDA, BAE, [DFPRW]. {usda 41}.

Keywords: World War II-impacts on rural areas; community. NE.

0709 Lynde, Lt. Samuel A., and Edgar A. Schuler.
1944. "The undereducated serviceman and the 'G.I. Bill of Rights'." *Adult Education Bulletin* 9(2): 35-40.

Keywords: Veterans; World War II; education.

0710 MacLeish, Kenneth, and Kimball Young.
1942. *Culture of a Contemporary Rural Community: Landaff, New Hampshire.* [DC]: USDA, BAE, [DFPRW]. Rural Life Studies No. 3.

Keywords: Community; rural life. NH.

0711 Mathews, M. Taylor.
1945. "Wheeler County Rural Health Services Association, Wheeler County, Texas." Mimeo. DC: USDA, Farm Security Administration, Health Services Division, and BAE, [DFPRW]. Rural Health Report No. 7.

Keywords: *Experimental health programs (USDA); Farm Security Administration. TX.

0712 Matthews, M. Taylor, David R. Jenkins, and Raymond F. Sletto.
1942. *Attitudes of Edgefield County Farmers Toward Farm Practices and Rural Programs.* Clemson, SC: Clemson Agricultural College, South Carolina AES. Bulletin No. 339. USDA, BAE, [DFPRW] cooperating.

0712 (continued).
Keywords: Attitudes/ opinions; agricultural agencies. Blacks. SC.

0713 Mayo, Selz C., R. E. L. Greene, C. Horace Hamilton, and G. W. Forster.
1944. *1944 Farm Labor Problems: Farm Manpower Situation in North Carolina.* Raleigh, NC: North Carolina State College of Agriculture and Engineering, North Carolina AES. Bulletin No. 344.

Keywords: Farm labor; labor requirements in agriculture; farm women. NC.

0714 McKain, Walter C., Jr.
1943. "The Share the Meat Program in Rhode Island: A study of the organization used in the Share the Meat Program in Rhode Island, and an analysis of the results of the program." Mimeo. [Upper Darby, PA]: USDA, BAE, [DFPRW]. Federal Security Agency, Office of Defense Health and Welfare Services, and Rhode Island Nutrition Council cooperating. {usda 27}.

Keywords: World War II-mobilization of local areas. RI.

0715 McKain, Walter C., Jr.
[1945?]. "Social Security: Southwest Intermountain Region." Mimeo. Berkeley, CA:USDA, BAE, [DFPRW]. {usda 42}.

Keywords: Social security; research.

0716 McKain, Walter C., Jr.
1945. "Too many workers--a post-war farm labor problem." Proceedings of the Pacific Sociological Society. Published in *Research Studies, State College of Washington* 13(1): 17-24.

Keywords: Farm labor; labor force; post-war II planning. Pacific Coast.

0717 McKain, Walter C., Jr.
1945. "Rural Life Trends Project." Mimeo. Berkeley, CA: USDA, BAE, [DFPRW].

Keywords: Division of Farm Population and Rural Life; research.

0718 McKain, Walter C., Jr., and William H. Metzler.
1945. "Measurement of turnover and retirement of farm owners and operators." *Rural Sociology* 10(1): 73-76.

Keywords: Farm operator turnover; methodology. CA.

0719 Metzler, William H.
1942. "The farm labor situation in the apricot harvest, Santa Clara County, California." Dittoed. [Berkeley, CA]: USDA, BAE, [DFPRW]. {usda 24}.

Keywords: Farm labor; World War II-impacts on rural areas. CA.

0720 Metzler, William H.
1945. "Wages and wage rates of farm workers in the citrus harvest, Los Angeles Area, California, April-June 1945." Mimeo. DC: USDA, BAE. Surveys of Wages and Wage Rates in Agriculture, Report No. 5.

Keywords: Farm wage rates. Mexican nationals; Mexicans. CA.

0721 Metzler, William H.
1945. "Wages and wage rates of seasonal farm workers in USDA Labor Supply Centers at Arvin, Linnell, and Shafter, California, June 1945." Mimeo. DC: USDA, BAE. Surveys of Wages and Wage Rates in Agriculture, Report No. 6.

Keywords: Farm wage rates. CA.

0722 Moe, Edward O., and Carl C. Taylor.
1942. *Culture of a Contemporary Rural Community: Irwin,*

0722 (continued).
Iowa. [DC]: USDA, BAE, [DFPRW]. Rural Life Studies No. 5.

Keywords: Community; rural life. IA.

0723 Montgomery, James E.
1944. "Newton County, Mississippi, Agricultural Health Association." Mimeo. DC: USDA, Farm Security Administration, Health Services Division, and BAE, [DFPRW], Rural Health Report No. 2.

Keywords: Experimental health programs (USDA); Farm Security Administration. Blacks. MS.

0724 Montgomery, James E.
1945. "Experimenting in rural health organization." *Rural Sociology* 10(3): 296-308.

Keywords: Experimental health programs (USDA); Farm Security Administration; evaluation. MS.

0725 Montgomery, James, and Olen Leonard.
1944. "Settlement and post-war planning." *Applied Anthropology* 3(2): 23-26.

Keywords: Post-war II planning; resettlement. TN.

0726 Motheral, Joe R.
1942. "Texas farm population changes during 1941." Part 1 of Progress Report No. 795, A. D. Jackson (ed.). Mimeo. College Station, TX: Agricultural and Mechanical College of Texas, Texas AES. [USDA], BAE, [DFPRW] cooperating.

Keywords: Farm population; farm population trends. TX.

0727 Neeley, Wayne C.
[1944]. "The impact of the war on a Mid-West rurban community." Undated mimeo. [DC: USDA, BAE, DFPRW]. {usda 28}.

0727 (continued).
Keywords: World War II-impacts on rural areas; attitudes\ opinions; community. IA.

0728 Nichols, Ralph R.
1942. "Granger Homesteads," pp. 106-118, and "Houston Gardens," pp. 118-135, in Russell Lord and Paul H. Johnstone (eds.), *A Place on Earth: A Critical Appraisal of Subsistence Homesteads*. DC: USDA, BAE.

Keywords: Subsistence homesteads; evaluation. IA; TX.

0729 Nichols, Ralph R., and Morton B. King, Jr.
1943. *Social Effects of Government Land Purchase*. State College, MS: Mississippi State College AES. Bulletin No. 390.

Keywords: Land purchase programs; evaluation. MS.

0730 Niederfrank, E. J.
1942. "A preliminary survey of the shift of manpower in Maine from rural areas to urban war industrial centers." Mimeo. [Orono, ME: University of Maine, College of Agriculture, Department of Agricultural Economics and Farm Management].

Keywords: World War II-impacts on rural areas; migration; labor force. ME.

0731 Niederfrank, E. J.
1945. "The Massachusetts hill towns in wartime." Mimeo. Upper Darby, PA: USDA, BAE, [DFPRW]. {usda 43}.

Keywords: World War II-impacts on rural areas; community. MA.

0732 Peterson, George R., and Lawrence B. Lyall.
1942. "Farm resources and farming systems needed to meet living needs of farm families in five type-of-farming areas: Part V--North Central South Dakota." Mimeo. Lincoln, NE: USDA, BAE.

0732 (continued).
Keywords: Level of living; farm systems; planning. SD.

0733 Peterson, Howard L.
1942. "Survey of communities in Buffalo County, Nebraska." Mimeo. Lincoln, NE: USDA, BAE, [DFPRW]. Buffalo County Agricultural Planning Commitee and Agricultural Extension Service cooperating.

Keywords: *Community. NE.

0734 Pryor, Herbert, and Theo L. Vaughn.
1945. "A rural community in wartime: Roby, Texas." Mimeo. Little Rock, AR: USDA, BAE, [DFPRW]. {usda 41}.

Keywords: World War II-impacts on rural areas; community. TX.

0735 Raper, Arthur F.
1944. "Shifts in the farm labor situation, 1942-43." Dittoed. DC: USDA, BAE, [DFPRW]. {NAL v.63}.

Keywords: *Farm labor.

0736 Raper, Arthur F.
1945. "What farmers want from their rural schools." *Land Policy Review* 8(3): 3-6.

Keywords: Schools; social change/ trends; attitudes/ opinions.

0737 Raper, Arthur F., and F. Howard Forsyth.
1943. "Cultural factors which result in artificial farm labor shortages." *Rural Sociology* 8(1): 3-14.

Keywords: Farm labor; culture of agriculture; farm women; social change/ trends; World War II.

0738 Raper, Arthur F., and Pearl Wheeler Tappan.
1943. "'Never too old to learn new tricks'; The canning

0738 (continued).
program in Greene County, Georgia." *Applied Anthropology* 2(3): 3-11.

Keywords: Culture of agriculture; rural rehabilitation; women; Farm Security Administration. Blacks. GA.

0739 Raper, Arthur F., and U. T. Summers.
1944. "What do farmers expect after the war?" *Agricultural Situation* 28(10): 20-23.

Keywords: Attitudes/ opinions; social change/ trends; World War II.

0740 Reagan, Barbara B., and William H. Metzler.
1945. "Wages and wage rates of seasonal farm workers in Maricopa County, Arizona and Imperial County, California, February-March, 1945." Mimeo. DC: USDA, BAE. Surveys of Wages and Wage Rates in Agriculture, Report No. 2.

Keywords: Farm wage rates. Spanish-American; Mexican nationals. AZ; CA.

0741 Roberts, Roy L.
1942. "Population changes in the Great Plains." *Rural Sociology* 7(1): 40-48.

Keywords: Population trends. Great Plains; KS.

0742 Roberts, Roy L.
1943. "Rural population in relation to agricultural resources." Dittoed. DC: USDA, BAE, [DFPRW].

Keywords: *Population; rural.

0743 Roberts, Roy L.
1944. "Differences in number of farm operators and number of farmers and farm managers reported in the U.S. Censuses of Agriculture and Population, 1940." *Rural Sociology* 9(2): 178-182.

0743 (continued).
Keywords: Methodology-population analysis.

0744 Roberts, Roy L., and Irwin Holmes.
1943. *Analysis of Specified Farm Characteristics for Farms Classified by Total Value of Products.* DC: U.S. Department of Commerce, Bureau of the Census, and USDA, BAE and Farm Security Administration, cooperating. Technical Monograph based on a 2% sample from the 1940 Census of Agriculture. Parts issued separately in Technical Releases No. 1-9.

Keywords: Agricultural production; land tenure; farm size; farm labor. Blacks. Appalachia; South.

0745 Roberts, Roy L., and W. S. Middaugh.
1943. "Agricultural manpower situation in the Northeast." Mimeo. Upper Darby, PA: USDA, BAE. {usda 32}.

Keywords: Farm labor. Northeast.

0746 Robertson, Lynn, Harry F. Ainsworth, O. E. Baker, and Nat T. Frame.
1942. *Rural Youth in Indiana (18-28 Years of Age).* Lafayette, IN: Purdue University AES. Bulletin No. 467. USDA, BAE, [DFPRW] cooperating.

Keywords: Youth; gender roles. IN.

0747 Rural Sociological Society Committee on Post-war Recruitment and Training (J. H. Kolb, Charles E. Lively, Dwight Sanderson, T. Lynn Smith, Conrad Taeuber, Carl C. Taylor, and Edmund deS. Brunner, Chairman).
1945. "Report of the Committee on Post-war Recruitment and Training of the Rural Sociological Society." *Rural Sociology* 10(1): 76-85.

Keywords: Sociology-rural sociology.

0748 Rush, Donald R., and Olaf F. Larson.
1942. "Farm resources and farming systems needed to

0748 (continued).
meet living needs of farm families in five type-of-farming areas: Part I--Summary." Mimeo. DC: USDA, BAE.

Keywords: Level of living; farm systems; planning.

0749 Rusinow, Irving.
1942. *A Camera Report on El Cerrito, a Typical Spanish-American Community in New Mexico*. DC: USDA, BAE, USDA Miscellaneous Publication 479.

Keywords: Community; graphic analysis. Spanish Americans. NM.

0750 Sanderson, Dwight, and S. Earl Grigsby.
1943. "The social characteristics of Erin--a rural town in Southern New York." Ithaca, NY: Cornell University AES, Department of Rural Sociology Mimeograph Bulletin No. 10. USDA, BAE, [DFPRW], and Cornell University, Department of Agricultural Economics cooperating. Revision of a September 1942 Cornell University Ph.D. thesis by S. Earl Grigsby titled "Erin: A socio-economic study of families living on marginal land."

Keywords: Population composition; income; socioeconomic status-individual/ family; social participation. NY.

0751 Schaefer, George T., Ross V. Baumann, and F. Howard Forsyth.
1942. "Farm resources and farming systems needed to meet living needs of farm families in five type-of-farming areas: Part VI--South Central Minnesota." Mimeo. Milwaukee, WI: USDA, BAE.

Keywords: Level of living; farm systems; planning. MN.

0752 Schuler, Edgar A.
1944. "Some regional variations in levels and standards of living." *Rural Sociology* 9(2): 122-141.

0752 (continued).
Keywords: Level of living; standard of living; graphic analysis.

0753 Schuler, Edgar A.
1944. "Suggestions for rural sociological research under wartime restrictions on travel." *Rural Sociology* 9(1): 59-62.

Keywords: Research; sociology-rural sociology; World War II.

0754 Schuler, Edgar A..
1945. "Farm family living prospects in 1946: Education." *Agricultural Situation* 29(11): 46.

Keywords: Education; social change/ trends.

0755 [Schuler, Edgar A., et al.]
1944. "Soldiers' plans for farming after they leave the army." Mimeo. [DC]: Army Service Forces, Information and Education Division Headquarters. Post-war Plans of the Soldier Series Report No. B-131.

Keywords: Veterans; World War II; post-war II planning; occupations. Blacks.

0756 Schuler, Edgar A., and Douglas Ensminger.
1945. "Counseling and education for the veteran in rural communities." *Bulletin of National Association of Secondary-School Principals* 29(129): 24-28.

Keywords: Veterans; education.

0757 Sitler, Harry G., and Paul J. Jehlik.
1942. "Farm resources and farming systems needed to meet living needs of farm families in five type-of-farming areas: Part IV--Southeastern Colorado and Northeastern New Mexico." Mimeo. Amarillo, TX: USDA, BAE.

0757 (continued).
Keywords: Level of living; farm systems; planning. CO; NM.

0758 Snyder, L. B., and A. H. Anderson.
1944. *Determinants of Levels of Living for Farmers of Lancaster County, Nebraska.* Lincoln, NE: University of Nebraska, College of Agriculture AES. Bulletin No. 368.

Keywords: Level of living. NE.

0759 Standing, T. G.
1942. "The problem of rural housing in the South." Adapted from a paper presented at the Southern Agricultural Workers Conference on February 5 at Memphis, TN. *Rural Sociology* 7(3): 267-275.

Keywords: Housing. Blacks. South.

0760 Standing, T. G.
1942. "The sociological aspects of farm tenure." Adapted from a paper presented at the meeting of the Southwestern Social Science Association on April 3, 1942 at Dallas, TX. *Southwestern Social Science Quarterly* 23(3): 264-274.

Keywords: Land tenure; uses of rural sociology research.

0761 Standing, T. G.
1942. "Some recent changes in agriculture, with particular reference to the Southwest." Adapted from a paper presented at the meeting of Section "K" of the American Association for the Advancement of Science on December 29, 1941 at Dallas, TX. *Southwestern Social Science Quarterly* 22(4): 273-286.

Keywords: Social change/ trends; level of living; land tenure; population; mechanization. Southwest.

0762 Standing, T. G., and T. Wilson Longmore.
1942. "Neighborhood discussion groups in relation to the Farm Security Administration program in Delaware

0762 (continued).
County, Oklahoma." Dittoed. Little Rock, AR: USDA, BAE, [DFPRW]. {usda 21}.

Keywords: Neighborhood discussion/ action groups (RR-FSA). OK.

0763 Standing, T. G., and T. Wilson Longmore.
1943. "Civilian organization for total war, Calhoun County, Arkansas." Mimeo. Little Rock, AR: USDA, BAE, [DFPRW]. {usda 30}.

Keywords: World War II-mobilization of local areas; social organization; evaluation; extension; Farm Security Administration; Agricultural Adjustment Administration. Blacks. AR.

0764 Standing, T. G., T. Wilson Longmore, and Herbert Pryor.
1943. "Civilian participation in war programs, Louisiana, 1943--Part I: An analysis of wartime programs in St. Landry, Madison, and Lincoln Parishes." Mimeo. Little Rock, AR: USDA, BAE, [DFPRW]. {usda 30}.

Keywords: World War II-mobilization of local areas; World War II-impacts on rural areas; evaluation. Blacks. LA.

0765 Standing, T. G., T. Wilson Longmore, and Herbert Pryor.
1943. "Civilian Participation in war programs, Louisiana, 1943--Part II: Structure and function of wartime organization in St. Landry, Madison, and Lincoln Parishes." Dittoed. Little Rock, AR: USDA, BAE, [DFPRW]. {usda 30}.

Keywords: World War II-mobilization of local areas; social organization; agricultural agencies. Blacks. LA.

0766 Standing, T. G., Herbert Pryor, and T. Wilson Longmore.

0766 (continued).
   1943. "Adjustments to wartime needs in the South Central Region." Mimeo. Little Rock, AR: USDA, BAE, [DFPRW]. {usda 32}.

   Keywords: World War II-impacts on rural areas. AR; OK; TX.

0767 Swiger, Rachel R. (see also Rowe), and Conrad Taeuber.
   1942. "They too--produce for victory (summarized from annual reports of twenty Farm Security Administration farm and home supervisors)." Mimeo. DC: USDA, BAE, [DFPRW]. Farm Security Administration cooperating.

   Keywords: Experimental rural rehabilitation program; Farm Security Administration; evaluation.

0768 Swiger, Rachel R. (see also Rowe), and Conrad Taeuber.
   1942. "Solving problems through cooperation (summarized from annual reports of twenty Farm Security Administration farm and home supervisors)." Mimeo. DC: USDA, BAE, [DFPRW]. Farm Security Administration cooperating.

   Keywords: Experimental rural rehabilitaion program; Farm Security Adminstration; evaluation.

0769 Swiger, Rachel R. (see also Rowe), and Conrad Taeuber.
   1942. "Ill fed, ill clothed, ill housed--five hundred families in need of help." Mimeo. DC: USDA, BAE, [DFPRW]. Farm Security Administration cooperating.

   Keywords: Experimental rural rehabilitation program; Farm Security Administration; evaluation.

0770 Swiger, Rachel R. (see also Rowe), and Olaf F. Larson.
   1943. "Yesterday, today, and tomorrow--Five hundred low-income farm families in wartime (summarized from

0770 (continued).
1941-42 annual reports of twenty Farm Security Administration farm and home supervisors)." Dittoed. DC: USDA, BAE, [DFPRW]. Farm Security Administration cooperating.

Keywords: Experimental rural rehabilitation program; Farm Security Administration; evaluation.

0771 Swiger, Rachel R. (see also Rowe), and Olaf F. Larson. 1944. "Climbing toward security." Mimeo. DC: USDA, BAE, [DFPRW]. Reprinted March 1966 on pp. 9-58 in *A Ten-county Program Experiment with 606 Low-income Rural Families*. Ithaca, NY: Cornell University, New York State College of Agriculture, Department of Rural Sociology Bulletin No. 68.

Keywords: Experimental rural rehabilitation program; Farm Security Administration; evaluation.

0772 Taeuber, Conrad.
1942. "Agricultural manpower." *Agricultural Situation* 26(9): 22-23.

Keywords: Farm labor; migration.

0773 Taeuber, Conrad.
1943. "Agricultural underemployment." Presented at Joint Session of the Rural Sociological Society and the American Farm Economic Association on September 15 at St. Louis, MO. *Rural Sociology* 8(4): 342-355.

Keywords: Farm labor.

0774 Taeuber, Conrad.
1944. "Replacement rates for rural-farm males aged 25-69 years, by counties, 1940-50." Mimeo. DC: USDA, BAE, [DFPRW].

Keywords: Replacement rates. Blacks.

0775 Taeuber, Conrad, and Irene B. Taeuber.
1942. "A research memorandum on internal migration resulting from the war effort." NY: Social Science Research Council Committee on Research on Social Aspects of the War.

Keywords: Methodology-population analysis; migration; World War II.

0776 Taylor, Carl C.
1942. "Rural life." *American Journal of Sociology* 47(6): 841-853.

Keywords: Social change/ trends; rural life.

0777 Taylor, Carl C.
1942. "Opportunities for rural sociologists in the present emergency." *Rural Sociology* 7(1): 3-9.

Keywords: Sociology-rural sociology; uses of rural sociology research; World War II.

0778 Taylor, Carl C.
[1943]. "Proposals to provide Social Security for farm people." Dittoed. [DC: USDA, BAE, DFPRW]. {usda 28}.

Keywords: Social security; public policy.

0779 Taylor, Carl C.
1943. "Land-ownership and status in Argentina." *Land Policy Review* 6(2): 25-30.

Keywords: Land tenure. Argentina.

0780 Taylor, Carl C.
1943. "Social Security for farm people." Dittoed. [DC: USDA, BAE, DFPRW]. {usda 28}.

Keywords: Social security; public policy.

0781 Taylor, Carl C.
1943. "Farming and farm life in the major production areas of Argentina." *Foreign Agriculture* 7(7): 147-159.

Keywords: Agricultural production; land tenure; rural life. Argentina.

0782 Taylor, Carl C.
1943. "Argentina loves her cattle." *Agriculture in the Americas* 3(3): 43-46.

Keywords: Culture of agriculture. Argentina.

0783 Taylor, Carl C.
1944. "Human resources of the Southern Appalachians." *Land Policy Review* 7(1): 3-6.

Keywords: Rural life. Appalachia.

0784 Taylor, Carl C.
1944. "Social Security for agricultural workers." Dittoed. DC: USDA, BAE, [DFPRW].

Keywords: *Social security; public policy.

0785 Taylor, Carl C.
1944. "Rural locality groups in Argentina." Presented at the 38th Annual Meeting of the American Sociological Society on December 4, 1943, at New York. *American Sociological Review* 9(2): 162-170.

Keywords: Locality groups. Argentina.

0786 Taylor, Carl C.
1944. "Attitudes of American farmers--International and provincial." Revised and reorganized version of a paper presented at the 38th Annual Meeting of the American Sociological Society on December 4, 1943, at New York. *American Sociological Review* 9(6): 657-664.

Keywords: Attitudes/ opinions; public policy.

0787 Taylor, Carl C.
1944. "Programs of colonization and resettlement in Argentina." Mimeo. {usda 36}.

Keywords: Colonization; evaluation. Argentina.

0788 Taylor, Carl C.
1945. "The cultural approach to extension." Pp. 194-198 in *Conference Report on the Contribution of Extension Methods and Techniques Toward the Rehabilitation of War-Torn Countries*, Washington, D. C., September 19-22, 1944. DC: USDA, Extension Service, and Office of Foreign Agricultural Relations.

Keywords: Sociology-rural sociology; cultural anthropology; extension.

0789 Taylor, Carl C.
1945. "The cultural approach to extension work." Pp. 225-227 in *Conference Report on the Contribution of Extension Methods and Techniques Toward the Rehabilitation of War-Torn Countries* at DC, September 19-22, 1944. DC: USDA, Extension Service, and Office of Foreign Agricultural Relations.

Keywords: Extension; sociology-rural sociology.

0790 Taylor, Carl C.
1945. "Farm family living prospects in 1946: Farm population." *Agricultural Situation* 29(11): 47.

Keywords: Farm population; social change/ trends.

0791 Taylor, Carl C.
1945. "The veteran in agriculture." *Annals of the American Academy of Political and Social Science* 238: 48-55.

Keywords: Veterans.

0792 Taylor, Carl C.
1945. "Critique of Lee M. Brooks' 'Some regional implica-

0792 (continued).
tions of sociological instruction'." *Social Forces* 24(1): 79-80.

Keywords: Uses of rural sociology research.

0793 Taylor, Carl C., and Conrad Taeuber.
1942. "Aid for low income workers in agriculture." *Monthly Bulletin of Agricultural Economics and Sociology (International Institute of Agriculture)* 33(1): 1E-17E.

Keywords: Income-low; rural rehabilitation. Appalachia; Southwest.

0794 Tetreau, E. D., and Varden Fuller.
1942. "Some factors associated with the school achievement of children in migrant families." *Elementary School Journal* 42(6): 423-431. [Arizona AES, Arizona State Department of Education, and USDA, BAE, DFPRW cooperating].

Keywords: Education; youth; migration; migrant farm labor; occupations. AZ; CA.

0795 Thomas, Howard E.
1945. "A study of the impact of the war upon a rural community." Cornell University Ph.D. thesis. [USDA, BAE, DFPRW cooperating].

Keywords: World War II-impacts on rural areas; population trends; occupations; community. NY.

0796 USDA, BAE.
1942. "Farm resources and farming systems needed to meet living needs of farm families in five type-of-farming areas: Part III--Delta of Mississippi, Louisiana and Arkansas." Mimeo. Little Rock, AR: USDA, BAE.

Keywords: Level of living; farm systems; planning. MS; LA; AR.

0797 [USDA, BAE, DFPRW?].
1942. "Delineation of communities and neighborhoods: Expanded organization of voluntary local leaders." Mimeo. State College: Mississippi State College. Circular. USDA, BAE, [DFPRW] cooperating.

Keywords: *Locality groups; leadership.

0798 [USDA, BAE, DFPRW?].
1942. "Neighborhood and community basis of rural organization." Mimeo. Lexington, KY: University of Kentucky AES, Agricultural Extension Service, and College of Agriculture and Home Economics, and USDA, BAE, [DFPRW] cooperating.

Keywords: *Locality groups.

0799 [USDA, BAE, DFPRW?].
1942. "Settlement possibilities--Backwater area of Issaquena County, Mississippi." Mimeo. State College: USDA, BAE, [DFPRW?], and Mississippi State College. Mississippi Backwater Areas Study--Yazoo Segment.

Keywords: *Planning; public policy; resettlement. MS.

0800 USDA, [BAE, DFPRW].
1942. "The agricultural manpower situation." Mimeo. [DC]: USDA, [BAE, DFPRW]. {usda 22}.

Keywords: Farm labor; labor force; World War II-impacts on rural areas.

0801 USDA, BAE, [DFPRW].
1942. "The farm labor situation on Wisconsin dairy farms." Mimeo. Milwaukee, WI: USDA, BAE, [DFPRW]. Federal-State Crop Reporting Service, Wisconsin AES and Extension Service, Wisconsin USDA War Board, Jefferson County USDA War Board, the U.S. Employment Service cooperating. {usda 24}.

0801 (continued).
Keywords: Farm labor; labor force; farm wage rates; World War II-impacts on rural areas. WI.

0802 USDA, BAE, [DFPRW].
1943. "Labor and other factors influencing dairy production in the Los Angeles milkshed, November 1942." Mimeo. DC: USDA, BAE, [DFPRW]. {usda 26}.

Keywords: Farm labor; farm wage rates; agricultural production. CA.

0803 USDA, BAE, [DFPRW].
1944. "Part-time farming." Chapter prepared for U.S. Armed Forces Institute textbook, *What Is Farming?* Mimeo. DC: USDA, BAE, [DFPRW?]. The book, written by specialists in the USDA under the editorial supervision of Gustav E. Larson, was issued in 1944. It was revised by Gustav E. Larson and Walter Magnes Teller and published under the same title. NY: D. van Nostrand Co., 1945.

Keywords: Part-time farming.

0804 USDA, BAE, [DFPRW].
1945. "The BAE general-purpose sample of 101 counties." Mimeo. DC: USDA, BAE, [DFPRW]. {usda 39}.

Keywords: Methodology-regional analysis.

0805 USDA, BAE, [DFPRW].
1945. "Technical supplement to 'The BAE general-purpose sample of 101 counties'." Mimeo. DC: USDA, BAE, [DFPRW]. {usda 39}.

Keywords: Methodology-regional analysis.

0806 USDA, BAE, [DFPRW].
1945. "Farm wage surveys of the Bureau of Agriculutral Economics." Mimeo. DC: USDA, BAE, [DFPRW]. {usda 43}.

0806 (continued).
Keywords: Farm wage rates; research.

0807 USDA, BAE, [DFPRW], and Farm Security Administration.
1942. "Backgrounds of the war farm labor problem." Mimeo. DC: USDA, [BAE, DFPRW]. {usda 22}.

Keywords: Farm labor; structure of agriculture; socioeconomic status-aggregate/ area; public policy; migrant farm workers; collective bargaining-farm workers; Farm Security Administration. Blacks.

0808 USDA, Committee VII on Social Security (Carl C. Taylor, chair).
[1943]. "Social security for farm people." Dittoed. [DC: USDA]. {usda 28}.

Keywords: Social security; research.

0809 U.S. Department of the Interior, Bureau of Reclamation [P. Hetherton et al., including Carl C. Taylor, investigators].
1945. *Columbia Basin Joint Investigations, Problem 9, Farm Improvement.* DC: GPO.

Keywords: Planning-Columbia River Basin; public policy; agricultural production; housing.

0810 U.S. Department of the Interior, Bureau of Reclamation [H. H. Johnson, E. G. Arnold, E. C. Johnson, O. H. Maughan, Edward Davis, and Carl C. Taylor, investigators].
1945. *Columbia River Basin Joint Investigations, Problem 14, Financial Aid for Settlers.* DC: GPO.

Keywords: Planning-Columbia River Basin; agricultural agencies; public policy; reclamation projects; irrigation. OR.

0811 USDA, Farm Security Administration.
1942. *How Neighborhoods and Communities Aid Farm*

0811 (continued).
Security Administration Group Programs. Prepared by the [USDA], BAE, [DFPRW]. Mimeo. [DC]: USDA, Farm Security Administration. Publication No. 108.

Keywords: Locality groups; Farm Security Administration.

0812 USDA, Inter-Bureau Committee on Postwar Programs (preparers, comprising an Inter-Bureau Working Group).
1945. *Agricultural Cooperatives in the Postwar Period.* [DC]: USDA.

Keywords: Post-war II planning; cooperatives.

0813 USDA, Inter-Bureau Committee on Post-War Programs.
1945. *Farmers Look at Post-War Prospects.* DC: USDA.

Keywords: Post-war II planning.

0814 USDA Inter-Bureau Committee on Post-war Programs, Surplus Property Work Group.
1945. *Disposal of War Surplus Medical and Hospital Supplies.* [DC]: USDA.

Keywords: Post-war II planning; health and medical care.

0815 USDA, Inter-Bureau Committee on Postwar Agricultural Programs, Land Settlement Work Group.
1945. *Farm Opportunities in the United States: Outlook, Problems, Policies.* DC: USDA.

Keywords: Post-war II planning; veterans; public policy; structure of agriculture.

0816 Vaughan, Theo L., and Herbert Pryor.
1945. *Nevada County Rural Health Services Association, Inc., 1942-44, Nevada County, Arkansas.* DC: USDA, Farm Security Administration, Health Services Division, and BAE, [DFPRW]. Rural Health Report No. 5.

0816 (continued).
Keywords: *Experimental health programs (USDA); Farm Security Administration. Blacks. AR.

0817 Whetten, Nathan L., and Henry W. Riecken, Jr.
1943. *The Foreign-Born Population of Connecticut, 1940.* Storrs, CT: Storrs AES. Bulletin No. 246. USDA, BAE, [DFPRW] cooperating.

Keywords: Population composition. CT.

0818 Williams, Robin M., and Howard W. Beers.
1943. *Farmers on Local Planning Committees in Three Kentucky Counties, 1939-1940.* Lexington, KY: University of Kentucky AES. Bulletin No. 443. USDA, [BAE], DFPRW cooperating.

Keywords: Leadership; land-use planning. KY.

0819 Wolaver, Howard W., and Nat T. Frame.
1942. "Austin Acres." Pp. 58-64 in Russell Lord and Paul H. Johnstone (eds.), *A Place on Earth: A Critical Appraisal of Subsistence Homesteads.* DC: USDA, BAE.

Keywords: Subsistence homesteads; evaluation. MN.

0820 Wynne, Waller, Jr.
[1942?]. "Report on field study of FSA Community and Cooperative Service Program, Bradley County, Arkansas, August 1942." Undated mimeo. [DC: USDA, BAE, DFPRW]. {usda 23}.

Keywords: Community and cooperative services (RR-FSA); evaluation. Blacks. AR.

0821 Wynne, Waller, Jr.
1942. "Report on field study of community and cooperative services of Farm Security Administration, Taylor County, Kentucky." Dittoed. DC: USDA, BAE, [DFPRW]. {usda 23}.

0821 (continued).
Keywords: Community and cooperative services (RR-FSA); evaluation. KY.

0822 Wynne, Waller, Jr.
[1943]. "Report on field study of community and cooperative services in Malheur County, Oregon." Mimeo. [DC]: USDA, BAE, [DFPRW]. {usda 30}.

Keywords: Community and cooperative services (RR-FSA); evaluation. OR.

0823 Wynne, Waller Jr.
1943. *Culture of a Contemporary Rural Community: Harmony, Georgia.* [DC]: USDA, BAE, [DFPRW]. Rural Life Studies No. 6.

Keywords: Community; rural life. Blacks. GA.

D. 1946-1953

0824 Adkins, William G., and Joe R. Motheral.
1953. "Life insurance protection of farm-operator families, Wharton County, Texas, 1952." Mimeo. College Station, TX: Texas A & M College System, Texas AES, Progress Report No. 1529.

Keywords: Social insurance; land tenure. TX.

0825 Adkins, William G., and Joe R. Motheral.
1953. "Retirement plans of farm operators, Wharton County, Texas, 1952." Mimeo. College Station, TX: Texas A & M College System, Texas AES, Progress Report No. 1565.

Keywords: Retirement. TX.

0826 Adkins, William G., and Joe R. Motheral.
1953. "Attitudes toward the Old-Age and Survivors Insurance program: Wharton County, Texas, farm operators, 1952." Mimeo. College Station, TX: Texas A & M College System, Texas AES. USDA, BAE, [DFPRL] cooperating.

0826 (continued).
Keywords: Social insurance; attitudes/ opinions. TX.

0827 Alexander, Frank D.
[1946?]. "Postwar employment problems and opportunities in agriculture in the South." Undated mimeo. Atlanta, GA: USDA, BAE, DFPRW. {usda 45}.

Keywords: Post-war II planning; labor force; veterans; World War II-impacts on rural areas. Blacks. South.

0828 Alexander, Frank D., and Robert E. Galloway.
1947. "Salient features of social organization in a typical county of the general and self-sufficing farm region." *Rural Sociology* 12(4): 395-405.

Keywords: Social organization; social change/ trends; population trends. Appalachia; GA.

0829 Alexander, Frank D., and Lowry Nelson.
1949. *Rural Social Organization: Goodhue County*. University Farm, St. Paul, MN: University of Minnesota AES, Bulletin No. 401. USDA, [BAE], DFPRL, and University of Minnesota AES, Division of Rural Sociology cooperating.

Keywords: Social organiztion; locality groups; community clubs/ organizations; agricultural agencies; social agencies. MN.

0830 Alexander, Frank, and Carl F. Kraenzel.
1953. *Rural Social Organization of Sweet Grass County, Montana, with Attention to the Sutland Characteristics*. Bozeman, MT: Montana State College AES, Bulletin No. 490. USDA, BAE, DFPRL cooperating.

Keywords: Social organization; locality groups; community clubs/ organizations; social agencies; agricultural agencies. MT.

0831 Almack, Ronald B., and Lawrence M. Hepple.

0831 (continued).
1950. *Rural Social Organization in Dent County, Missouri.* Columbia, MO: University of Missouri, College of Agriculture AES, Research Bulletin No. 458.

Keywords: Social organization; culture of agriculture; rural life; extension; World War II-impacts of rural areas. MO.

0832 Anderson, A. H.
1946. "Some practical implications of farm-population density in the Northern Great Plains." Mimeo. Lincoln, NE: USDA, BAE, [DFPRW]. {usda 45}.

Keywords: Farm population. Northern Great Plains.

0833 Anderson, A. H.
1947. "Population distribution and rural services in the Northern Great Plains." Fort Collins, CO: Colorado A & M College Library, Library Bulletin No. 18.

Keywords: Planning-community services; farm population; World War II-impacts on rural areas. Northern Great Plains.

0834 Anderson, A. H.
1950. "Space as a social cost: An approach toward community design in the sparsely populated areas of the Great Plains." *Journal of Farm Economics* 32(3): 411-430.

Keywords: Planning-community services. Great Plains.

0835 Anderson, A. H.
1951. *A Study of Rural Communities and Organizations in Seward County, Nebraska.* Lincoln, NE: University of Nebraska, College of Agriculture AES, Bulletin No. 405. USDA, BAE, DFPRL cooperating.

Keywords: Locality groups; community clubs/ organizations; social agencies; agricultural agencies; social participation. NE.

0836 Anderson, A. H.
1952. *Changes in Farm Population and Rural Life in Four North Dakota Counties.* Fargo, ND: North Dakota Agricultural College AES, Bulletin No. 375. USDA, BAE, [DFPRL] cooperating.

Keywords: Farm population; farm populatioon trends; attitudes/ opinions; migration; population composition; rural life. ND.

0837 Anderson, A. H.
1952. "Community changes with coming of irrigation." *Nebraska Agricultural Extension Service News* 41(1): 2.

Keywords: Irrigation; community; social change/ trends. NE.

0838 Anderson, A. H., and Randall C. Hill.
1948. *Rural Communities and Organizations: A Study of Group Life in Ellis County, Kansas.* Manhattan, KS: Kansas AES, Department of Agricultural Economics, Circular No. 143. USDA, BAE, DFPRL cooperating.

Keywords: Social organization; locality groups; community clubs/ organizations; agricultural agencies; social participation. KS.

0839 Anderson, A. H., and Glen V. Vergeront.
1948. *Rural Communities and Organizations: A Study of Group Life in Wells County, North Dakota.* Fargo, ND: North Dakota Agricultural College AES, Bulletin No. 351. USDA, BAE, DFPRL cooperating.

Keywords: Locality groups; agricultural agencies; community clubs/ organizations; social agencies; social participation. ND.

0840 Anderson, A. H., and Paul J. Jehlik.
1952. *Irrigation and the Community (Some Aspects of Irrigation Development in Established Farming Areas of Nebraska).* Lincoln, NE: University of Nebraska, College

0840 (continued).
of Agriculture AES, Agricultural Economics Progress Report No. 6. USDA, BAE, [DFPRL] cooperating.

Keywords: Irrigation; farm size; farm population trends. NE.

0841 Anderson, A. H., and C. J. Miller.
1953. *The Changing Role of the Small Town in Farm Areas (a Study of Adams, Nebraska).* Lincoln, NE: University of Nebraska, College of Agriculture AES, Bulletin No. 419. USDA, BAE, [DFPRL] cooperating.

Keywords: Villages; trade centers; level of living; population composition; social change/ trends. NE.

0842 Anderson, A. H., and C. J. Miller.
1953. "Our small towns do have a future." Lincoln, NE: University of Nebraska, College of Agriculture. *Nebraska Experiment Station Quarterly* 2(1): 6-7.

Keywords: Villages; social change/ trends. NE.

0843 Bachman, K. L., J. C. Ellickson, W. D. Goodsell, and Ray Hurley.
1948. "Appraisal of the economic classification of farms." *Journal of Farm Economics* 30(4): 680-702.

Keywords: Farm size-economic class; methodology.

0844 Bogue, Donald J., and Margaret Jarman Hagood, assisted by Gladys K. Bowles, Ruth W. Smith, and Elizabeth J. Bogue.
1953. *Subregional Migration in the United States, 1935-40. Volume 2, Differential Migration in the Corn and Cotton Belts: A Pilot Study of the Selectivity of Intrastate Migration to Cities from Nonmetropolitan Areas.* Oxford, OH: Miami University, Scripps Foundation. Scripps Foundation Studies in Population Distribution No. 6.

Keywords: Migration; methodology-population analysis;

0844 (continued).
population composition. Blacks.

0845 Bowles, Gladys K., Louis J. Ducoff, and Margaret Jarman Hagood.
1950. "The hired farm working force, 1948 and 1949, with special reference to coverage of hired farm workers under Old-Age and Survivors Insurance." Mimeo. DC: USDA, BAE, [DFPRL].

Keywords: Farm labor; social insurance; aging; population composition; women in agriculture.

0846 Bright, Margaret L., and Donald G. Hay.
1952. "Health resources and their use by rural people: Ulster County." Mimeo. Ithaca, NY: Cornell University, New York State College of Agriculture, Department of Rural Sociology, Mimeograph Bulletin No. 32. USDA, BAE, [DFPRL] cooperating.

Keywords: Health and medical care. NY.

0847 Burnight, Robert G., Walter C. McKain, Jr., Paul L. Putnam, Louis J. Ducoff, and Margaret Jarman Hagood.
1952. "Turn-over of regular hired workers on Connecticut dairy farms, 1950-52 (A preliminary report)." Mimeo. Storrs, CT: University of Connecticut, College of Agriculture, Storrs AES. USDA, BAE, [DFPRL] cooperating.

Keywords: Farm labor; social change/ trends. CT.

0848 Burnight, Robert G., and Walter C. McKain, Jr.
1953. *Regular Hired Workers on Commercial Dairy Farms in Connecticut, April 1950-April 1952.* Storrs, CT: University of Connecticut, College of Agriculture, Storrs AES, Bulletin No. 267. USDA, BAE, [DFPRL] cooperating.

Keywords: Farm labor; social change/ trends. CT.

0849 Clark, Helen M.
1946. "Wages and wage rates of grape harvest workers in

0849 (continued).
Chautauqua and Erie Counties, New York, week ended October 14, 1945." Mimeo. DC: USDA, BAE, [DFPRW]. Surveys of Wages and Wage Rates in Agriculture, Report No. 15.

Keywords: Farm wage rates; farm labor; population composition; women in agriculture; prisoners of war. Blacks; Indians; Jamaican Nationals. NY.

0850 Conference on Extension Experiences Around the World, Committee on Social Sciences in Relation to Extension Work (Carl C. Taylor, chairman).
1949. *Experience with Human Factors in Agricultural Areas of the World.* Conference held May 16-20. [DC]: USDA, Extension Service and Office of Foreign Agricultural Relations, cooperating.

Keywords: Rural development-less developed countries; extension; social organization.

0851 Dahlke, H. Otto, and Harvey V. Stonecipher.
1946. "A wartime back-to-land movement of old age groups." *Rural Sociology* 11(2): 148-152.

Keywords: Aging; migration; retirement. CA.

0852 Draper, C. R., and Daniel Russell.
1951. "Rural organization in Val Verde County, Texas." Mimeo. College Station, TX: Texas Agricultural and Mechanical College System, Texas AES, Miscellaneous Publication No. 71. USDA, [BAE, DFPRL] cooperating.

Keywords: Social organization; locality groups; community clubs/ organizations; social agencies. TX.

0853 Ducoff, Louis J.
1947. "Migratory farm workers in the United States." *Journal of Farm Economics* 29(3): 711-722.

Keywords: Migrant farm workers; social change/ trends.

0853 (continued).
Blacks.

0854 Ducoff, Louis J.
1948. "Farm laborers: 4.1 million drew wages in '47." *Agricultural Situation* 32(7): 13-14.

Keywords: Farm labor; farm wage rates.

0855 Ducoff, Louis J.
1950. *Migratory Farm Workers in 1949*. DC: USDA, BAE. Agriculture Information Bulletin No. 25.

Keywords: Migrant farm workers; farm labor; population composition; women in agriculture; labor force. Blacks; Mexicans; Orientals.

0856 Ducoff, Louis J.
1951. "Migratory farm workers: A problem in migration analysis." Paper presented at the annual meeting of the Population Association of America on May 12-13, at Chapel Hill, NC. *Rural Sociology* 16(3): 217-224.

Keywords: Methodology-population analysis; migration; migrant farm workers; population composition.

0857 Ducoff, Louis J.
1952. "How defense affects farm manpower." *Agricultural Situation* 36(9): 7.

Keywords: Farm labor. CT; TX; KY.

0858 Ducoff, Louis J.
1953. "Employment in agriculture." Pp.367-382, in W. S. Woytinsky and Associates, *Employment and Wages in the United States*. New York: The Twentieth Century Fund.

Keywords: Farm labor; structure of agriculture; sociology of agriculture; agricultural technology.

0859 Ducoff, Louis J.

0859 (continued).
1953. "Wages in agriculture." Pp. 482-492, in W. S. Woytinsky and Associates, *Employment and Wages in the United States*. New York: The Twentieth Century Fund.

Keywords: Farm wage rates; farm labor; World War II-impacts on rural areas.

0860 Ducoff, Louis J.
1953. "The hired farm working force of 1952, with special information on migratory workers." Mimeo. DC: USDA, BAE, [DFPRL].

Keywords: Farm labor; migrant farm workers; population composition; women in agriculture. Blacks.

0861 Ducoff, Louis J., and Margaret Jarman Hagood.
1946. "Veterans returning to farm work." Mimeo. DC: USDA, BAE, [DFPRW]. {usda 46}.

Keywords: Veterans; labor force; farm labor.

0862 Ducoff, Louis J., and Margaret Jarman Hagood.
1946. "Employment and wages of the hired farm working force in 1945 with special reference to its population composition." Mimeo. DC: USDA, BAE, [DFPRW]. {usda 47}.

Keywords: Farm labor; farm wage rates.

0863 Ducoff, Louis J., and Margaret Jarman Hagood.
1946. "Objectives, uses, and types of labor force data in relation to economic policy." Presented at the 105th Annual Meeting of the American Statistical Association on January 24, at Cleveland, OH. *Journal of the American Statistical Association* 41(235): 293-302. Also published February 20 with the same authors and title. Mimeo. DC: U.S. Department of Commerce, Bureau of the Census.

Keywords: Methodology-labor force analysis.

0864 Ducoff, Louis J., and Louis Persh.
1946. "Wages and wage rates of harvesters of special crops in selected areas of 13 states, 1945: A statistical summary." Mimeo. DC: USDA, BAE. Surveys of Wages and Wage Rates in Agriculture, Report No. 17.

Keywords: Farm wage rates; farm labor; population composition; women in agriculture. Blacks; Mexicans, Indians, Mexican Nationals.

0865 Ducoff, Louis J., and Barbara B. Reagan.
1946. "Wages and wage rates of hired farm workers, United States and major regions, May 1945." Mimeo. DC: USDA, BAE. Surveys of Wages and Wage Rates in Agriculture, Report No. 7.

Keywords: Farm wage rates; farm labor; women in agriculture; population composition. Blacks.

0866 Ducoff, Louis J., and Barbara B. Reagan.
1946. "Wages and wage rates of hired farm workers, United States and major regions. September 1945." Mimeo. DC: USDA, BAE. Surveys of Wages and Wage Rates in Agriculture, Report No. 16.

Keywords: Farm wage rates; farm labor; population composition; women in agriculture. Blacks.

0867 Ducoff, Louis J., and Margaret Jarman Hagood.
1947. "Farm and nonfarm wage income of the hired farm working force in 1946." Mimeo. DC: USDA, BAE, [DFPRW]. {usda 45}.

Keywords: Farm labor; farm wage rates; World War II-impacts on rural areas.

0868 Ducoff, Louis J., and Margaret J. Hagood.
1947. "Wage income of hired farm labor." *Agricultural Situation* 31(8): 7-8.

Keywords: Farm labor; farm wage rates.

0869 Ducoff, Louis J., and Margaret Jarman Hagood (preparers; for the Subcommittee on Labor Force Statistics of the Committee on Labor Market Research).
1947. *Labor Force Definition and Measurement: Recent Experience in the United States.* New York: Social Science Research Council, Bulletin No. 56.

Keywords: Methodology-labor force analysis.

0870 Ducoff, Louis J., and Margaret Jarman Hagood.
1948. "The hired farm working force of 1947." Mimeo. DC: USDA, BAE, [DFPRL]. {usda 51}.

Keywords: Farm labor; labor force; income.

0871 Ducoff, Louis J., and Eleanor M. Birch.
1952. "The hired farm working force of 1951 with special information on regular workers in 1950." Mimeo. DC: USDA, BAE, [DFPRL].

Keywords: Farm labor; population composition; women in agriculture. Blacks.

0872 Ellickson, J. C., and John M. Brewster.
1947. "Technological advance and the structure of American agriculture." *Journal of Farm Economics* 29(4) (Part 1): 827-847.

Keywords: Agricultural technology; structure of agriculture; social change/ trends.

0873 Ensminger, Douglas.
1946. "Rural sociology in extension." Presented at the Rural Sociological Society on March 1-3 at Cleveland, Ohio. Mimeo. [DC]: USDA, Cooperative Extension Work in Agriculture and Home Economics. Extension Service Circular 437. Revision of report presented February 20 in the Federal Extension staff seminar on rural sociology.

Keywords: Extension; uses of rural sociology research.

0874 Ensminger, Douglas (Conference Chairman).
1951. "Summary of the Conference." Pp. 200-207 in *Conference Report on Extension Experiences Around the World*, Washington, D.C., May 16-20, 1949. DC: USDA, Extension Service, and Office of Foreign Agricultural Relations.

Keywords: Extension; rural development-less developed countries.

0875 Ensminger, Douglas, and Robert A. Polson.
1946. "The concept of the community." *Rural Sociology* 11(1): 43-51.

Keywords: Locality groups; social organization.

0876 [Frame, Nat T.]
1946. "Wartime influence on Jasper County, Illinois and community programs following the war: A study by the Jasper County Community Council assisted by the College of Agriculture, University of Illinois and [DFPRW], BAE, USDA." Mimeo. Milwaukee, WI: USDA, BAE. {usda 44}.

Keywords: Social organization; social change/ trends; rural life. IL.

0877 F[rame], N[at] T.
1947. "How to score your community." Dittoed. [DC: USDA, BAE, DFPRW]. {usda 50}.

Keywords: Community development.

0878 Federal Interagency Committee on Migrant Labor.
1947. *Migrant Labor... A Human Problem: Report and Recommendations*. DC: U.S. Department of Labor, Retraining and Reemployment Administration.

Keywords: Migrant farm workers; public policy; children.

0879 Fisher, Lloyd.
1947. "Standards and levels of living of prospective

0879 (continued).
settlers on new irrigation projects." Pp. 1-27 in U.S. Department of the Interior, Bureau of Reclamation, Columbia Basin Joint Investigations, *Standards and Levels of Living. Studies by the USDA for Problem 9.* DC: GPO.

Keywords: Planning-Columbia River Basin; level of living; standard of living; public policy. Columbia Basin.

0880 Flagg, Grace L., and T. Wilson Longmore.
1949. *Trends in Rural and Urban Levels of Living.* DC: USDA, BAE. Agriculture Information Bulletin No. 11.

Keywords: Level of living; levels of living indicators; rural-urban population comparisons; social change/ trends.

0881 Flagg, Grace L., and T. Wilson Longmore.
1952. *Trends in Selected Facilities Available to Farm Families.* DC: USDA, BAE. Agriculture Information Bulletin No. 87.

Keywords: Level of living; social change/ trends.

0882 Folsom, Josiah C.
1950. "Wage ceiling in Florida citrus groves, season of 1943-44." Mimeo. [DC]: USDA, BAE, [DFPRL]. {usda 53}.

Keywords: Farm wage ceilings and stabilization; farm labor; World War II-impacts on rural areas. Blacks. FL.

0883 Galloway, Robert E.
1947. *The Level of Living of Farm Operators in Washington Counties, 1940 and 1945.* Pullman, WA: State College of Washington, Institute of Agricultural Sciences, [Washington] AES. Station Circular No. 57. Contributed by Division of Rural Sociology. USDA, BAE, [DFPRW] cooperating.

Keywords: Levels of living indicators. WA.

0884 Galloway, Robert E.

0884 (continued).
1948. "A contrast in the rural social organization of Rabun County, Georgia, and Franklin County, Washington." *Rural Sociology* 13(4): 384-400.

Keywords: Social organization; level of living; rural family; schools; church; locality groups; leadership. Blacks. Appalachia; GA; WA.

0885 Galloway, Robert E., and Harold F. Kaufman.
1950. *Health Practices of Rural People in Lee County*. State College, MS: Mississippi State College AES. Sociology and Rural Life Series No. 1. USDA, BAE, [DFPRL] cooperating.

Keywords: Health and medical care. Blacks. MS.

0886 Galloway, Robert E., and Harold F. Kaufman.
1950. *Health Practices in Choctaw County*. State College, MS: Mississippi State College AES. Sociology and Rural Life Series No. 2. USDA, BAE, [DFPRL] cooperating.

Keywords: Health and medical care. Blacks. MS.

0887 Galloway, Robert E., Paul M. Houser, and Harold Hoffsommer.
1951. *Community Aspects of Library Planning (A Study of Social Organization in Relation to County Public Library Planning in Prince Georges County, Maryland)*. College Park, MD: University of Maryland, Maryland AES. Station Bulletin No. A-56. University of Maryland, Department of Sociology and AES, and USDA, BAE, [DFPRL] cooperating.

Keywords: Libraries; planning-community services. MD.

0888 Galloway, Robert E. and Marion T. Loftin.
1951. *Health Practices of Rural Negroes in Bolivar County*. State College, MS: Mississippi State College AES. Sociology and Rural Life Series No. 3. USDA, BAE, [DFPRL] cooperating.

0888 (continued).
Keywords: Health and medical care. Blacks. MS.

0889 Galloway, Robert E., and Marion T. Loftin.
1951. *Health Practices of Rural People in Forrest County.* Mimeo. State College, MS: Mississippi State College AES. Sociology and Rural Life Series No. 4. USDA, BAE, [DFPRL] cooperating.

Keywords: Health and medical care. Blacks. MS.

0890 Galloway, Robert E., and Harold F. Kaufman.
1952. *Use of Hospitals by Rural People in Four Mississippi Counties.* State College, MS: Mississippi State College AES. Circular No. 174. USDA, BAE, [DFPRL] cooperating.

Keywords: Hospitals; evaluation. Blacks. MS.

0891 Galloway, Robert E., and Howard W. Beers.
1953. *Utilization of Rural Manpower in Eastern Kentucky: A Study of Economic Area Eight.* Lexington, KY: University of Kentucky, Kentucky AES, Department of Rural Sociology. USDA, BAE, [DFPRL] cooperating.

Keywords: Labor force; farm labor; migration. KY.

0892 Grigsby, S. Earl, and Harold Hoffsommer.
1949. *Rural Social Organization of Frederick County, Maryland.* College Park, MD: University of Maryland AES. Bulletin No. A-51. University of Maryland, Department of Sociology and AES, and USDA, BAE, [DFPRL] cooperating.

Keywords: Social organization; locality groups; community clubs/ organizations; social agencies; agricultural agencies. MD.

0893 Hagood, Margaret Jarman.
1946. "Trends in agricultural population." Pp. 15-18 in Section 1: Trends of Population in the United States, of *Some Aspects of Population and Manpower.* A conference

0893 (continued).
sponsored by the Industrial College of the Armed Forces, the Academy of World Economics, the National Social Science Honor Society, Pi Gamma Mu, and the American Association for the Advancement of Science, Section K, May 2-3. Mimeo. DC: The Industrial College of the Armed Forces, Department of Research. Publication No. S121.

Keywords: Labor force; farm labor; farm population trends.

0894 Hagood, Margaret Jarman (summarizer).
1946. "Farm-population adjustments following the end of the war." Mimeo. [DC]: USDA, BAE, [DFPRW]. {usda 45}.

Keywords: Migration; farm population; World War II-impacts on rural areas.

0895 Hagood, Margaret Jarman.
1947. "Farmer's living conditions improve." *Agricultural Situation* 31(7): 1-3.

Keywords: Level of living; social change/ trends.

0896 Hagood, Margaret Jarman.
1947. "Farm operator family level of living indexes for counties of the United States, 1940 and 1945." Mimeo. DC: USDA, BAE, [DFPRW].

Keywords: Levels of living indicators; World War II-impacts on rural areas; social change/ trends.

0897 Hagood, Margaret Jarman.
1947. "Construction of county indexes for measuring change in level of living of farm operator families, 1940-45." *Rural Sociology* 12(2): 139-150.

Keywords: Methodology-levels of living indicators/ scales.

0898 Hagood, Margaret Jarman.

0898 (continued).
1947. "More people on farms." *Agricultural Situation* 31(9): 1-2.

Keywords: Farm population; farm population trends; veterans.

0899 Hagood, Margaret Jarman.
1947. "Recent contributions of statistics to research methodology in sociology." *Social Forces* 26(1): 36-40.

Keywords: Methodology; research; sociology-rural sociology.

0900 Hagood, Margaret Jarman.
1948. "Changing fertility differentials among farm-operator families in relation to economic size of farm." *Rural Sociology* 13(4): 363-373.

Keywords: Fertility; farm size-economic class.

0901 Hagood, Margaret Jarman.
1949. "Big baby crop, low death rate boost farm population." *Agricultural Situation* 33(8): 9.

Keywords: Farm population; farm population trends.

0902 Hagood, Margaret Jarman.
1949. "Prospects for regional distribution of the population of the United States." Mimeo. DC: USDA, BAE, [DFPRL]. {usda 52}.

Keywords: Population projections.

0903 Hagood, Margaret Jarman.
1951. "Farm population down." *Agricultural Situation* 35(10): 13.

Keywords: Farm population; farm population trends; agricultural technology.

0904 Hagood, Margaret Jarman.
1951. "New research resources for rural sociologists in the 1950 Census." *Rural Sociology* 16(1): 63-66.

Keywords: Research; sociology-rural sociology.

0905 Hagood, Margaret Jarman.
1952. "Farm operator families are living better, report shows." *Agricultural Situation* 36(7): 4-6.

Keywords: Level of living; social change/ trends.

0906 Hagood, Margaret Jarman.
1952. "Farm-operator family level-of-living indexes for counties of the United States: 1930, 1940, 1945, and 1950." Mimeo. DC: USDA, BAE, [DFPRL].

Keywords: Level of living; farm family; social change/ trends.

0907 Hagood, Margaret Jarman, and Louis J. Ducoff.
1946. "Million veterans on farms of U.S." *Agricultural Situation* 30(8): 1-3.

Keywords: Veterans; farm population; farm labor; gender roles; social change/ trends.

0908 Hagood, Margaret Jarman, and Louis J. Ducoff.
1946. "Some measurement and research problems arising from sociological aspects of a full employment policy." Presented at 40th Annual Meeting of the American Sociological Society on March 1-3, at Cleveland, OH. *American Sociological Review* 11(5): 560-567.

Keywords: Methodology-labor force analysis.

0909 Hagood, Margaret Jarman, and Gladys K. Bowles.
1947. "Low income farms in Virginia: Increase in average farm income and level of living, 1939-44." Charlottesville, VA: University of Virginia. *School of Rural Social Economics, Newsletter* 23 (18): 1.

0909 (continued).
Keywords: Income-low; income. VA.

0910 Hagood, Margaret Jarman, and Jacob S. Siegel.
1951. "Projections of the regional distribution of the population of the United States to 1975." *Agricultural Economics Research* 3(2): 41-52.

Keywords: Population projections; population composition; methodology-population analysis.

0911 Hagood, Margaret Jarman, and Emmit F. Sharp.
1951. *Rural-Urban Migration in Wisconsin, 1940-1950.* Madison, WI: University of Wisconsin AES. Research Bulletin No. 176.

Keywords: Population trends; fertility; mortality; migration; population projections. WI.

0912 Hagood, Margaret Jarman, and Jacob S. Siegel.
1952. "Population projections for sales forecasting." Presented at the 111th Annual Meeting of the American Statistical Association on December 27, 1951, at Boston, MA. *Journal of the American Statistical Association* 47(259): 524-540.

Keywords: Population projections; uses of rural sociology research.

0913 Hanger, Michael R., and William H. Metzler.
1946. "Farm wage stabilization in the Pacific states." Mimeo. Berkeley, CA: USDA, BAE, [DFPRW]. {usda 46}.

Keywords: Farm wage ceilings and stabilization.

0914 Hay, Donald G.
1948. "A scale for the measurement of social participation of rural households." *Rural Sociology* 13(3): 285-294.

Keywords: Methodology-social participation scales.

0915 Hay, Donald G.
1950. "The social participation of households in selected rural communities of the Northeast." *Rural Sociology* 15(2): 141-148.

Keywords: Social participation. ME; NY.

0916 Hay, Donald G.
1951. "Social participation of individuals in four rural communities of the Northeast." *Rural Sociology* 16(2): 127-135.

Keywords: Social participation; gender roles; age roles. ME; NY.

0917 Hay, Donald G., and Douglas Ensminger.
1949. "Leader-follower patterns in selected Maine towns." *Rural Sociology* 14(2):160-163.

Keywords: Methodology-local leader identification. ME.

0918 Hay, Donald G., Douglas Ensminger, Stacy R. Miller, and Edmond J. Lebrun.
1949. *Rural Organizations in Three Maine Towns.* Orono, ME: University of Maine. Maine Extension Bulletin No. 391.

Keywords: Social organization; locality groups; community clubs/ organizations; farm organizations; social participation; leadership; farm family; extension; women. ME.

0919 Hay, Donald G., and M. E. John.
1950. *Rural Organization of Bradford County, Pennsylvania.* State College, PA: Pennsylvania State College, School of Agriculture AES. Bulletin No. 524. USDA, BAE, [DFPRL] cooperating.

Keywords: Social organization; locality groups; community clubs/ organizations; social agencies; agricultural agencies; evaluation. PA.

0920 Hay, Donald G., and Olaf F. Larson.
1950. "Medical and health care resources available in Cortland County, New York,1949." Mimeo. Ithaca, NY: Cornell University, New York State College of Agriculture, Department of Rural Sociology Mimeograph Bulletin No. 24. USDA, BAE, [DFPRL] cooperating.

Keywords: Health and medical care. NY.

0921 Hay, Donald G., and Olaf F. Larson.
1950. "Medical and health care resources available in Oswego County, New York, 1949." Mimeo. Ithaca, NY: Cornell University, New York State College of Agriculture. Department of Rural Sociology Mimeograph Bulletin No. 25. USDA, BAE, [DFPRL] cooperating.

Keywords: Health and medical care. NY.

0922 Hay, Donald G., and Robert A. Polson.
1951. *Rural Organizations in Oneida County, New York*. Ithaca, NY: Cornell University, New York State College of Agriculture AES. Bulletin No. 871. USDA, BAE, [DFPRL] cooperating.

Keywords: Social organization; locality groups; community clubs/ organizations; agricultural agencies; social agencies. NY.

0923 Hay, Donald G., and Margaret L. Bright.
1952. "Health resources and their use by rural people in Clinton County, New York, 1951." Mimeo. Ithaca, NY: Cornell University, New York State College of Agriculture. Department of Rural Sociology Mimeograph Bulletin No. 33. USDA, BAE, [DFPRL] cooperating.

Keywords: Health and medical care. NY.

0924 Hay, Donald G., and Olaf F. Larson.
1952. "Use of health resources by rural people in two western New York counties, 1950." Mimeo. Ithaca, NY: Cornell University, New York State College of Agricul-

0924 (continued).
ture. Department of Rural Sociology Mimeograph Bulletin No. 31. USDA, BAE, [DFPRL] cooperating. Statistical supplement issued separately as Statistical Supplement to Department of Rural Sociology Mimeograph Bulletin No. 31. USDA, BAE [DFPRL] cooperating.

Keywords: Health and medical care. NY.

0925 Hay, Donald G. and Olaf F. Larson.
1952. "Medical and health care resources available in Chautauqua County, New York, 1950." Mimeo. Ithaca, NY: Cornell University, New York State College of Agriculture. Department of Rural Sociology Mimeograph Bulletin No. 29. USDA, BAE [DFPRL] cooperating.

Keywords: Health and medical care. NY.

0926 Hay, Donald G. and Olaf F. Larson.
1952. "Medical and health care resources available in Livingston County, New York, 1950." Mimeo. Ithaca, NY: Cornell University, New York State College of Agriculture. Department of Rural Sociology Mimeograph Bulletin No. 30. USDA, BAE [DFPRL] cooperating.

Keywords: Health and medical care. NY.

0927 Houser, Paul M., and Robert E. Galloway.
1949. "Use and acceptance of public library services in a rural area." *Rural Sociology* 14(3): 233-243.

Keywords: Libraries. MD.

0928 Houser, Paul M., Robert E. Galloway, and Harold Hoffsommer.
1952. *Rural Reading Habits: A Study of County Library Planning, Prince Georges County, Md.* College Park, MD: University of Maryland AES. Bulletin No. A-69. USDA, BAE, DFPRL, and the Prince Georges County Memorial Library cooperating.

0928 (continued).
Keywords: Information sources; libraries; planning-community services. MD.

0929 Interagency Committee on Migratory Workers, Committee VIII, (Carl C. Taylor, chairman).
1946. "Recruitment, employment and transportation of migratory workers." Dittoed. [DC]: USDA, BAE, [DFPRW]. {usda 46}.

Keywords: Migrant farm workers; children; public policy.

0930 Jehlik, Paul J.
1951. "Iowa loses more farm people." *Iowa Farm Science* 5(8): 124-126.

Keywords: Migration; farm population trends. IA.

0931 Jehlik, Paul J.
1952. "Iowa farmers using less hired help." *Iowa Farm Science* 6(12): 198-199.

Keywords: Farm labor; social change/ trends; agricultural technology. IA.

0932 Jehlik, Paul J.
1953. "What the census shows about Iowa farms and farm families." *Iowa Farm Science* 7(9): 161-162.

Keywords: Uses of rural sociology research. IA.

0933 Jehlik, Paul J.
1953. "How high are we living?" *Iowa Farm Science* 7(11): 209-210.

Keywords: Level of living; social change/ trends. IA.

0934 Jehlik, Paul J., and Wakeley, Ray E.
1949. *Rural Organization in Process: A Case Study of Hamilton County, Iowa.* Ames, IA: Iowa State College of Agriculture and Mechanic Arts. AES Research Bulletin

0934 (continued).
No. 365. Economics and Sociology Section, Sociology Subsection, and USDA, BAE, DFPRL cooperating.

Keywords: Social organization; locality groups; community clubs/ organizations; agricultural agencies. IA.

0935 Jehlik, Paul J., and J. Edwin Losey.
1951. *Rural Social Organization in Henry County, Indiana.* Lafayette, IN: Purdue University AES. Station Bulletin No. 568. USDA, BAE, DFPRL cooperating.

Keywords: Social organization; locality groups; community clubs/ organizations; social agencies; agricultural agencies; social participation. IN.

0936 Jehlik, Paul J., and Robert L. McNamara.
1952. "The relation of distance to the differential use of certain health personnel and facilities and to the extent of bed illness." *Rural Sociology* 17(3): 261-265.

Keywords: Health and medical care. MO.

0937 Larson, Olaf F.
1946. "The rural rehabilitation program as an instrument of social change." Proceedings of the Pacific Sociological Society. *Research Studies, State College of Washington* 14: 121-127.

Keywords: Rural rehabilitation; Farm Security Administration.

0938 Larson, Olaf F.
1946. "Farm veterans in the Pacific Northwest." *Rural Sociology* 11(3): 270-274.

Keywords: World War II-impacts on rural areas; post-war II planning; veterans.

0939 Larson, Olaf F.
1946. "Lessons from rural rehabilitation experience." *Land*

0939 (continued).
Policy Review 9(3): 13-18. Reprinted in *Farm Policy Forum* 1 (July 1948): 54-57, and on pp. 271-277 in *Readings in Agricultural Economics: Rehabilitation of Low-Income Groups in Agriculture.* Bombay: Indian Society of Agricultural Economics, 1951.

Keywords: Rural rehabilitation; Farm Security Administration; evaluation; public policy.

0940 Larson, Olaf F.
1946. "War and post-war adjustments of families who participated in the Farm Security Administration non-commercial project: Thurston County, Washington. A follow-up study." Pp. 59-68 in "A ten-county program experiment with 606 low-income rural families." Mimeo. Ithaca, NY: Cornell University, New York State College of Agriculture. Department of Rural Sociology Bulletin No. 68, March 1966.

Keywords: Experimental rural rehabilitation programs; Farm Security Administration; evaluation; World War II. WA.

0941 Larson, Olaf F.
1947. "Rural rehabilitation--theory and practice." *Rural Sociology* 12(3): 223-237.

Keywords: Rural rehabilitation; Farm Security Administration; social change/ trends; public policy.

0942 Larson, Olaf F.
1950. "Health services used by rural families." *Farm Research* 16(3): 6.

Keywords: Health and medical care. NY.

0943 Larson, Olaf F., and Michael R. Hanger.
1946. "Some postwar rural trends in the Pacific Northwest." Mimeo. Portland, OR: USDA, BAE, [DFPRW]. {usda 45}.

0943 (continued).
Keywords: Population trends; migration; farm labor; veterans; income. Pacific Northwest.

0944 Larson, Olaf F., assisted by Paul J. Jehlik, Ralph R. Botts, Elco Greenshields, Donald C. Horton, Giles Hubert, T. Wilson Longmore, Orlin J. Scoville, and Rachel Rowe Swiger.
1947. "Ten years of rural rehabilitation in the United States." Mimeo. DC: USDA,BAE, [DFPRW]. Also abridged by Sri B. S. Mavinkurve and published under the same author and title, Bombay, India: The Indian Society of Agricultural Economics, 1951.

Keywords: Rural rehabilitation; Farm Security Administration; social change/ trends; evaluation. Blacks.

0945 Larson, Olaf F., and Donald G. Hay.
1951. "Hypotheses for sociological research in the field of rural health." Revised version of paper presented at the annual meeting of the Rural Sociological Society on September 3-7, 1950, at Denver, CO. *Rural Sociology* 16(3): 225-237.

Keywords: Health and medical care; methodology-health research. NY.

0946 Larson, Olaf F., Donald G. Hay, Walter C. Levy, and William E. Mosher.
1951. "Family utilization of health resources in rural areas." *New York State Journal of Medicine* 51(3): 335-340.

Keywords: Health and medical care; farm family; methodology-health research. NY.

0947 Larson, Olaf F., and Donald G. Hay.
1952. "Differential use of health resources by rural people." Presented by invitation at the 144th Annual Meeting of the Medical Society of the State of New York on May 2, 1951, at Buffalo, NY. *New York State Journal of Medicine* 52(1): 43-48.

0947 (continued).
Keywords: Health and medical care. NY.

0948 Larson, Olaf F., and Donald G. Hay.
1952. "Use of health resources by rural people in two central New York counties, 1949." Mimeo. Ithaca, NY: Cornell University, New York State College of Agriculture. Department of Rural Sociology Mimeograph Bulletin No. 27. USDA, BAE, [DFPRL] cooperating. Statistical supplement issued separately as Statistical Supplement to Department of Rural Sociology Bulletin No. 27.

Keywords: Health and medical care. NY.

0949 Lewis, Oscar.
1946. "Bumper crops in the desert." *Harper's Magazine* 193(1159): 525-528.

Keywords: Agricultural production; mechanization. WA.

0950 Longmore, T. Wilson.
1953. "Special agencies within the Department of Agriculture." Pp.146-169, in *Rural Social Systems and Adult Education*, a committee report sponsored by the Association of Land Grant Colleges and Universities and the Fund for Adult Education established by the Ford Foundation. East Lansing, MI: Michigan State College Press.

Keywords: Farmer's Home Administration; soil conservation service; education.

0951 Longmore, T. Wilson, and Grace L. Flagg.
1949. "Farm living varies with distance to city." *Agricultural Situation* 33(10):2-4.

Keywords: Level of living; rural-urban population comparisons.

0952 Longmore, T. Wilson, and Carl C. Taylor.
1951. "Elasticities of expenditures for farm family living, farm production, and savings, United States, 1946."

0952 (continued).
Journal of Farm Economics 33(1): 1-19.

Keywords: Level of living; farm family; income.

0953 Longmore, T. Wilson and Frank C. Nall.
1953. "Service, professional and other civic clubs." Pp. 122-146, in *Rural Social Systems and Adult Education*, a committee report sponsored by the Association of Land Grant Colleges and Universities and the Fund for Adult Education established by the Ford Foundation. East Lansing, MI: Michigan State College Press.

Keywords: Community clubs/ organizations; women.

0954 Lyall, Lawrence B.
[1946]. "Some current trends in the Northern Great Plains." Undated mimeo. [Lincoln, NE]: USDA, BAE, [DFPRW]. {usda 45}.

Keywords: World War II-impacts on rural areas; veterans; social change/ trends; Northern Great Plains.

0955 Manny, Elsie S.
1947. "Dun and Bradstreet as a source of sociological data." *Rural Sociology* 12(1): 58-59.

Keywords: Trade centers; social change/ trends; depression; World War II; research; sociology-rural sociology.

0956 Manny, Elsie S.
1949. "Days lost from work by farm operators because of illness, January-April, 1948." Mimeo. [DC]: USDA, BAE, [DFPRL]. {usda 52}.

Keywords: Health.

0957 Matthews, M. Taylor.
1946. "The Wheeler County, Texas, Rural Health Services Association." *Rural Sociology* 11(2): 128-137.

0957 (continued).
Keywords: Experimental health programs (USDA); health and medical care; attitudes/ opinions; evaluation. TX.

0958 McKain, Walter C., Jr.
1947. "Farm-city living compared." *Agricultural Situation* 31(9): 9-10.

Keywords: Level of living; rural-urban population comparisons.

0959 McKain, Walter C., Jr., and H. Otto Dahlke.
1946. *Turn-Over of Farm Owners and Operators, Vale and Owyhee Irrigation Projects*. Berkeley, CA: USDA, BAE, [DFPRW]. {usda 46}.

Keywords: Farm operator turnover; irrigation. OR.

0960 McKain, Walter C., Jr., and Sara Miles.
1946. "Santa Barbara County between two social orders." *California Historical Society Quarterly* 25(4): 311-318.

Keywords: Population; population composition; migration. Mexicans. CA.

0961 McKain, Walter C., Jr., and Grace L. Flagg.
1948. "Differences between rural and urban levels of living: Part I--Nationwide comparisons." Mimeo. [DC]: USDA, BAE, [DFPRW].

Keywords: Levels of living indicators; rural-urban population comparisons.

0962 McKain, Walter C., Jr., and Grace L. Flagg.
1948. "Differences between rural and urban levels of living: Part II--Regional variations." Mimeo. [DC]: USDA, BAE, [DFPRW].

Keywords: Levels of living indicators; rural-urban population comparisons.

0963 McKain, Walter C., Jr., and Nathan L. Whetten.
1949. *Occupational and Industrial Diversity in Rural Connecticut.* Storrs, CT: University of Connecticut, College of Agriculture, Storrs AES. Bulletin No. 263.USDA, BAE [DFPRL] cooperating.

Keywords: Industries; labor force. CT.

0964 McKain, Walter C., Jr., Elmer D. Baldwin, and Louis J. Ducoff.
1952. *Economic Security in Old Age: Connecticut Farm Operators--1951 (A Preliminary Report).* Storrs, CT: University of Connecticut, College of Agriculture, Storrs AES INF-43. USDA, BAE, [DFPRL] cooperating.

Keywords: Aging; retirement; social insurance. CT.

0965 McKain, Walter C., Jr., Elmer D. Baldwin, and Louis J. Ducoff.
1953. *Old Age and Retirement in Rural Connecticut--2: Economic Security of Farm Operators and Farm Laborers.* Storrs, CT: University of Connecticut, College of Agriculture, Storrs AES. Bulletin No. 299. USDA, BAE, [DFPRL] cooperating.

Keywords: Aging; retirement; social insurance. CT.

0966 McNamara, Robert L., and Paul J. Jehlik.
1950. "Some observations noted during the course of a field sample on changes in farm population." *Rural Sociology* 15(1): 63-64.

Keywords: Farm population; housing. MO.

0967 Metzler, William H.
1946. "Wages and wage rates of seasonal farm workers at selected USDA labor supply centers in North Central California, August-October 1945." Mimeo. DC: USDA, BAE. Surveys of Wages and Wage Rates in Agriculture, Report No. 9.

0967 (continued).
Keywords: Farm wage rates; farm labor; population composition; women in agriculture. CA.

0968 Metzler, William H.
1946. *Two Years of Farm Wage Stabilization in California.* Berkeley, CA: USDA, BAE, [DFPRW]. {usda 46}.

Keywords: Farm wage ceilings and stabilization; World War II; social change/ trends. CA.

0969 Metzler, William H.
1946. "Wages and wage rates of seasonal farm workers in the harvest of selected truck crops, California, 1945." Mimeo. DC: USDA, BAE. Surveys of Wages and Wage Rates in Agriculture, Report No. 10.

Keywords: Farm wage rates; farm labor; population composition. Mexicans; Mexican Nationals; Filipino. CA.

0970 Metzler, William H.
1946. "Wages and wage rates of seasonal farm workers in USDA labor supply centers at Arvin, Woodville, and Firebaugh, California, November 1945." Mimeo. DC: USDA, BAE. Surveys of Wages and Wage Rates in Agriculture, Report No. 13.

Keywords: Farm wage rates; farm labor; population composition; women in agriculture. CA.

0971 Metzler, William H.
1946. "Wages and wage rates of seasonal farm workers in the harvest of selected deciduous fruits, California, May-Sept. 1945." Mimeo. DC: USDA, BAE. Surveys of Wages and Wage Rates in Agriculture, Report No. 12.

Keywords: Farm wage rates; farm labor; population composition; women in agriculture. Blacks; Mexicans; Mexican Nationals; Filipino. CA.

0972 Metzler, William H.

0972 (continued).
1946. "Wages and wage rates of farm workers in the potato, sugar beet, and cotton harvests, California, 1945." Mimeo. DC: USDA, BAE. Surveys of Wages and Wage Rates in Agriculture, Report No. 14.

Keywords: Farm wage rates; farm labor; population composition; women in agriculture; prisoners of war. Blacks; Mexicans; Mexican Nationals; Filipino. CA.

0973 Metzler, William H., and Afife F. Sayin.
1950. "The agricultural labor force in the San Joaquin Valley, California: Characteristics, employment, mobility, 1948." Mimeo. DC: USDA, BAE, [DFPRL]. University of California Institute of Industrial Relations cooperating.

Keywords: Farm labor; migrant farm workers; population composition; women in agriculture. Blacks; Mexicans; Filipino. CA.

0974 Montgomery, Mary, and Marion Clawson.
1946. *History of Legislation and Policy Formation of the Central Valley Project.* Berkeley, CA: USDA, BAE.

Keywords: Planning-Central Valley, California; reclamation projects; public policy. CA.

0975 Motheral, Joe R., William H. Metzler, and Louis J. Ducoff.
1951. "Recruitment of cotton-harvest workers, Texas High Plains, 1951." Mimeo. College Station, TX: Texas AES. Progress Report No. 1502.

Keywords: Farm labor. TX.

0976 Motheral, Joe R., William H. Metzler, and Louis J. Ducoff.
1952. "Sources of cotton labor, Texas High Plains." Mimeo. College Station, TX: Texas AES. Progress Report No. 1491.

Keywords: Farm labor. Blacks; Mexican Nationals. TX.

0977 Motheral, Joe R., William H. Metzler, and Louis J. Ducoff.
1952. "Men and machines in the cotton harvest, Texas High Plains, 1951." Mimeo. College Station, TX: Texas AES. Progress Report No. 1501.

Keywords: Mechanization; irrigation; farm size; land tenure. TX.

0978 Motheral, Joe R., William H. Metzler, and Louis J. Ducoff.
1952. "Labor turnover in cotton production, Texas High Plains, 1951." Mimeo. College Station, TX: Texas AES. Progress Report No. 1506.

Keywords: Farm labor. TX.

0979 Motheral, Joe R., William H. Metzler, and Louis J. Ducoff.
1953. *Cotton and Manpower--Texas High Plains.* College Station, TX: Texas Agricultural and Mechanical College System, Texas AES. Bulletin No. 762. USDA, BAE, [DFPRL] cooperating.

Keywords: Farm labor; mechanization; farm wage rates. Blacks; Mexican Nationals. TX.

0980 National Conference for the Prevention and Control of Juvenile Delinquency, Rural Aspects Panel (Carl C. Taylor chaired the rural aspects panel).
1947. "Report No. 17 of the conference." November 20-22, 1946, in DC at call of U.S. Attorney General. DC: GPO. Recommendations of the panel summarized pp. 122-136 in [U.S.] Department of Justice, *Recomendations for Action for the Panels of the National Conference on Prevention and Control of Delinquency.* DC: GPO, 1947.

Keywords: Juvenile delinquency; public policy. Blacks.

0981 Niederfrank, E. J., with contributions from Donald G. Hay, Henry W. Riecken, Jr., and Ralph R. Nichols.

0981 (continued).
1946. "Some postwar social trends in the rural Northeast." Mimeo. Upper Darby, PA: USDA, BAE, [DFPRW]. {usda 41}.

Keywords: Social change/ trends; veterans; post-war II planning. Northeast.

0982 Pedersen, Harald A.
1952. "Attitudes relating to mechanization and farm labor changes in the Yazoo-Mississippi Delta." Revised version of paper presented at the 15th Annual Meeting of the Southern Sociological Society on March 27-28 as Mississippi AES Journal Article No. 280, at Atlanta, GA. *Land Economics* 28(4): 353-361.

Keywords: Mechanization; farm labor; plantations; attitudes/ opinions; social change/ trends. Blacks. MS.

0983 Pedersen, Harald A., and Arthur F. Raper.
1954. *The Cotton Plantation in Transition: The Case Studies of a Mechanized and an Unmechanized Cotton Plantation in the Yazoo-Mississippi Delta.* State College: Mississippi State College AES. Bulletin No. 508 USDA, BAE, [DFPRL] cooperating.

Keywords: Plantations; mechanization; social change/ trends. MS.

0984 Raper, Arthur F.
1946. "Future of the family-sized farm." *Social Action* 12(4): 4-19.

Keywords: Structure of agriculture; land tenure.

0985 Raper, Arthur F.
1946. "The role of agricultural technology in Southern social change." Presented at the 9th Annual Meeting of the Southern Sociological Society on May 17, at Atlanta, GA. *Social Forces* 25(1): 21-30. The paper was also revised and published as "Machines in the cotton fields," *New South*

0986 (continued).
(Southern Regional Council, Inc.) 1(9): 1-34.

Keywords: Agricultural technology; rural life; social change/ trends; land tenure; Blacks; South.

0986 Raper, Arthur F.
1946. "Farm life and mechanization." *Agricultural Situation* 30(10): 4-5.

Keywords: Mechanization; farm size; farm labor; level of living; social organization; social change/ trends. Blacks.

0987 Raper, Arthur F. (summarizer).
1946. "Uses being made by rural families of increased wartime incomes: Based on current field reports made by professional trained observers in a national sample of 71 counties." Mimeo. [DC]: USDA, BAE, [DFPRW]. {usda 45}.

Keywords: World War II-impacts on rural areas; income; level of living.

0988 Raper, Arthur F. (chairman).
1948. *Land Policy and Church Stability*. Report of Commission Number 3 of the National Methodist Rural Life Conference on July 29-31, 1947, at Lincoln, NE. New York: Extension of the Methodist Church, Division of Home Missions and Church, Department of Town and Country Work.

Keywords: Structure of agriculture; public policy; church.

0989 Raper, Arthur F.
1950. "Evaluation of Rural Life Conference." Pp. 117-125 in *The Changing Status of the Negro in Southern Agriculture*, Proceedings of the Tuskegee Rural Life Conference, ed. by Lewis W. Jones. Tuskegee Institute, Rural Life Council, Rural Life Information Series, Bulletin No. 3.

Keywords: Rural life; social change/ trends; sociology-rural sociology. Blacks. South.

0990 Raper, Arthur F.
1950. "Southern agricultural trends and their effect on Negro farmers." Pp. 12-36 in *The Changing Status of the Negro in Southern Agriculture,* Proceedings of the Tuskegee Rural Life Conference, ed. by Lewis W. Jones. Tuskegee Institute, Rural Life Council, Rural Life Information Series, Bulletin No. 3.

Keywords: Rural life; social change/ trends; population trends; mechanization; land tenure; level of living. Blacks. South.

0991 Raper, Arthur F.
1951. "Some recent changes in Japanese village life." *Rural Sociology* 16(1): 3-16.

Keywords: Land tenure; social change/ trends. Japan.

0992 Raper, Arthur F.
1951. "Some effects of land reform in 13 Japanese villages." *Journal of Farm Economcs* 33(2): 177-182.

Keywords: Land tenure; social change/ trends; attitudes/ opinions. Japan.

0993 Raper, Arthur F.
1952. *A Graphic Presentation of Rural Trends.* DC: USDA, BAE, and Extension Service.

Keywords: Graphic analysis; rural life; social change/ trends.

0994 Raper, Arthur F., Tamie Tsuchiyama, Herbert Passin, and David L. Sills.
1950. *The Japanese Village in Transition.* Tokyo: Supreme Commander for the Allied Powers, General Headquarters. Report No. 136.

Keywords: Culture of agriculture; social change/ trends; land tenure; social organization; leadership; farm family;

0994 (continued).
women in agriculture; women; religion; education; rural life. Japan.

0995 Raper, Arthur F., and Martha J. Raper.
1951. *Guide to Agriculture, U.S.A.* [DC]: USDA. Agriculture Information Bulletin No. 30. USDA, Office of Foreign Agricultural Relations and BAE cooperating.

Keywords: Structure of agriculture; farm population; culture of agriculture; social agencies; social change/ trends.

0996 Raper, Arthur F., and Martha Jarrell Raper.
1951. "Economic and social facts about town and country." Pp. 6-21 in *Methodists in Town and Country*, proceedings of National Methodist Town and Country Conference at Sioux City, IA. Mount Vernon, IA: Cornell College Press for the National Methodist Town and Country Conference.

Keywords: *Rural life; social change/ trends.

0997 Reagan, Barbara B. (under the direction of Louis J. Ducoff).
1946. "Perquisites furnished hired farm workers, United States and major regions, 1945." Mimeo. DC: USDA, BAE. Surveys of Wages and Wage Rates in Agriculture, Report No. 18.

Keywords: Farm wage rates; farm labor; population composition; women in agriculture.

0998 Reagan, Barbara B.
1947. "Wages by type of farm and type of farm work, United States and major regions, 1945." Mimeo. DC: USDA, BAE. Surveys of Wages and Wage Rates in Agriculture, Report No. 19.

Keywords: Farm wage rates; farm labor; population composition; women in agriculture. Blacks.

0999 Reid, Margaret G., and Walter C. McKain.
1946. "Farm family living prospects in 1947." *Agricultural Situation* 30(11): 30-32.

Keywords: Level of living; farm family; World War II-impacts on rural areas.

1000 Riecken, Henry W., Jr., and Nathan L. Whetten.
1948. *Rural Social Organization in Litchfield County, Connecticut.* Storrs, CT: University of Connecticut, College of Agriculture, Storrs AES. Bulletin No. 261. USDA, BAE [DFPRL] cooperating.

Keywords: Social organization; community clubs/ organizations; agricultural agencies; level of living. CT.

1001 Roberts, Roy L.
1946. "Some postwar rural trends in Kentucky, North Carolina, Tennessee, Virginia, and West Virginia." Mimeo. [DC]: USDA, BAE, [DFPRW]. {usda 45}.

Keywords: World war II-impacts on rural areas; veterans; income. Appalachia; KY;NC; TN; VA; WV.

1002 Roberts, Roy L.
1946. "Getting started in life." *Mountain Life and Work* 22(2): 1-2, 23, 27.

Keywords: Replacement rates. Appalachia.

1003 Rohrer, Wayne C.
1949. "Trends in the Texas farm population, 1949." Mimeo. College Station, TX: Texas A & M College System, Texas AES. Progress Report No. 1184. USDA, [BAE, DFPRL] cooperating.

Keywords: Resettlement. CA.

1004 Rohrer, Wayne C., and Carl C. Taylor.
1953. "Adult educational programs or activities of the general farmers' organizations and cooperatives." Pp. 100-

1004 (continued).
122, in *Rural Social Systems and Adult Education*, a committee report sponsored by the Association of Land Grant Colleges and Universities and the Fund for Adult Education established by the Ford Foundation. East Lansing, MI: Michigan State College Press.

Keywords: Farm organizations; education.

1005 Schuler, Edgar A.
1946. "A workshop that worked." *Extension Service Review* 17(10): 134-135.

Keywords: Libraries.

1006 Schuler, Edgar A., and Rachel Rowe Swiger (see also Rowe).
1946. "Trends in farm family levels and standards of living." Dittoed. Revised in August, 1947 by Walter C. McKain Jr. Mimeo. DC: USDA, BAE, [DFPRW].

Keywords: Level of living; standard of living; social change/ trends.

1007 Schuler, Edgar A., and Selz C. Mayo.
1946. "Measuring unmet needs for medical care: An experiment in method." Dittoed. [DC: USDA, BAE, DFPRW]. {usda 46}.

Keywords: Methodology-health research.

1008 Schuler, Edgar A., Selz C. Mayo, and Henry B. Makeover.
1946. "Measuring unmet needs for medical care: An experiment in method." *Rural Sociology* 11(2): 152-158.

Keywords: Methodology-health research. NC.

1009 Senf, Catherine (preparer).
1946. "Wages and wage rates of potato harvest workers on Long Island, New York, week ended September 1, 1945."

1009 (continued).
Mimeo. DC: USDA, BAE. Surveys of Wages and Wage Rates in Agriculture, Report No. 8.

Keywords: Farm wage rates; farm labor; population composition; women in agriculture; prisoners of war. Blacks; JamaicanNationals. NY.

1010 Senf, Catherine, Helen Clark, and Elizabeth Christen (preparers).
1946. "Wages and wage rates of seasonal farm workers in the harvest of tomatoes, beets, and strawberries in selected areas of New York State, 1945." Mimeo. DC: USDA, BAE. Surveys of Wages and Wage Rates in Agriculture, Report No. 11.

Keywords: Farm wage rates; farm labor; population composition; women in agriculture; prisoners of war. Blacks; Jamaican Nationals. NY.

1011 Sewell, William H., Charles E. Ramsey, and Louis J. Ducoff.
1953. *Farmers['] Conceptions and Plans for Economic Security in Old Age.* Madison, WI: University of Wisconsin AES. Research Bulletin No. 182. USDA, BAE, DFPRL cooperating.

Keywords: Social security; retirement; attitudes/ opinions. WI.

1012 Stonecipher, Harvey V., and H. Otto Dahlke.
1946. "Rural settlement in the foothill areas of Butte County, California." Mimeo. Berkeley, CA: USDA, BAE, [DFPRW]. {usda 46}.

Keywords: Resettlement. CA.

1013 Swiger, Rachel Rowe, and Edgar A. Schuler.
1947. "Farm family levels and standards of living in the Plains and the Northwest." Pp. 29-48 in U.S. Department of the Interior, Bureau of Reclamation, Columbia Basin

1013 (continued).
Joint Investigations, *Standards and Levels of Living. Studies by the USDA for Problem 9*. DC: GPO.

Keywords: Planning-Columbia River Basin; level of living; standard of living; public policy. KS; ND; OR; WA.

1014 Taylor, Carl C.
1946. "Dwight Sanderson--social scientist." *Rural Sociology* 11(1): 14-23.

Keywords: Sociology-rural sociology.

1015 Taylor, Carl C.
1946. "The sociologists' part in planning the Columbia Basin." Presented at the Annual Meeting of the American Sociological Society on March 1, at Cleveland, OH. *American Sociological Review* 11(3): 321-330.

Keywords: Uses of rural sociology research; planning-Columbia River Basin. Columbia Basin.

1016 Taylor, Carl C.
1946. "The social responsibilities of the social sciences--the national level." Presented at the Annual Meeting of the American Sociological Society on March 1-3, at Cleveland, OH. *American Sociological Review* 11(4): 384-392.

Keywords: Uses of rural sociology research; sociology-rural sociology.

1017 Taylor, Carl C.
1947. "Sociology and common sense." Presidential address, annual meeting of the American Sociological Society, December 28-30, 1946 at Chicago, IL. *American Sociological Review* 12(1): 1-9.

Keywords: Research; sociology-rural sociology; evaluation.

1018 Taylor, Carl C.

1018 (continued).
1948. "Dr. Galpin at Washington." *Rural Sociology* 13(2): 145-155.

Keywords: Sociology-rural sociology.

1019 Taylor, Carl C.
1948. "Current research projects of Division of Farm Population and Rural Life, Bureau of Agricultural Economics, U.S. Department of Agriculture, April 27, 1948." *Rural Sociology* 13(3): 315-324.

Keywords: Division of Farm Population and Rural Life.

1020 Taylor, Carl C.
1950. "Summary of open discussion of 'Needed Research in Rural Sociology,' by Wm. H. Sewell." *Rural Sociology* 15(2): 129-130.

Keywords: Sociology-rural sociology; evaluation.

1021 Taylor, Carl C.
1950. "Profitable areas of socio-economic research in land-grant colleges." Pp. 57-63 in *The Changing Status of the Negro in Southern Agriculture*, Proceedings of the Tuskegee Rural Life Conference. Tuskegee Institute, Alabama; Lewis W. Jones (ed). Tuskegee Institute, AL: Tuskegee Institute, Rural Life Council, Rural Life Information Series, Bulletin No. 3.

Keywords: Sociology-rural sociology; research. Blacks. South.

1022 Taylor, Carl C.
1950. "Conservation as a movement." *Journal of Soil and Water Conservation* 5(3):103-105, 114.

Keywords: Soil conservation; social change/ trends.

1023 Taylor, Carl C.
1951. "Conservation: A social and moral problem." Presen-

1023 (continued).
tation at the Soil Conservation Society of America on October 27, 1950, at Detroit, MI. *Journal of Soil and Water Conservation* 6(1): 7-14.

Keywords: Soil conservation; rural life.

1024 Taylor, Carl C.
1951. "The stewardship of natural resources." Pp. 65-70 in *Methodists in Town and Country*, proceedings of National Methodist Town and Country Conference on July 21, at Sioux City, IA. Mount Vernon, IA: Cornell College Press for the National Methodist Town and Country Conference.

Keywords: *Soil conservation; rural life.

1025 Taylor, Carl C.
1951. "Summaries of panel discussions held at the 1950 annual meeting: The Point-Four Program." *American Sociological Review* 16(1): 73-74.

Keywords: Rural development-less developed countries; research; sociology-rural sociology; cultural anthropology.

1026 Taylor, Carl C.
1951. "Some rural situations and the responsibilities of rural churches." *Town and Country Church* 68: 7, 16.

Keywords: Church; rural life.

1027 Taylor, Carl C.
1951. "Rural community responsibility and world tensions." Pp. 125-129 in *Home and Community Responsibilities in a World of Tension*, Proceedings of the 30th Conference of the American Country Life Association on September 18-20 at Urbana, IL. Des Moines, IA: Wallace-Homestead Publishing Co. for American Country Life Association.

Keywords: Rural life.

1028 Taylor, Carl C., Louis J. Ducoff, and Margaret Jarman Hagood.
1948. *Trends in the Tenure Status of Farm Workers in the United States Since 1880.* DC: USDA, BAE, [DFPRL].

Keywords: Land tenure; social change/ trends; agricultural ladder.

1029 Taylor, Carl C., and Wayne C. Rohrer.
1953. "General farmers' organizations and cooperatives." Pp. 80-99, in *Rural Social Systems and Adult Education,* a committee report sponsored by the Association of Land Grant Colleges and Universities and the Fund for Adult Education established by the Ford Foundation. East Lansing, MI: Michigan State College Press.

Keywords: Farm organizations; American Farm Bureau Federation; cooperatives.

1030 USDA, BAE, [DFPRL], and U.S. Department of Labor, Bureau of Employment Security.
1953. *Unemployment and Partial Employment of Hired Farm Workers in Four Areas, May 1951-May 1952 (summary Report).* DC: USDA, BAE, [DFPRL], and U.S. Department of Labor, Bureau of Employment Security.

Keywords: Farm labor; population composition; women in agriculture; social change/ trends. NM; AR; LA; GA.

1031 U.S. Department of Commerce, Bureau of the Census.
1953. *Farms and Farm People: Population, Income, and Housing Characteristics by Economic Class of Farms; a Special Cooperative Report.* DC: GPO. USDA, BAE, DFPRL, Division of Statistical and Historical Research and Division of Farm Management and Costs; and Bureau of Human Nutrition and Home Economics, Family Economics Division cooperating.

Keywords: Farm population; population composition; women; income; housing; occupations; farm size-economic class. Blacks.

1032 U.S. Department of the Interior, Bureau of Reclamation and USDA, BAE [Carl C. Taylor, chairman investigating committee].
    1946. *Columbia Basin Joint Investigations, Problem 27 [Rural Community Centers].* Dittoed. DC: U.S. Department of the Interior, Bureau of Reclamation and USDA, BAE.

    Keywords: Planning-Columbia River Basin; community; trade centers; social agencies; public policy. Columbia Basin.

1033 U.S. Department of the Interior, Bureau of Reclamation [Carl C. Taylor et al., investigators].
    1947. *Columbia Basin Joint Investigations, Problem 10, Pattern of Rural Settlement.* DC: GPO.

    Keywords: Planning-Columbia River Basin; land division/settlement patterns; public policy. Columbia Basin.

1034 U.S. Department of the Interior, Bureau of Reclamation [Marion Clawson et al., investigators].
    1949. *Central Valley Studies, Problem 24, The Effect of the Central Valley Project on the Agricultural and Industrial Economy and on the Social Character of California: A report on Problem 24.* DC: GPO.

    Keywords: Planning-Central Valley, California; reclamation projects. CA.

1035 U.S. Department of Labor, Bureau of Employment Security.
    1952. "Four area survey shows employment pattern of seasonal farm workers." *The Labor Market and Employment Security.* October: 41-45.

    Keywords: Farm labor. South; Southwest.

1036 Vaughan, Theo L., and Herbert Pryor.
    1946. "Prepayment medical care in Nevada County, Arkansas." *Rural Sociology* 11(2): 137-147.

1036 (continued).
Keywords: Experimental health programs (USDA); health and medical care; evaluation; attitudes/ opinions. Blacks. AR.

1037 Wakeley, Ray E.
1947. "The culture of Corn-Belt County." *Mid-West Sociologist* 10(1): 15-16.

Keywords: Social organization; rural life. IA.

1038 Wakeley, Ray E., and Paul J. Jehlik.
1953. "Regional research in population dynamics." Revision of paper presented at the Annual Meeting of the American Sociological Society on September 4, 1952, at Atlantic City, NJ. *Rural Sociology* 18(2): 166-169.

Keywords: Research; population. North Central.

1039 Wallrabenstein, Paul P.
1947. "Wages and wage rates of hired farm workers: United States and major regions, July 1946." Mimeo. DC: USDA, BAE. Surveys of Wages and Wage Rates in Agriculture, Report No. 20.

Keywords: Farm wage rates; farm labor; population composition; women in agriculture. Blacks.

1040 Wallrabenstein, Paul P.
1948. "Wages and wage rates of hired farm workers, United States and major regions, January 1947." Mimeo. DC: USDA, BAE. Surveys of Wages and Wage Rates in Agriculture, Report No. 21.

Keywords: Farm wage rates; farm labor; population composition; women in agriculture. Blacks.

1041 Wallrabenstein, Paul P. and David O. Mesick.
1950. "Wages and wage rates of hired farm workers, United States and major regions, January 1947." Mimeo. DC: USDA, BAE. Surveys of Wages and Wage Rates in

1041 (continued).
Agriculture, Report No. 22.

Keywords: Farm wage rates; farm labor. Blacks.

1042 White, Helen R.
1952. "Potential 4-H membership." Prepared at the request of the Extension Service. Mimeo. DC: USDA, BAE, [DFPRL]. {usda 55}.

Keywords: Population trends; 4-H clubs.

1043 White, Helen R.
1953. "Population in farm-operator households." Pp. 45-64 in *Farms and Farm People: Population, Income, and Housing Characteristics by Economic Class of Farms; a Special Cooperative Report.* DC: GPO. USDA, BAE, DFPRL, Division of Statistical and Historical Research, and Division of Farm Management and Costs; and USDA Bureau of Human Nutrition and Home Economics, Family Economics Division cooperating.

Keywords: Farm family; population composition; farm size-economic class; women; fertility. Blacks.

1044 White, Helen R., Jacob S. Siegel, and Beatrice M. Rosen.
1953. "Short cuts in computing ratio projections of population." *Agricultural Economics Research* 5(1): 5-11.

Keywords: Methodology-population analysis; population projections.

1045 Woytinsky, W. S., and Louis J. Ducoff.
1953. "Employers." Pp. 342-347, in W. S. Woytinsky and Associates, *Employment and Wages in the United States.* New York: The Twentieth Century Fund.

Keywords: Farm labor; structure of agriculture.

Restricted, 1919-1934 215

V. Restricted use reports and manuscripts

A. 1919-1934

1046 Ajure, Oscar, and Ilena M. Bailey.
1921. "The labor and leisure year of the farmer and his wife." Typed. DC: USDA, Office of Farm Management and Farm Economics, Section of Farm Life Studies, and Office of Home Economics cooperating. (Manuscript intended for USDA bulletin, not approved for publication as a USDA bulletin). {National Archives RG83}.

1047 Manny, Theodore B., and R. C. Smith.
1931. "The Farm Bureau situation in Adams County, Ohio." A confidential report not for public use. Typed. DC: USDA, BAE, [DFPRL]. Ohio State University and the Federal Farm Board cooperating. {usda 2}.

1048 Manny, Theodore B., and R. C. Smith.
1931. "The Farm Bureau situation in Allen County, Ohio." A confidential report not for public use. Typed. DC: USDA, BAE, [DFPRL]. Ohio State University and the Federal Farm Board cooperating. {usda 2}.

1049 Manny, Theodore B., and R. C. Smith.
1931. "The Farm Bureau situation in Ashtabula County, Ohio." A confidential report not for public use. Typed. DC: USDA, BAE, [DFPRL]. Ohio State University and the Federal Farm Board cooperating. {usda 2}.

1050 Manny, Theodore B., and R. C. Smith.
1931. "The Farm Bureau situation in Athens County, Ohio." A confidential report not for public use. Typed. DC: USDA, BAE, [DFPRL]. Ohio State University and the Federal Farm Board cooperating. {usda 2}.

1051 Manny, Theodore B., and R. C. Smith.
1931. "The Farm Bureau situation in Auglaize County, Ohio." A confidential report not for public use. Typed.

1051 (continued).
DC: USDA, BAE, [DFPRL]. Ohio State University and the Federal Farm Board cooperating. {usda 2}.

1052 Manny, Theodore B., and R. C. Smith.
1931. "The Farm Bureau situation in Butler County, Ohio." A confidential report not for public use. Typed. DC: USDA, BAE, [DFPRL]. Ohio State University and the Federal Farm Board cooperating. {usda 2}.

1053 Manny, Theodore B., and R. C. Smith.
1931. "The Farm Bureau situation in Fayette County, Ohio." A confidential report not for public use. Typed. DC: USDA, BAE, [DFPRL]. Ohio State University and the Federal Farm Board cooperating. {usda 2}.

1054 Manny, Theodore B., and R. C. Smith.
1931. "The Farm Bureau situation in Franklin County, Ohio." A confidential report not for public use. Typed. DC: USDA, BAE, [DFPRL]. Ohio State University and the Federal Farm Board cooperating. {usda 2}.

1055 Manny, Theodore B., and R. C. Smith.
1931. "The Farm Bureau situation in Henry County, Ohio." A confidential report not for public use. Typed. DC: USDA, BAE, [DFPRL]. Ohio State University and the Federal Farm Board cooperating. {usda 2}.

1056 Manny, Theodore B., and R. C. Smith.
1931. "The Farm Bureau situation in Mahoning County, Ohio." A confidential report not for public use. Typed. DC: USDA, BAE, [DFPRL]. Ohio State University and the Federal Farm Board cooperating. {usda 2}.

1057 Manny, Theodore B., and R. C. Smith.
1931. "The Farm Bureau situation in Miami County, Ohio." A confidential report not for public use. Typed. DC: USDA, BAE, [DFPRL]. Ohio State University and the Federal Farm Board cooperating. {usda 2}.

1058 Manny, Theodore B., and R. C. Smith.

1058 (continued).
1931. "The Farm Bureau situation in Muskingum County, Ohio." A confidential report not for public use. Typed. DC: USDA, BAE, [DFPRL]. Ohio State University and the Federal Farm Board cooperating. {usda 2}.

1059 Manny, Theodore B., and R. C. Smith.
1931. "The Farm Bureau situation in Richland County, Ohio." A confidential report not for public use. Typed. DC: USDA, BAE, [DFPRL]. Ohio State University and the Federal Farm Board cooperating. {usda 2}.

1060 Manny, Theodore B., and R. C. Smith.
1931. "The Farm Bureau situation in Tuscarawas County, Ohio." A confidential report not for public use. Typed. DC: USDA, BAE, [DFPRL]. Ohio State University and the Federal Farm Board cooperating. {usda 2}.

1061 Taylor Carl C., Fred R. Yoder, and Carle C. Zimmerman.
[1920?]. "Tenants on reclaimed land in Southeastern Missouri--Living conditions of farm residents in the white sections of the Upper Mississippi Delta." Typed. [DC: USDA, Division of Farm Management and Farm Economics, Section of Farm Life Studies. University of Missouri AES cooperating]. (Manuscript intended for USDA bulletin, not approved for publication). {CU Archives}.

B. 1935-1941

1062 Aaronson, Franklin M., and Olaf F. Larson.
1941. "Paid-up and inactive borrowers." Dittoed. [DC]: USDA, BAE, [DFPRW]. Administrative Memorandum No. 7, Based upon Study of FSA Standard Loan RR Borrowers. {NAL}.

1063 DFPRW.
1941. "Effect of Iowa ordnance plant on local rural labor situation." [For administrative use]. Typed. DC: USDA, BAE, DFPRW.

1064 DFPRW.

1064 (continued).
1941. "Effect of Indiana ordnance plant on local rural labor situation." [For administrative use]. Typed. DC: USDA, BAE, DFPRW.

1065 DFPRW.
1941. "Effect of Ohio ordnance plant on local rural labor situation." [For administrative use]. Typed. DC: USDA, BAE, DFPRW.

1066 Hoffsommer, Harold C.
1941. "New ground farmers in the Mississippi River Delta (social study of 500 former cotton tenants and croppers)." Preliminary--for review. Dittoed. DC: USDA, BAE, [DFPRW], Lousiana State University cooperating. {usda 20}.

1067 Larson, Olaf F., and Dorothy F. McCamman.
1941. "Purpose and method of study: the sample." Dittoed. [DC]: USDA, BAE, [DFPRW]. Administrative Memorandum No. 1. Based upon Study of FSA Standard Loan RR Borrowers. {NAL}.

1068 Larson, Olaf F., and Roy L. Roberts.
1941. "Grants in relation to repayments." Dittoed. [DC]: USDA, BAE, [DFPRW]. Administrative Memorandum No. 2. Based upon Study of FSA Standard Loan RR Borrowers. {NAL}.

1069 Larson, Olaf F., and Roy L. Roberts.
1941. "Age of borrowers." Dittoed. [DC]: USDA, BAE, [DFPRW]. Administrative Memorandum No. 8. Based upon Study of FSA Standard Loan RR Borrowers. {NAL}.

1070 Larson, Olaf F., and Roy L. Roberts.
1941. "Frequency and amount of grants." Dittoed. [DC]: USDA, BAE, [DFPRW]. Administrative Memorandum No. 10. Based upon Study of FSA Standard Loan RR Borrowers. {NAL}.

1071 Larson, Olaf F., with the assistance of Roy L. Roberts

1071 (continued).
and the collaboration of Fred L. Garlock and George Y. Jarvis.
1941. "Study of FSA standard loan RR borrowers: Region 1: Characteristics of borrowers, progress of borrowers, and action for rehabilitation. Tabulated data for administrative use only." This was the first of a series, one for each of the 12 FSA regions issued September 1941 through April 1943. Dittoed. DC: USDA, BAE, [DFPRW]. {NAL}.

1072 McCamman, Dorothy F., and Olaf F. Larson.
1941. "Completeness and adequacy of records available for study." Dittoed. [DC]: USDA, BAE, [DFPRW]. Administrative Memorandum No. 5. Based upon Study of FSA Standard Loan RR Borrowers. {NAL}.

1073 McCamman, Dorothy F., and Olaf F. Larson.
1941. "Net worth." Dittoed. [DC]: USDA, BAE, [DFPRW]. Administrative Memorandum No. 6. Based upon Study of FSA Standard Loan RR Borrowers. {NAL}.

1074 Metzler, William H.
1941. "Labor situation in sugar beets, Malheur County, Oregon, and vicinity." Preliminary--For official use only. Dittoed. [DC]: USDA, BAE, [DFPRW]. {usda 18}.

1075 Roberts, Roy L., and Olaf F. Larson.
1941. "Education of borrowers." Dittoed. [DC]: USDA, BAE, [DFPRW]. Administrative Memorandum No. 3. Based upon Study of FSA Standard Loan RR Borrowers. {NAL}.

1076 Roberts, Roy L., and Olaf F. Larson.
1941. "Family composition and size." Dittoed. [DC]: USDA, BAE, [DFPRW]. Administrative Memorandum No. 4. Based upon Study of FSA Standard Loan RR Borrowers. {NAL}.

1077 Roberts, Roy L., and Olaf F. Larson.
1941. "Tenure status of borrowers." Dittoed. [DC]: USDA, BAE, [DFPRW]. Administrative Memorandum No. 9. Based upon Study of FSA Standard Loan RR Borrowers. {NAL}.

1078 Taylor, Carl C., Charles Loomis, John Provinse, J. E. Hulett, Jr., and Kimball Young.
1940. "Cultural, structural, and social-psychological study of selected American farm communities. Field manual (preliminary and confidential)." For administrative use only. Mimeo. DC: [USDA], BAE, DFPRW. {usda 14}.

C. 1942-1945.

1079 Alexander, Frank D.
1943. "Rural Life Trends Report No. 5: Claiborne County, Mississippi. For administrative use only." Dittoed. DC: USDA, BAE, [DFPRW]. {usda 31}.

1080 Alexander, Frank D.
1944. "Cultural reconnaissance survey of Coahoma County, Mississippi (summary). For administrative use." Attached are "Current and anticipated rural migration problems" and "A summary of current problems and post-war prospects." (Note: cover page has December 1944 date, first page of text has March 1944 date). Dittoed. Atlanta, GA: USDA, BAE, [DFPRW]. {NAL}.

1081 Almack, Ronald B.
1944. "Cultural reconnaissance: Crawford County, Iowa." [For administrative use.] Typed. Milwaukee, WI: USDA, BAE, [DFPRW]. {NAL}.

1082 Anderson, Anton H.
1945. "The culture of the wheat area: A summary of reconnaissance surveys in six sample counties." Typed. Lincoln, NE: USDA, BAE, [DFPRW]. {NAL}.

1083 Beers, Howard W., John H. Bondurant, James C. Downing, and Olaf F. Larson.
1943. "Manpower for war work: Eastern Kentucky. Preliminary for review." Dittoed. DC: USDA, BAE, [DFPRW]. University of Kentucky, Kentucky AES, Lexington cooperating. {usda 31}.

1084 Bell, Earl H. (Chairman of the Subcommittee on Medical and Hospital Equipment and Supplies).

1084 (continued).
1944. "Principles for the disposal of war surplus medical and hospital supplies." For administrative use. [With cover memo from the subcommittee.] Mimeo. [DC: USDA, Interbureau Committee on Post-war Programs]. {usda 36}.

1085 Burchfield, Laverne, Nat T. Frame, Julia Wright Morrill, and Floyd W. Reeves.
1944. "Postwar planning for farm and rural life: A selected list of materials and digest of activities designed to furnish useful information to planners and discussants. For review purposes only--not for publication." Prepared by a committee representative of the American Library Association, the Rural Educational Project of the University of Chicago, and the DFPRW, USDA, for the American Country Life Conference on April 11-13, at Chicago, IL. Undated mimeo. [DC]: American Country Life Association. {usda 36}.

1086 Christensen, Harold T.
1945. "A cultural reconnaissance of Rutland County, Vermont." For administrative use only. Dittoed. Upper Darby, PA: [USDA, BAE, DFPRW]. {NAL}.

1087 Dahlke, H. Otto.
[1945]. "The Negro problem enters Clark County [Washington]." For administrative use. Typed. [Berkeley, CA]: USDA, BAE, [DFPRW]. {NAL}.

1088 Dahlke, H. Otto.
1945. "Cultural reconnaissance survey, Bingham County [Idaho]." [Administrative use]. Typed. Berkeley, CA: USDA, BAE, [DFPRW]. {NAL}.

1089 Dahlke, H. Otto.
1945. "Clark County, Washington, cultural reconnaissance survey." Administrative use. Typed. [Berkeley, CA]: USDA, BAE, [DFPRW]. {NAL}.

1090 Dahlke, H. Otto.
1945. "Present and anticipated rural migration trends,

1090 (continued).
Clark County, Washington." For administrative use. Typed. Berkeley, CA: USDA, BAE, [DFPRW]. {NAL}.

1091 Dahlke, H. Otto.
1945. "Current problems and post-war prospects, Clark County, Washington." For administrative use. Typed. [Berkeley, CA]: USDA, BAE, [DFPRW]. {NAL}.

1092 Derr, David E., James C. Downing, Louis J. Ducoff, John C. Ellickson, Margaret Jarman Hagood, Orlin J. Scoville, Everett C. Weitzell, and William T. Ham (project leader).
1943. "Manpower and agricultural resources in the Appalachian Region." For administrative use. Mimeo. DC: USDA, BAE, [DFPRW]. {usda 30}.

1093 Dodson, Linden S.
[1944]. "An approach to the study of a 'laboratory' county in the Appalachian region: Pocahontas County, West Virginia." [For administrative use]. Undated. Dittoed. [DC: USDA, BAE, DFPRW]. {usda 35}.

1094 Ducoff, Louis J.
1944. "Agricultural employment trends, 1940-44." Prepared for a meeting of the Washington Chapter of the American Statistical Association on April 14, at DC. Dittoed. [DC]: USDA, BAE, [DFPRW]. {usda 35}.

1095 [Ducoff, Louis J., and Margaret J. Hagood].
1943. "Recent developments in the 1943 agricultural manpower situation." For administrative use. Mimeo. DC: USDA, BAE, [DFPRW]. {usda 28}.

1096 [Folsom, Josiah C.].
1945. "Social Security, present and proposed." [For administrative use]. Dittoed. DC: USDA, BAE, [DFPRW]. {usda 42}.

1097 [Frame, Nat T.].
1944. "Preliminary cultural reconnaissance: Nobles County,

1097 (continued).
Minnesota." [For administrative use]. Typed. Milwaukee, WI: USDA, BAE, [DFPRW]. {NAL}.

1098 Frame, Nat T.
1944. "Report of a cultural reconnaissance of Goodhue County, Minnesota." [For administrative use]. Typed. [Milwaukee, WI: USDA], BAE, [DFPRW]. {NAL}.

1099 Frame, Nat T., J. Edwin Losey, and Ronald B. Almack.
1944. "Rural Life Trends Report No. 7--North Central Region, Milwaukee: Mid-West Rural Life Trends, April 1944." Preliminary statement for administrative use. Mimeo. Milwaukee, WI.: USDA, BAE, DFPRW. {usda 34}.

1100 Hagood, Margaret J.
1943. "Possible uses of the 'master sample' by the DFPRW in the Rural Life Trends Project." [For administrative use]. Dittoed. DC: USDA, BAE, [DFPRW]. {usda 34}.

1101 [Hagood, Margaret J.].
1944. "The Corn Belt sample." For administrative use. Dittoed. DC: USDA, BAE, [DFPRW]. {NAL}.

1102 [Hagood, Margaret J.].
[1944]. "Tables basic to stratification of counties in the major type-of-farming regions." [For administrative use]. Dittoed. DC: USDA, BAE, [DFPRW]. {NAL}.

1103 Hagood, Margaret J., and Louis J. Ducoff.
1944. "Farm population and utilization of resources in the post-war period." Preliminary and not for release. Dittoed. DC: USDA, BAE, [DFPRW]. {usda 27}.

1104 [Ham, William T.].
[1943]. "Methods and criteria for determining farm wage rates." For administrative use only. Dittoed. DC: [USDA, BAE, DFPRW]. {usda 27}.

1105 [Ham, William T., and Louis J. Ducoff].
1943. "Selected list of material relating to farm wage rates

1105 (continued).
and wartime farm labor problems." For administrative use--preliminary. [DC]: USDA, BAE, [DFPRW]. {usda 27}.

1106 [Ham, William T., and Josiah C. Folsom].
1943. "Wartime use of women in agriculture." [For administrative use]. Dittoed. [DC]: USDA, BAE, [DFPRW]. {usda 28}.

1107 [Hanger, M. Reid].
[1945]. "Current and anticipated rural migration problems and current problems and post-war prospects: Franklin County, Washington." [For administrative use]. Typed. [Portland, OR: USDA, BAE, DFPRW]. {NAL}.

1108 Hay, Donald G.
1944. "Cultural reconnaissance of Oneida County, New York." For administrative use only. Typed. [Upper Darby, PA: USDA, BAE, DFPRW]. {NAL}.

1109 Hay, Donald G.
1945. "Rural reconnaissance: Bradford County, Pennsylvania." [For administrative use]. Typed. Upper Darby, PA: USDA, BAE, [DFPRW].

1110 Hill, George W., Glen T. Barton, and Gilbert Sanborn.
1942. "Labor recruitment in the Wisconsin Cut-Over Area." Preliminary--for administrative use only. Mimeo. Milwaukee, WI: USDA, BAE, [DFPRW]. {usda 26}.

1111 Jehlik, Paul J.
[1943]. "Rural Life Trends Report No. 5: Dallas County, Alabama." For administrative use only. Dittoed. DC: USDA, BAE, [DFPRW]. {usda 31}.

1112 Jehlik, Paul J.
1944. "A cultural reconnaissance report of Jasper County, Illinois." [For administrative use]. Typed. Milwaukee, WI: USDA, BAE, [DFPRW]. {NAL}.

1113 Jehlik, Paul J.

1113 (continued).
1945. "Cultural reconnaissance: Henry County, Indiana." [For administrative use]. Typed. Milwaukee, WI: USDA, BAE, [DFPRW]. {NAL}.

1114 Jehlik, Paul J.
1945. "Cultural reconnaissance of Monroe County, Wisconsin." [For administrativeuse]. Typed. [Milwaukee, WI: USDA, BAE, DFPRW]. {NAL}.

1115 Jehlik, Paul J.
1945. "Rural cultural reconnaissance: Sawyer County, Wisconsin." [For administrative use]. Typed. [Milwaukee, WI: USDA, BAE, DFPRW]. {NAL}.

1116 Johansen, John P.
1945. "The Red River Valley farms, North Dakota, 1936-1944: A study of a Farm Security infiltration and rehabilitation project." [For administrative use]. Typed. Lincoln, NE: USDA, BAE, [DFPRW]. {usda 40}.

1117 Jones, Ronald W.
1942. "Some effects of the war on Louisiana's farm population and on-farm labor supply." Not for publication--for administrative use. Dittoed. Little Rock, AR: USDA, BAE, DFPRW and Agricultural Statistics Division. {usda 24}.

1118 Jones, Ronald W.
1942. "Some effects of the war on Arkansas farm population and on-farm labor supply." For administrative use. Dittoed. Little Rock, AR: USDA, BAE, [DFPRW].

1119 Jones, Ronald W.
1943. "An approach to farm manpower adjustments." For administrative use--not for publication. Dittoed. Little Rock, AR: USDA, BAE, [DFPRW]. {usda 32}.

1120 Jones, Ronald W.
1944. "Texas farm population 1940-1942-43." [For administrative use]. Undated mimeo. College Station, TX: Texas AES. {usda 38}.

1121 Jones, Ronald W., John R. Wenmohs, and Joe R. Motheral.
[1943?]. "Texas farm labor: An analysis of demand and on-farm supply in four major types of farming areas, 1943." Not for publication--preliminary, for review only. Undated mimeo. [College Station, TX]: USDA, BAE, [DFPRW]. The Agricultural and Mechanical College of Texas, Texas Agricultural Extension Service and Texas AES cooperating. {usda 30}.

1122 Larson, Olaf F.
1942. "Status of borrowers on February 28, 1939." Typed. [DC: USDA, BAE, DFPRW]. Special Report No. 1 [to Farm Security Administration], Based upon Study of FSA Standard Loan RR Borrowers. {NAL}.

1123 Larson, Olaf F.
1942. "Changes in working capital associated with changes in net worth." Typed. DC: USDA, BAE, [DFPRW]. Special Report No. 3 [to Farm Security Administration], Based upon Study of FSA Standard Loan RR Borrowers. {NAL}.

1124 Larson, Olaf F.
1942. "Disabilities of RR borrowers and their families." Typed. DC: USDA, BAE, [DFPRW]. Special Report No. 5 [to Farm Security Administration], Based upon Study of FSA Standard Loan RR Borrowers. {NAL}.

1125 Larson, Olaf F.
1942. "Report on reconnaissance work in Ohio and Kentucky for pilot project on mobilizing unproductively used rural manpower, with special reference to a dairy labor program." Preliminary. DC: USDA, BAE, [DFPRW]. {NAL}.

1126 Larson, Olaf F.
1945. "Population changes: Second report--Ada County, Idaho." For administrative use only--not to be released for general distribution. Typed. Portland, OR: USDA, BAE, [DFPRW]. {NAL}.

1127 Larson, Olaf F.

1127 (continued).
1945. "Current and anticipated rural migration problems: Ada County, Idaho." For administrative use only--not to be released for general distribution. Typed. Portland, OR: [USDA], BAE, [DFPRW]. {NAL}.

1128 Larson, Olaf F.
1945. "Current problems and postwar prospects: Ada County, Idaho." For administrative use only--not to be released for general distribution. Typed. Portland, OR: USDA, BAE, [DFPRW]. {NAL}.

1129 Larson, Olaf F.
1945. "Use of savings accumulated during the war period by farm families: AdaCounty, Idaho." For administrative use only--not to be released for general distribution. Typed. [Portland, OR]: USDA, BAE, [DFPRW]. {NAL}.

1130 Larson, Olaf F.
1945. "Population changes: Second Report--Clark County, Washington." For administrative use only--not to be released for general distribution. Typed. [Portland, OR]: USDA, BAE, [DFPRW]. {NAL}.

1131 Larson, Olaf F.
1945. "Use of savings accumulated during the war period by farm families: Clark County, Washington." For administrative use only--not to be released for general distribution. Typed. [Portland, OR]: USDA, BAE, [DFPRW]. {NAL}.

1132 Larson, Olaf F.
1945. "A reconnaissance survey of Ada County, [Idaho]." For administrative use only--not to be released for general distribution. Typed. Portland, OR: [USDA], BAE, [DFPRW]. {NAL}.

1133 Larson, Olaf F., and Rachel R. Swiger (see also Rowe).
1942. "White and colored borrowers." Dittoed. [DC]: USDA, BAE, [DFPRW]. Administrative Memorandum No. 23 [to Farm Security Administration], Based upon Study of FSA

1133 (continued).
Standard Loan RR Borrowers. {NAL}.

1134 Larson, Olaf F., and Rachel R. Swiger (see also Rowe). 1942. "Relief aid before acceptance on RR." Typed. DC: USDA, BAE, [DFPRW]. Special Report No. 4 [to Farm Security Administration], Based upon Study of FSA Standard Loan RR Borrowers. {NAL}.

1135 Larson, Olaf F., and Rachel R. Swiger (see also Rowe). 1942. "Farm leases." Typed. DC: USDA, BAE, [DFPRW]. Special Report No. 7 [to Farm Security Adminstration], Based upon Study of FSA Standard Loan RR Borrowers. {NAL}.

1136 Leonard, Olen E.
1943. "Rural Life Trends Report No. 5: Broward County, Florida." For administrative use. Dittoed. DC: USDA, BAE, [DFPRW]. {usda 31}.

1137 Leonard, Olen E., and Myra Reagon.
1943. "The Share the Meat Campaign in South Carolina." For administrative use. Mimeo. [DC]: USDA, BAE, [DFPRW]. Office of Defense Health and Welfare Service, Nutrition Division cooperating. {usda 27}.

1   1138 Lewis, Oscar.
1945. "Cultural reconnaissance: Bell County, Texas." For administrative use only. Dittoed. Little Rock, AR: USDA, BAE, [DFPRW]. {NAL}.

1139 Lewis, Oscar.
1945. "Current and anticipated rural migration problems: Bell County, Texas." [For administrative use]. Dittoed. [Little Rock, AR: USDA, BAE, DFPRW]. {NAL}.

1140 Lewis, Oscar.
1945. "Current problems and postwar prospects: Bell County, Texas." [For administrative use]. Dittoed. [Little Rock, AR: USDA, BAE, DFPRW]. {NAL}.

1141 Lewis, Oscar.
1945. "A reconnaissance survey of Franklin County, Washington." For administrative use only. Typed. [Berkeley, CA: USDA, BAE, DFPRW]. {NAL}.

1142 Longmore, T. Wilson.
1943. "Rural Life Trends Report No. 5: Desha County, Arkansas--the manpower situation." For administrative use. Mimeo. DC: USDA, BAE, [DFPRW]. {usda 31}.

1143 Longmore, T. Wilson.
1943. "Rural Life Trends Report No. 4: Desha County, Arkansas--agricultural production 1943." For administrative use. Mimeo. [DC: USDA, BAE, DFPRW]. {usda 32}.

1144 Longmore, T. Wilson, and Herbert Pryor.
1945. "Cultural reconnaissance: Desha County, Arkansas." For administrative use only. Typed. Little Rock, AR: USDA, BAE, [DFPRW]. {NAL}.

1145 Lyall, Lawrence.
1944. "Cultural reconnaissance: Custer County, Montana." [For administrative use]. Typed. Lincoln, NE: USDA, BAE, [DFPRW]. {NAL}.

1146 Lyall, Lawrence, and Donald G. Hay.
1943. "Farm manpower adjustments in the Great Plains, 1943." For administrative use only. Dittoed. Lincoln, NE: [USDA], BAE, [DFPRW]. {usda 29}.

1147 Matthews, M. Taylor.
[1944?]. "How people change their minds or adopt new ways of doing things--as illustrated in Wheeler County, Texas, by replies of 153 family heads to the question: 'Why do you approve or disapprove of federal participation in health costs?'." For review only. Mimeo. [DC: USDA, BAE, DFPRW]. {usda 34}.

1148 [Matthews, M. Taylor].
1945. "Current problems and postwar prospects: Woods

1148 (continued).
County, Oklahoma." [For administrative use]. Dittoed. [Little Rock, AR: USDA, BAE, DFPRW]. {NAL}.

1149 [Matthews, M. Taylor].
[1945]. "Current and anticipated rural migration problems [Woods County, Oklahoma]." [For administrative use]. Dittoed. [Little Rock, AR: USDA, BAE, DFPRW]. {NAL}.

1150 Matthews, M. Taylor.
1945. "Cultural reconnaissance: Woods County, Oklahoma." For administrative use only. Dittoed. Little Rock, AR: USDA, BAE, [DFPRW]. {NAL}.

1151 McCamman, Dorothy F., and Olaf F. Larson.
1942. "Receipts from government benefit payments." Dittoed. [DC]: USDA, BAE, [DFPRW]. Administrative Memorandum No. 11 [to Farm Security Administration], Based upon Study of FSA Standard Loan RR Borrowers. {NAL}.

1152 McCamman, Dorothy F., and Olaf F. Larson.
1942. "Gardens." Dittoed. [DC]: USDA, BAE, [DFPRW]. Administrative Memorandum No. 12 [to Farm Security Administration], Based upon Study of FSA Standard Loan RR Borrowers. {NAL}.

1153 McCamman, Dorothy F., and Olaf F. Larson.
1942. "Major source of cash receipts." Dittoed. [DC]: USDA, BAE, [DFPRW]. Administrative Memorandum No. 14 [to Farm Security Administration], Based upon Study of FSA Standard Loan RR Borrowers. {NAL}.

1154 McCamman, Dorothy F., and Olaf F. Larson.
1942. "Receipts from off-farm work." Dittoed. [DC]: USDA, BAE, [DFPRW]. Administrative Memorandum No. 16 [to Farm Security Administration], Based upon Study of FSA Standard Loan RR Borrowers. {NAL}.

1155 McCamman, Dorothy F., and Olaf F. Larson.
1942. "Cash receipts and net cash income." Dittoed. [DC]:

1155 continued).
USDA, BAE, [DFPRW]. Administrative Memorandum No. 17 [to Farm Security Administration], Based upon Study of FSA Standard Loan RR Borrowers. {NAL}.

1156 McCamman, Dorothy F., and Olaf F. Larson.
1942. "Major purposes for which loans were made." Dittoed. [DC]: USDA, BAE, [DFPRW]. Administrative Memorandum No. 20 [to Farm Security Administration], Based upon Study of FSA Standard Loan RR Borrowers. {NAL}.

1157 [McKain, Walter C., Jr.].
1943. "Rural Life Trends Project--Study No. 6--Luzerne County, Pennsylvania." For administrative use only. Dittoed. [Upper Darby, PA: USDA, BAE, DFPRW]. {NAL}.

1158 McKain, Walter C., Jr.
1943. "Rural Life Trends Report No. 5: Luzerne County, Pennsylvania." For administrative use only. Dittoed. DC: USDA, BAE, [DFPRW]. {usda 31}.

1159 McKain, Walter C., Jr.
1943. "Rural Life Trends Project Study No. 3: Farmers' use of 1943 income." For administrative use. Dittoed. Upper Darby, PA: USDA, BAE, [DFPRW]. {usda 33}.

1160 McKain, Walter C., Jr.
1945. "Post-war intentions of West Coast workers." For administrative use. Dittoed. Berkeley, CA: USDA, BAE, [DFPRW]. {usda 42}.

1161 McKain, Walter C., Jr.
1945. "Cultural reconnaissance: Imperial County, California." For administrative use. Typed. [Berkeley, CA]: USDA, BAE, [DFPRW]. {NAL}.

1162 McKain, Walter C., Jr., and William H. Metzler.
1945. "Measurement of turnover and retirement of farm owners and operators." [For administrative use]. Dittoed. Berkeley, CA: USDA, BAE, [DFPRW]. {usda 43}.

1163 Metzler, William H.
[1942]. "Labor situation in the apricot harvest, Brentwood, California." Preliminary: For official use only. Dittoed. [Berkeley, CA]: USDA, BAE, [DFPRW]. {usda 26}.

1164 Metzler, William H.
[1942]. "The labor situation in the peach harvest, Sutter and Yuba Counties, California, August 28, 1942." Confidential--for official use only. Dittoed. [Berkeley, CA]: USDA, BAE, [DFPRW]. {usda 26}.

1165 Metzler, William H.
1943. "Underemployed farmers in Clark County, Washington." For administrative use. Dittoed. [Berkeley, CA]: USDA, BAE, [DFPRW]. {usda 28}.

1166 Metzler, William H.
1943. "Planning for effective use of new types of farm labor in 1943." [For administrative use]. Dittoed. Berkeley, CA: USDA, BAE, [DFPRW]. {usda 28}.

1167 Metzler, William H.
1943. "Analysis of the operation of the wage ceiling in the asparagus industry, Sacramento-San Joaquin Delta, 1943." [For administrative use]. Mimeo. Berkeley, CA: USDA, BAE, [DFPRW]. {usda 32}.

1168 Metzler, William H.
1944. "An example of worker representation in the wage stabilization program." [For administrative use]. Dittoed. Berkeley, CA: USDA, BAE, [DFPRW]. {usda 34}.

1169 Metzler, William H.
1944. "Analysis of operation of the wage ceiling order for harvesting cannery tomatoes: California, 1943." [For administrative use]. Mimeo. Berkeley, CA: USDA, BAE, [DFPRW]. {usda 35}.

1170 Metzler, William H.
1944. "Analysis of the operation of the wage ceiling on picking sun-dried raisin grapes: California, 1943." [For

1170 (continued).
administrative use]. Mimeo. Berkeley, CA: USDA, BAE, [DFPRW]. {usda 35}.

1171 Metzler, William H.
1944. "Operation of the wage ceiling on picking cotton, California, 1943." For administrative use only. Mimeo. Berkeley, CA: USDA, BAE, [DFPRW]. {usda 36}.

1172 Mighell, Ronald L., Russell S. Kifer, Conrad Taeuber, et al.
1942. "Regional patterns of American agriculture: Actual 1940 and 1941, goals 1942, estimated 1944 and 1954." Statement submitted to the National Resources Planning Board (for administrative use only). Typed. DC: [USDA, BAE]. {NAL}.

1173 Montgomery, James E.
1944. "Newton County, Mississippi, Agricultural Health Association." [For administrative use]. Mimeo. DC: USDA, BAE, [DFPRW]. {usda 34}.

1174 Nichols, Ralph R.
1945. "Reconnaissance report, Frederick County, Maryland." For administrative use. Dittoed. DC: USDA, BAE, [DFPRW]. {usda 40}.

1175 [Niederfrank, E. J.].
1943. "Rural Life Trends Project--Study No. 6--Hampshire County, Massachusetts." For administrative use only. Dittoed. [Upper Darby, PA: USDA, BAE, DFPRW]. {NAL}.

1176 Niederfrank, E. J.
1943. "Rural Life Trends Report No. 5: Oneida County, New York." For administrative use. Dittoed. DC: USDA, BAE, [DFPRW]. {usda 31}.

1177 Niederfrank, E. J.
1943. "Rural Life Trends Report No. 5: Hampshire County, Massachusetts." For administrative use only. Dittoed. DC: USDA, BAE, [DFPRW]. {usda 31}.

1178 Niederfrank, E. J.
1943. "Rural Life Trends Report No. 5: Belknap County, New Hampshire." For administrative use only. Dittoed. DC: USDA, BAE, [DFPRW]. {usda 31}.

1179 Niederfrank, E. J.
1945. "Cultural reconnaissance of Litchfield County, Connecticut." Not for publication--for administrative use only. Dittoed. Upper Darby, PA: [USDA, BAE, DFPRW]. {NAL}.

1180 [Page, John S.].
1944. "Plans for using demountable defense houses for post-war rural housing in California." A progress report for administrative use only. Mimeo. [Berkeley, CA: USDA, BAE, DFPRW]. {usda 36}.

1181 Persh, Louis.
[1944]. "The master sample for farms." [For administrative use]. Typed. [DC: USDA, BAE, DFPRW]. {usda 35}.

1182 Pryor, Herbert.
1942. "Community and cooperative services, Desha County, Arkansas." [For administrative use]. Mimeo. Little Rock: USDA, BAE, DFPRW. {usda 23}.

1183 Pryor, Herbert.
1943. "Community and cooperative services and discussion groups: Acadia Parish, Louisiana." For administrative use. Mimeo. Little Rock, AR: USDA, BAE, [DFPRW]. {usda 30}.

1184 Pryor, Herbert.
1943. "Community and cooperative services and neighborhood action groups, Madison County, Arkansas." For administrative use. Mimeo. Little Rock, AR: USDA,BAE, [DFPRW]. {usda 30}.

1185 Pryor, Herbert.
1943. "Rural Life Trends Report No. 5: McCulloch County, Texas." For administrative use. Mimeo. DC: USDA, BAE, [DFPRW]. {usda 31}.

1186 Pryor, Herbert.
1943. "Rural Life Trends Report No. 5: Johnson County, Texas--the farm manpower situation." For administrative use. Mimeo. DC: USDA, BAE, [DFPRW]. {usda 31}.

1187 Pryor, Herbert.
1943. "Rural Life Trends Report No. 5: Fisher County, Texas--the manpower situation." For administrative use. Mimeo. DC: USDA, BAE, [DFPRW]. {usda 31}.

1188 [Pryor, Herbert].
1945. "Current problems and postwar prospects: Avoyelles Parish, Louisiana." [For administrative use]. Dittoed. [Little Rock, AR: USDA, BAE, DFPRW]. {NAL}.

1189 [Pryor, Herbert].
1945. "Current and anticipated rural migration problems: Izard County, Arkansas." [For administrative use]. Dittoed. [Little Rock, AR: USDA, BAE, DFPRW]. {NAL}.

1190 [Pryor, Herbert].
1945. "Current problems and postwar prospects: Izard County, Arkansas." [For administrative use]. Dittoed. [Little Rock, AR: USDA, BAE, DFPRW]. {NAL}.

1191 [Pryor, Herbert].
1945. "Current and anticipated rural migration problems: Pottawatomie County, Oklahoma." [For administrative use]. Dittoed. [Little Rock, AR: USDA, BAE, DFPRW]. {NAL}.

1192 [Pryor, Herbert].
1945. "Current problems and postwar prospects: Pottawatomie County, Oklahoma." [For administrative use]. Dittoed. [Little Rock, AR: USDA, BAE, DFPRW]. {NAL}.

1193 Pryor, Herbert.
[1945]. "Current and anticipated rural migration problems: Avoyelles Parish, Louisiana." [For administrative use]. Dittoed. [Little Rock, AR]: USDA, BAE, [DFPRW]. {NAL}.

1194 Pryor, Herbert.
1945. "Cultural reconnaissance: Avoyelles Parish, Louisiana." For administrative use only. Dittoed. Little Rock, AR: USDA, BAE, [DFPRW]. {NAL}.

1195 Pryor, Herbert.
1945. "Cultural reconnaissance: Izard County, Arkansas." For administrative use only. Dittoed. Little Rock, AR: USDA, BAE, [DFPRW]. {NAL}.

1196 Pryor, Herbert.
1945. "Cultural reconnaissance: Pottawatomie County, Oklahoma." [For administrative use]. Dittoed. Little Rock, AR: USDA, BAE, [DFPRW]. {NAL}.

1197 Pryor, Herbert.
1945. "Cultural reconnaissance: Fisher County, Texas." For administrative use only. Dittoed. Little Rock, AR: USDA, BAE, [DFPRW]. {NAL}.

1198 [Raper, Arthur F.].
1943. "Use of urban high school and college students on farms: Summary." For administrative use. Dittoed. DC: USDA, BAE, [DFPRW]. {usda 28}.

1199 [Raper, Arthur F.].
1943. "The farmers' slant on farm labor." For administrative use. Dittoed. DC: USDA, BAE, [DFPRW]. {usda 30}.

1200 Raper, Arthur F.
1943. "Farmers at work in wartime." For administrative use. Dittoed. DC: USDA, BAE, [DFPRW]. {usda 29}.

1201 Raper, Arthur F.
1943. "Rural Life Trends Report No. 5: Pittsylvania County, Virginia." For administrative use. Dittoed. DC: USDA, BAE, [DFPRW]. {usda 31}.

1202 Raper, Arthur F.
1943. "Rural [Life] Trends Project Study No. 5: Salem County, New Jersey." For administrative use only. Dittoed.

1202 (continued).
[DC: USDA, BAE, DFPRW]. {usda 33}.

1203 Raper, Arthur F.
1944. "Cultural reconnaissance: Greene County, Georgia."
[For administrative use]. Dittoed. [DC: USDA, BAE, DFPRW]. {NAL}.

1204 Raper, Arthur F., and F. Howard Forsyth.
[1943]. "Traditional practices and farm labor shortages: Summary." For administrative use. . DC: USDA, BAE, [DFPRW]. {usda 30}.

1205 [Raper, Arthur F., et al.].
1944. "Farmers' opinions about post-war conditions, spring-summer 1944." For administrative use. Dittoed. DC: USDA, BAE, [DFPRW]. Reprinted October 5, 1944, by the BAE under same title. {usda 35}.

1206 [Raper, Arthur F., et al.].
1944. "The farm labor situation eases up." For administrative use. Dittoed. DC: USDA, BAE, [DFPRW]. {usda 36}.

1207 Raper, Arthur F., and U. T. Miller Summers.
1944. "Shifts in the farm labor situation, 1942-43." For administrative use only. Dittoed. DC: USDA, BAE, [DFPRW]. {usda 34}.

1208 Roberts, Roy L., and Olaf F. Larson.
1942. "Size of farm and acres in crops." Dittoed. [DC]: USDA, BAE, [DFPRW]. Administrative Memorandum No. 13 [to Farm Security Administration], Based upon Study of FSA Standard Loan RR Borrowers. {NAL}.

1209 Roberts, Roy L., and Olaf F. Larson.
1942. "Livestock numbers: Cows, sows, and hens." Dittoed. [DC]: USDA, BAE, [DFPRW]. Administrative Memorandum No. 15 [to Farm Security Administration], Based upon Study of FSA Standard Loan RR Borrowers. {NAL}.

1210 Roberts, Roy L., and Olaf F. Larson.

1210 (continued).
1942. "Number of male youths." Dittoed. [DC]: USDA, BAE, [DFPRW]. AdministrativeMemorandum No. 18 [to Farm Security Administration], Based upon Study of FSA Standard Loan RR Borrowers. {NAL}.

1211 Roberts, Roy L., and Olaf F. Larson.
1942. "Number and size of loans." Dittoed. [DC]: USDA, BAE, [DFPRW]. Administrative Memorandum No. 19 [to Farm Security Administration], Based upon Study of FSA Standard Loan RR Borrowers. {NAL}.

1212 Roberts, Roy L., and Olaf F. Larson.
1942. "Assets (including farm real estate, livestock and equipment) and liabilities." Dittoed. [DC]: USDA, BAE, [DFPRW]. Administrative Memorandum No. 21 [to Farm Security Administration], Based upon Study of FSA Standard Loan RR Borrowers. {NAL}.

1213 Roberts, Roy L., and Olaf F. Larson.
1942. "Cash farm receipts and diversification of receipts from crops and livestock." Dittoed. [DC]: USDA, BAE, [DFPRW]. Administrative Memorandum No. 22 [to Farm Security Administration], Based upon Study of FSA Standard Loan RR Borrowers. {NAL}.

1214 [Roberts, Roy L., and W. S. Middaugh].
1943. "Factors affecting agricultural production in the Northeast." [For administrative use]. Mimeo. Upper Darby, PA: USDA, BAE, [DFPRW]. {usda 29}.

1215 Standing, T. G.
1943. "Rural Life Trends Report No. 5: Latimer County, Oklahoma--the current farm manpower situation." For administrative use. Mimeo. DC: USDA, BAE, [DFPRW].{usda 31}.

1216 Standing, T. G., and Herbert Pryor.
1943. "Community and cooperative services and discussion groups, West Carroll Parish, Louisiana." For administrative

1216 (continued).
use. Mimeo. Little Rock, AR: USDA, BAE, [DFPRW]. {usda 30}.

1217 Swiger, Rachel R. (see also Rowe), and Olaf F. Larson. 1942. "Actual versus planned cash receipts during the 1938 crop year." Typed. DC: USDA, BAE, [DFPRW]. Special Report No. 2 [to Farm Security Administration], Based upon Study of FSA Standard Loan RR Borrowers. {NAL}.

1218 Swiger, Rachel R. (see also Rowe), and Olaf F. Larson. 1942. "Mobility of RR borrowers." Typed. DC: USDA, BAE, [DFPRW]. Special Report No. 6 [to Farm Security Administration], Based upon Study of FSA Standard Loan RR Borrowers. {NAL}.

1219 Taylor, Carl C.
1943. "Community organization--intensive study of the rural community after two years of war." A memorandum to "Area Leaders." [For administrative use]. Dittoed. DC: USDA, BAE, DFPRW. {NAL}.

1220 Taylor, Carl C.
1943. "General instructions for schedules used in study of rural community in wartime (Bureau of the Budget No. 40-43194): Schools survey, family survey, community services survey, social and economic organizations survey." [For administrative use]. Dittoed. DC: USDA, BAE, DFPRW. {NAL}.

1221 [Taylor, Carl C.].
1944. "Guide for reconnaissance survey of sample counties." [For administrative use]. Dittoed. DC: USDA, BAE, [DFPRW]. {NAL}.

1222 [Taylor, Carl C.].
1944. "Notes on measuring the long time culture changes in rural communities." Accompanied by an "Introduction" for the July 1944 conference of Division staff at which the "Notes" were used. For administrative use only. Dittoed. DC: USDA, BAE, [DFPRW]. {usda 38}.

1223 Taylor, Carl C.
1944. "The issue of Social Security for farm people as a part of post-war planning." [For administrative use]. Dittoed. [DC: USDA, BAE, DFPRW]. {usda 34}.

1224 Taylor, Carl C.
1944. "Social Security for farm people." [For administrative use]. Dittoed. [DC: USDA, BAE, DFPRW]. {usda 36}.

1225 Taylor, Carl C.
1944. "[Memorandum to Regional Leaders:] Social Security for farm people." [For administrative use]. Dittoed. DC: USDA, BAE, [DFPRW]. {usda 36}.

1226 Taylor, Carl C.
1944. "Report of a cultural reconnaissance of Shelby County, Iowa." [For administrative use]. Dittoed. DC: USDA, BAE, DFPRW. {NAL}.

1227 [Taylor, Carl C.].
1945. "Field instructions for work in sample counties." [For administrative use]. Dittoed. [DC: USDA, BAE, DFPRW]. {usda 39}.

1228 [Taylor, Carl C.].
1945. "Report on hired farm laborers." For review purposes only. Dittoed. [DC]: USDA, BAE, [DFPRW]. {usda 42}.

1229 Taylor, Carl C., Pauline S. Schloesser and Louis Persh.
1943. "Rural newspapers record attitudes and activities on the farm production front, January-March 1943." [For administrative use]. Dittoed. [DC]: USDA, BAE, [DFPRW]. {usda 27}.

1230 Taylor, Carl C. (forwarder), and J. C. Folsom (preparer).
1944. "[Memorandum to H. R. Tolley:] Summary of preliminary post-war planning reports." [For administrative use]. Dittoed. DC: USDA, BAE, [DFPRW]. {usda 36}.

1231 [Taylor, Carl C., and Josiah C. Folsom].

1231 (continued).
1945. "Social Security for farm people." [For administrative use]. Dittoed. [DC:USDA, BAE, DFPRW]. {usda 42}.

1232 USDA, BAE.
1943. "Memorandum on manpower in agriculture for 1943 For administrative use." Mimeo. {usda 27}.

1233 USDA, BAE [DFPRW].
[1943?]. "Study of six-county experimental rural health programs and FSA health associations and groups." [For administrative use]. Dittoed. DC: USDA, BAE, DFPRW. {NAL}.

1234 USDA, BAE, [DFPRW].
1943. "Shifts of males of military age to agricultural work during the first quarter of 1943 and of 1942." For administrative use. Mimeo. DC: USDA, BAE, [DFPRW].

1235 USDA, BAE, [DFPRW].
1943. "Recent shifts in rural medical facilities: Summary." For administrative use. Dittoed. DC: USDA, BAE, [DFPRW]. {usda 28}.

1236 USDA, BAE, [DFPRW].
1943. "Memorandum on manpower in agriculture for 1943." For administrative use. Mimeo. DC: USDA, BAE, [DFPRW]. A revision and expansion of material issued August 1942 by [USDA], BAE, [DFPRW], entitled "Manpower in agriculture for 1943." {usda 31}.

1237 USDA, BAE, [DFPRW].
1943. "How farmers are spending their increased income: Summary." For administrative use. Dittoed. DC: USDA, BAE, [DFPRW]. {usda 32}.

1238 USDA, BAE, [DFPRW].
1945. "Instructions to enumerators in surveys of farm wage rates--Preliminary draft." [For administrative use]. Mimeo. DC: USDA, BAE, [DFPRW]. {usda 41}.

1239 USDA, BAE, [DFPRW].
1945. "Strata identifications of counties of the United States for BAE samples."[For administrative use]. Dittoed. DC: USDA, BAE, [DFPRW]. {usda 41}.

1240 USDA, BAE, [DFPRW].
1945. "The BAE special-purpose sample of 158 counties for farm-wage surveys." [For administrative use]. Mimeo. DC: USDA, BAE, [DFPRW]. {usda 42}.

1241 USDA, BAE, [DFPRW].
1945. "Studies of wages and wage rates." [For administrative use]. Dittoed. DC: USDA, BAE, [DFPRW]. {usda 43}.

1242 [USDA, BAE, DFPRW].
[1943]. "Factors affecting achievement of the 1943 production goals." For administrative use. Undated. Dittoed. [DC: USDA, BAE, DFPRW]. Summary issue of county reports: Rural Life Trends Report No. 4. {usda 29}.

1243 [USDA, BAE, DFPRW].
1943. "Memorandum on opportunities for occupational adjustments in agricultural populations." Prepared for the United Nations Conference on Food and Agriculture on May 18, at Hot Springs, VA. Mimeo. {usda 28}.

1244 [USDA, BAE, DFPRW].
1943. "Factors in the 1944 agricultural manpower situation--preliminary." For administrative use. Dittoed. [DC]: USDA, BAE, DFPRW]. {usda 29}.

1245 [USDA, BAE, DFPRW].
1943. "The BAE 'master sample'." [For administrative use]. Dittoed. [DC: USDA, BAE, DFPRW]. {usda 31}.

1246 [USDA, BAE, DFPRW].
1945. "Field instructions for work in sample counties." [For administrative use]. Dittoed. [DC: USDA, BAE, DFPRW]. {NAL}.

1247 USDA, BAE, DFPRW.

Restricted, 1942-1945 243

1247 (continued).
1942. "Farm labor situation in New Jersey." [For administrative use]. Typed. DC: USDA, BAE, DFPRW.

1248 USDA, BAE, DFPRW.
1942. "Formulae for farm wage rate determination." Memorandum prepared for R. C. Smith of the BAE. [For administrative use]. Typed. DC: USDA, BAE, DFPRW.

1249 USDA, BAE, DFPRW.
1942. "Possible cotton wage rates in Southwest, 1942 season." [For administrative use]. Typed. DC: USDA, BAE, DFPRW.

1250 USDA, BAE, DFPRW.
1942. "Farm labor conditions in a typical Corn Belt county, Atchison County, Missouri." [For administrative use]. Typed. DC: USDA, BAE, DFPRW.

1251 USDA, BAE, DFPRW.
1942. "Farm labor situation--irrigated valley composed of Dona Ana County, New Mexico, El Paso and Hudspeth Counties, Texas." [For administrative use]. Typed. DC: USDA, BAE, DFPRW.

1252 USDA, BAE, DFPRW.
1942. "Labor in 1942 and 1943 by 12 manpower regions." [For administrative use]. Typed. DC: USDA, BAE, DFPRW.

1253 USDA, BAE, DFPRW.
1942. "Farm labor situation--Southwest Missouri strawberry area." [For administrative use]. Typed. DC: USDA, BAE, DFPRW and U.S. Employment Service cooperating.

1254 USDA, Inter-bureau Working Group on Post-War Programs, Sub-group on Surplus War Property.
1945. "Disposal of war surplus medical and hospital supplies." For administrative use. Mimeo. [DC]: USDA. {usda 43}.

1255 USDA, Interbureau Coordinating Committee on War-

1255 (continued).
time Farm Production Adjustments.
    1942. "Wartime adjustments on Southern farms." Prepared under the general leadership of the USDA, BAE, [DFPRW]. For administrative use. Mimeo. Atlanta, GA, and Little Rock, AR: USDA, BAE. {usda 26}.

1256 USDA, Interbureau Committee on Post-War Programs, Working Group on Land Settlement.
    1944. "Guiding principles for successful establishment of veterans and others on farms." Preliminary draft, for review. Dittoed. [DC]: USDA, Interbureau Committee on Post-War Programs. {usda 34}.

1257 USDA, Interbureau Committee on Postwar Programs, Working Group on Farm Tenure.
    1945. "Farm tenure improvement in the United States: Policy objectives, problems and recommendations." Preliminary copy for review and administrative use. Mimeo. DC: USDA. {usda 43}.

1258 [Vaughan, Theo L.].
    1945. "Current and anticipated rural migration problems: Val Verde County, Texas." For administrative use only. Dittoed. [Little Rock, AR: USDA, BAE, DFPRW]. {NAL}.

1259 Vaughan, Theo L.
    1945. "Cultural reconnaissance: Val Verde County, Texas." For administrative use only. Dittoed. Little Rock, AR: USDA, BAE, [DFPRW]. {NAL}.

1260 Vaughan, Theo L.
    1945. "Current problems and postwar prospects: Val Verde County, Texas." [For administrative use]. Dittoed. [Little Rock, AR: USDA, BAE, DFPRW]. {NAL}.

1261 Wynne, Waller, Jr.
    1943. "Report on field study of the neighborhood action group program in a county in southern Illinois." For administrative use. Mimeo. [DC]: USDA, BAE [DFPRW]. {usda 27}.

1262   Young, Gladwin E., Nat T. Frame, J. Edwin Losey, Ronald B. Almack, Frank T. Hady, Ross V. Baumann, Raymond J. Penn, Howard W. Mayne, and George H. Walter.
1943. "The state of the area: North Central area." Preliminary--for administrative use only. Dittoed. Milwaukee, WI: USDA, BAE, [DFPRW]. Summary issue for region: Rural Life Trends Report No. 4. {usda 28}.

D. 1946-1953

1263 Ducoff, Louis J., and Margaret Jarman Hagood.
1946. "Veterans returning to farm work." For administrative use only. Dittoed. DC: USDA, BAE, [DFPRW]. {usda 47}.

1264   Ducoff, Louis J., with the assistance of Margaret Jarman Hagood.
1951. "Considerations basic to development of agricultural wage stabilization policy and program." Prepared for the Economic Stabilization Agency, Wage Stabilization Board. Preliminary draft--not for publication. Dittoed. [DC: USDA,BAE, DFPRL]. {usda 54}.

1265 Frame, Nat T.
1947. "A history: Country life program West Virginia." Working data--preliminary--for review only. Dittoed. [DC: USDA, BAE, DFPRW]. {usda 50}.

1266 Hagood, Margaret Jarman, and Louis J. Ducoff.
1946. "Recent changes in farm population with reference to the farm labor supply for 1946." For administrative use only. Dittoed. DC: USDA, BAE, [DFPRW]. {usda 45}.

1267 Jehlik, Paul J.
1946. "Some post-war trends in the Midwest." For administrative use only. Typed. Milwaukee, WI: USDA, BAE, North Central Region Office. {NAL}.

1268 Leonard, Olen E.
1946. "Walton County Agricultural Health Association: An experiment in rural health, Georgia, 1942-43." For admin

1268 (continued).
istrative use. Mimeo. DC: USDA, BAE, [DFPRW]. {usda 44}.

1269 Metzler, William H., and Arthur Raper.
1946. "Rural life in the Western Specialty Crop Areas. Preliminary--for review only." [For administrative use]. Typed. [Berkeley, CA: USDA, BAE, DFPRW]. {NAL}.

1270 Persh, Louis J., and Josiah C. Folsom.
1947. "Unusual wage arrangements for hired farm laborers." Working data--restricted. Dittoed. DC: USDA, BAE, [DFPRW]. {usda 48}.

1271 USDA, BAE, DFPRW.
1947. "Tentative supplement to publications and releases of the Division of Farm Population and Rural Welfare and its staff members between July 1944 and June 1946." [For administrative use]. Dittoed. DC: USDA, BAE, [DFPRW]. {usda 48}.

Addresses (unpublished)

A. 1919-1934
1272 Galpin, Charles J.
1920. "The village in relation to the surrounding country." Presentation at a conference regarding the village and town school of the National Education Association on February 26. at Cleveland, OH. Undated mimeo. DC: USDA, BAE, [DFPRL]. {NAL v.63}.

1273 Galpin, Charles J.
1921. "Farm population studies." Presentation for the Directors Experiment Stations, Conference of Land-Grant Colleges on November 8 at New Orleans, LA. Undated mimeo. DC: USDA, BAE, DFPRL.

1274 Galpin, Charles J.
1921. "The role of rural education in community life." Presentation at Pennsylvania Schoolmen's Conference on

1274 (continued).
April 8 at University of Pennsylvania, Philadelphia, PA. Undated mimeo. DC: USDA, BAE, [DFPRL]. {NAL v.63}.

1275 Galpin, Charles J.
1922. "The American farm community--what it is and how it functions." Presentation at the Annual Extension Service [Conference] on October 20 at Ohio State University, Columbus, OH. Undated mimeo. DC: USDA, BAE, [DFPRL]. {NAL v.63}.

1276 Galpin, Charles J.
1922. "Sociological aspects of highway transportation." Presentation at a Conference on Highway Transportation on October 26 at DC. Undated mimeo. DC: USDA, BAE, [DFPRL]. {NAL v.63}.

1277 Galpin, Charles J.
1923. "Rural and urban life in America." Presentation at Commencement on June 7 at the State Agricultural College of Colorado. Undated mimeo. DC: USDA, BAE, [DFPRL]. {NAL v.63}.

1278 Galpin, Charles J.
1924. "Where the farm manager and the home manager meet and join hands." Presentation at conference of Eastern States extension workers in farm management demonstrations and home management on February 19 at Springfield, MA. Undated mimeo. DC: USDA, BAE, [DFPRL].

1279 Galpin, Charles J.
1924. "The country--the economic basis of national life." Presentation at the annual meeting of the Rural Section of the National Education Association on July 3 at DC. Undated mimeo. DC: USDA, BAE, [DFPRL]. {NAL v.63}.

1280 Galpin, Charles, J.
1924. "Rural boys and the Boy Scouts." Presentation at an annual meeting of Boy Scout executives on September 9 at

1280 (continued).
Estes Park, CO. Undated mimeo. DC: USDA, BAE, [DFPRL]. {NAL v.63}.

1281 Galpin, Charles J.
1928. "The 4-H Club work as a sociologist sees it." Outline of a presentation for the leaders of the Boys' and Girls' 4-H Club work on June 26 at U.S. National Museum, DC. Undated mimeo. DC: USDA, BAE, [DFPRL].

1282 Galpin, Charles J.
1928. "An income-spending farm program." Presentation at the Third Annual Bankers' Farm School of the University of Arkansas in cooperation with the Arkansas Bankers' Association on January 17 at Fayetteville, AR. Undated mimeo. DC: USDA, BAE, [DFPRL]. {NAL v.63}.

1283 Galpin, Charles J.
1928. "A high standard of living." Radio address on November 29 at DC. Undated mimeo. DC: USDA, BAE, [DFPRL]. {NAL v.63}.

1284 Galpin, Charles J.
1929. "Reduce the detours in farm life." Presentation at the Second Annual Neighborhood Day on January 15 at North Dakota Agricultural College, Fargo, ND. Undated mimeo. DC: USDA, BAE, [DFPRL]. {NAL v.63}.

1285 Galpin, Charles J.
1929. "A single farm community." Radio address broadcast on May 31 by Station WRC and 16 other stations associated with the National Broadcasting Company. Undated mimeo. DC: USDA, BAE, [DFPRL]. {NAL v.63}.

1286 Galpin, Charles J.
1930. "Trends in farm population movements." Radio address broadcast on February 26 by Station WRC and 32 other stations associated with the National Broadcasting Company. Undated mimeo. DC: USDA, BAE, [DFPRL].

1287 Galpin, Charles, J.

1287 (continued).
1930. "Is the purchasing power of the farmer's town declining?" Presentation at the Country Newspaper Department, Advertising Federation of America on May 20 at DC. Undated mimeo. DC: USDA, BAE, [DFPRL]. {NAL v.63}.

1288 Galpin, Charles J.
1930. "The 4-H Club work. Part 1: Old objectives. Part 2: A new emphasis." Presentation for the leaders of 4-H Club work at the National 4-H Club Camp on June 19 at DC. Undated mimeo. DC: USDA, BAE, [DFPRL].

1289 Galpin, Charles J.
1931. "Farm population starts gaining." Radio address broadcast on February 19 by Station WRC and 39 other stations associated with the National Broadcasting Company. Undated mimeo. DC: USDA, BAE, [DFPRL].

1290 Galpin, Charles J.
1931. "A changing farm life; what it is parting with; what gaining; what holding fast; struggles in evolving a new rural civilization." Presentation at 19th Annual Farm and Home Convention on March 6 at Western State Teachers College, Kalamazoo, MI. Undated mimeo. DC: USDA, BAE, [DFPRL]. {NAL v.63}.

1291 Galpin, Charles J.
1933. "Educational values that come to the 4-H Club member." Radio address (to 4-H Club boys and girls) broadcast on February 4 by 57 stations associated with the National Broadcasting Company. DC: USDA, BAE, DFPRL. Extract published under same title in Farm Population and Rural Life Activities 7(2):13.

1292 Manny, Theodore B.
1930. "Some Ohio trends in membership relations." Presentation at the annual meeting of the American Institute of Cooperation on July 12 at Columbus, OH. Undated mimeo. DC: USDA, BAE, [DFPRL]. {NAL v.63}.

1293 Manny, Theodore B.
1932. "Farmer opinions as factors in cotton acreage determination." Presentation at the USDA 1932 National Outlook Conference in DC. Summary published in *Farm Population and Rural Life Activities* 6(1):9.

1294 Manny, Theodore B.
1933. "Adjusting research in farm population to present conditions." Presentation at the Third Conference of Purnell Research Specialists in Rural Sociology. Excerpt published in *Farm Population and Rural Life Activities* 7 (2): 1-2.

1295 Manny, Theodore B.
1934. "The Roosevelt Country Life Commission's report after twenty-five years." Presentation at the State-Wide Conference of Farm Young Folks on May 5 at Richmond, VA.

1296 Manny, Theodore B.
1934. "Local government in New Jersey: (1) Functions of townships, villages, and boroughs; (2) The rural municipality idea; (3) Ways of reorganizing county government; and (4) Relations of state and county governments." Series of addresses at Institute of Rural Economics on February 26-March 2 at Rutgers University, New Brunswick, NJ and at four New Jersey farmers' meetings. Undated mimeo. DC: USDA, BAE, [DFPRL]. {NAL v.63}.

1297 Manny, Theodore B.
1934. "Local government." Presentation at the Institute of Economics on May 15 at Rutgers University, New Brunswick, NJ.

1298 Manny, Theodore B., and Mary A. Rokahr.
1934. "What cooperation in the new agriculture will mean to the farm home." Summarizes a forum dialogue between Manny and Rokahr before the National 4-H Club delegates on June 19 at DC. Undated mimeo. DC: USDA, BAE, [DFPRL].

B. 1935-1941

1299 Baker, Oliver E.
1935. "Some attempts to change rural life." Presented at Farm Forum Discussion Topic Number 7--"What kind of a rural life can be looked forward to in the United States?" Undated mimeo. [DC: USDA, BAE, DFPRL]. Reprinted in mimeo form as supplementary data for a paper on German land tenure given at the Annual Conference of the Southern Sociological Society in April 1936 at Atlanta, GA. {usda 4}.

1300 Baker, Oliver E.
1935. "The population prospect and some agricultural implications." A radio talk broadcast during the "National Farm and Home Hour" by NBC and a network of 61 associated radio stations on March 29, Undated mimeo. DC: [USDA, BAE, DFPRL]. {usda 4}.

1301 Baker, Oliver E.
1935. "The population prospect: [Part] 2--Regional." Lecture at Summer Session at Iowa State College. Undated mimeo. Ames, IA: Iowa State College of Agriculture and Machanic Arts, Extension Service. {usda 4}.

1302 Baker, Oliver E.
1935. "Better land utilization in the Great Lakes states." Presentation at the Extension Conference on November 7, at Michigan State College, Lansing, MI. Undated mimeo. [DC: USDA, BAE, DFPRL]. {usda 4}.

1303 Baker, Oliver E.
1935. "Relation of population trends to commercial agriculture, especially to production of animal products." Presentation at the American Society of Animal Production on November 29, 1935, at Chicago, IL. Undated mimeo. DC: USDA, BAE, [DFPRL]. {usda 4}.

1304 Baker, Oliver E.
[1935]. "The other half of our farmers and the outlook for their children." Presentation at the Institute of Rural Economics, sponsored by New Jersey State College of Agricul-

1304 (continued).
ture and AES at Rutgers University, New Brunswick, NJ. Undated mimeo. [DC: USDA, BAE, DFPRL]. {usda 4}.

1305 Baker, Oliver E.
[1937]. "Two trends of significance to farmers." Presented at Fort Collins, CO. Undated mimeo. Fort Collins, CO: Colorado Agricultural College ([Division of] Cooperative Extension Work in Agriculture and Home Economics). USDA, [BAE, DFPRL] cooperating. {usda 7}.

1306 Baker, Oliver E.
1938. "Some factors affecting the outlook for rural youth." Presentation at the New York State 4-H Club Leaders Conference on November 16, at Buffalo, NY. Undated mimeo. [DC: USDA, BAE, DFPRL]. {usda 8}.

1307 Baker, Oliver E.
1939. "America's stake in rural life." Presentation at the Iowa State College Farm and Home Week Christian Rural Fellowship dinner on February 13, at Ames, IA. Undated mimeo. [DC: USDA, BAE, DFPRW]. {usda 11}.

1308 Baker, Oliver E.
1940. "Where do Americans live?" The second radio address in the Homemakers Forum Series, America's Human Wealth, by the Rutgers University Home Economics Extension Service, in cooperation with the USDA, BAE, [DFPRW], and the Population Association of America, broadcast over Station WOR in DC and stations associated with the Mutual Broadcasting System. Undated mimeo. [DC]: USDA, BAE, [DFPRW]. {usda 16}.

1309 Baker, Oliver E.
1940. "Population trends and Christian education." Presentation at the Joint Conference of Professional Advisory Sections of the International Council of Religious Education on February 5, at Chicago, IL. Undated mimeo. Chicago, IL: International Council of Religious Education. {usda 16}.

Addresses, 1935-1941

1310 Baker, Oliver E.
1941. "The population prospect in the South." Presentation at the Second Annual Convention of the Catholic Conference of the South on April 21, at Birmingham, AL. Undated mimeo. [DC]: USDA, BAE, [DFPRW]. {usda 18}.

1311 Baker, Oliver E.
1941. "Rural youth in the farm picture." Presentation at the 54th annual convention of the Association of Land-Grant Colleges and Universities on November 12, 1940, at Chicago, Il. Undated mimeo. DC: USDA, Extension Service, and State Agricultural colleges cooperating. {usda 16}.

1312 Ham, William T.
1940. "Seasonal farm labor in the Southeast." Presentation at the Interstate Conference on Migratory Labor on December 17-18, at Atlanta, GA. Mimeo. DC: USDA, BAE, [DFPRW]. {usda 17}.

1313 Hamilton, C. Horace.
1939. "Significance of recently proposed farm tenancy legislation in Texas." Presentation at a meeting of the Southwestern Agricultural Economists and Rural Sociologists on December 8, at Texarkana, TX. Undated mimeo. DC: USDA, BAE, [DFPRW]. {usda 10}.

1314 Hamilton, C. Horace.
1940. "Charting needed areas of rural sociological research in the South." Presentation at the Southern Conference-Seminar on Teaching and Research in Rural Sociology on August 26-30, 1939, at Blue Ridge, NC. Undated mimeo. [DC]: USDA, BAE, [DFPRW]. {usda 14}.

1315 Hoffsommer, Harold C.
1940. "Population and community problems in county planning." Presentation at the University of Arkansas College of Agriculture Summer Session on June 14, Undated mimeo. [DC]: USDA, BAE, [DFPRW]. {usda 5}.

1316 Janow, Seymour J.

1316 (continued).
1939. "Some characteristics of the population engaged in agriculture in the western states." Presentation at BAE regional seminar on November 10, at Berkeley, CA. Undated mimeo. [Berkeley, CA]: USDA, BAE, [DFPRW]. {usda 11}.

1317 Loomis, Charles P.
1940. "A review of some recent studies of Southern culture." Presentation at the Southern Conference on Teaching and Research in Sociology on August 28, at Blue Ridge, NC. Undated mimeo. [DC]: USDA, BAE, [DFPRW]. {usda 11}.

1318 Taeuber, Conrad.
1937. "Some rural problems." Presentation at Fairfax Hall College on January 16, at Waynesboro, VA. Typed. {NAL}.

1319 Taylor, Carl C.
1935. "Farm housing." Presentation at the Joint National Conference on Housing on October 18, at DC. Typed. DC: USDA, BAE, DFPRL. {CU Archives}.

1320 Taylor, Carl C.
1935. "Relatioship of extension with resettlement administration." Presentation at meeting of the Land Grant Colleges Association on November 18, at DC. Typed. DC: USDA, BAE, DFPRL. {CU Archives}.

1321 Taylor, Carl C.
1936. "The contribution of sociology to the field of parent education." Presentation at meeting of the National Council of Parent Education on November 11, at Chicago, Il. Typed. DC: USDA, BAE, DFPRL. {CU Archives}.

1322 Taylor, Carl C.
1936. "Rural rehabilitation and resettlement." Radio speech given over KFAB on January 10, at Lincoln, NE. Typed. DC: USDA, BAE, DFPRL. {CU Archives}.

1323 Taylor, Carl C.

1323 (continued).
1936. "Stabilizing American agriculture and rural life." Presentation at Farm and Home Convention on January 28, at Lexington, KY. Typed. DC: USDA, BAE, DFPRL. Adaptations also presented at the North Carolina Crop Improvement Association on February 12 at High Point, NC, and the Illinois Farmer's Institute on February 19 at Belleville, IL. {CU Archives}.

1324 Taylor, Carl C.
1936. "The social aspects of land adjustment problems." Presentation at the 27th Annual Meeting of the American Farm Economics Association on December 29, at Chicago, IL. Typed. DC: USDA, BAE, [DFPRL]. {NAL}.

1325 Taylor, Carl C.
1936. "The contribution of sociology to the field of parent education." Presentation at a meeting of the National Council of Parent Education on November 11, at Chicago, IL. Typed. DC: USDA, BAE, [DFPRL]. {NAL}.

1326 Taylor, Carl C.
1937. "Population prospect and some agricultural implications." Outline of address for the Montgomery County Agricultural Extension Service on January 6, at Norristown, PA. Typed. DC: USDA, BAE, DFPRL. {CU Archives}.

1327 Taylor, Carl C.
1937. "Home relationships." Radio address during the Farm and Home Hour program on January 11, at DC. Typed. DC: USDA, BAE, DFPRL. {CU Archives}.

1328 Taylor, Carl C.
1937. "The American farm home." Outline of address at the East Tennessee Farmers' Institute on May 19, at Knoxville, TN. Same address given May 20 before the Middle Tennessee Farmers' and Home-Makers' Institute, Columbia, TN. Typed. DC: USDA, BAE, DFPRL. {CU Archives}.

1329 Taylor, Carl C.
1937. "Seeking security in agriculture." Presentation at the 6th Annual Farm andHome Week Conference, Washington State University on June 15, at Pullman, WA. Typed. DC: USDA, BAE, DFPRL. {CU Archives}.

1330 Taylor, Carl C.
1937. "Family aspects of population trends." Presentation at Virginia Polytechnic University on July 28, at Blacksburg, VA. Typed. DC: USDA, BAE, DFPRL. {CU Archives}.

1331 Taylor, Carl C.
1937. "National problems and their effect on Connecticut agricultural living." Presentation at the Annual Extension Conference on December 16, at Storrs. CT. Mimeo. DC: USDA, BAE, [DFPRL]. {NAL}.

1332 Taylor, Carl C.
1937. "Trends in rural life facing older youth." Presentation at the Conference of State Leaders of Older Rural Youth on November 14-17, at DC. Mimeo. DC: USDA, Extension Service, BAE, [DFPRL]. {NAL}.

1333 Taylor, Carl C.
1937. "Leadership in agriculture and rural life." Presentation at the 6th Annual Farm and Home Week Conference, Washington State University, on June 17, at Pullman, WA. Typed. DC: USDA, BAE, [DFPRL]. {NAL}.

1334 Taylor, Carl C.
1937. "The farmers' movement in the South." Presentation at the Southern Sociological Society Meeting on April 2, at Birmingham, AL. Typed. DC: USDA, BAE, [DFPRL]. {NAL}.

1335 Taylor, Carl C.
1937. "The social significance of recent developments." Presentation at Rutgers University on February 22, at New Brunswick, NJ. Typed. DC: USDA, BAE, [DFPRL]. {NAL}.

1336 Taylor, Carl C.
1937. "Recent population changes in the Southern states with comparisons and relations to other sections." Presentation at the Southern Conference of Agricultural Workers on February 4, at Nashville, TN. Typed. DC: USDA, BAE, [DFPRL]. {NAL}.

1337 Taylor, Carl C.
1937. "The restoration of rural culture." Presentation at the National Catholic Rural Life Conference on November 9, at Richmond, VA. Undated mimeo. [DC]: USDA, BAE, [DFPRL]. {NAL}.

1338 Taylor, Carl C.
1937. "Family life as a fundamental factor in effective farm living." Presentation for the staff of the Extension Service on December 17, at DC. Mimeo. DC: USDA, Extension Service, Division of Cooperative Extension [Work in Agriculture and Home Economics]. {usda 7}.

1339 Taylor, Carl C.
1938. "How farm communities can get together." Radio address on the FFA Radio Program on January 10, at DC. Typed. DC: USDA, BAE, DFPRW. {CU Archives}.

1340 Taylor, Carl C.
1938. "Land use and tenancy: A short course: "The land and the people", "Tenancy in foreign countries", "Tenancy and the problem of standards of living", "Problems and issues involved in attacking the tenancy problem in the United States." Four lectures given May 16-20 at a short course for home demonstration agents, University of Arkansas, Fayetteville, AR. Typed. USDA cooperating. {CU Archives}.

1341 Taylor, Carl C.
1938. "Our new interest in conservation." Presentation at FSA Project in Starkville, MS on April 25, Also given on April 27 at Okolomo, MS. Typed. DC: USDA, BAE, DFPRL. {CU Archives}.

1342 Taylor, Carl C.
1938. "Land program of the Bureau of Agricultural Economics." Radio address, WFBM, on October 7, at Indianapolis, IN. Typed. DC: USDA, BAE, DFPRL. {CU Archives}.

1343 Taylor, Carl C.
1938. "The issues of democracy." Outline of a presentation to the meeting of the Virginia Social Science Association on April 20, at Fredricksburg, VA. Typed. DC: USDA, BAE, [DFPRL]. Also given at the College of William and Mary, Williamsburg, VA, on March 16, 1939. {NAL}.

1344 Taylor, Carl C.
1938. "What is rural youth's interest?" Presentation at the American Farm Bureau Federation on December 12, at New Orleans, LA. Typed. DC: USDA, BAE, [DFPRL]. {NAL}.

1345 Taylor, Carl C.
1938. "Rural rehabilitation and resettlement." Presentation at the International Conference of Agricultural Economists on August 27, at Montreal, Canada. Typed. DC: USDA, BAE, [DFPRL]. {NAL}.

1346 Taylor, Carl C.
1938. "A national plan for handicrafts." Outline of address given before Federated Women's Clubs of America on January 14, at DC. Typed. DC: USDA, BAE, [DFPRL]. {NAL}.

1347 Taylor, Carl C.
1938. "Social classes in the United States." Outline of presentation at the Lester F. Ward Chapter, George Washington University on January 12, at DC. Typed. DC: USDA, BAE, [DFPRL]. {NAL}.

1348 Taylor, Carl C.
1938. "Human relations in land use planning." Presentation at the First Missouri Valley Planning Conference on February 11-12, at Omaha, NB. Mimeo. [DC]: USDA, BAE,

1348 (continued).
[DFPRL]. {usda 9}.

1349 Taylor, Carl C.
1939. "How health conditions have affected the economies of the South," "The land problem in the South," and "Population problems of the South,"; three presentations at the Regional meeting of the Farm Security Administration on June 27-29, at Fayetteville, AR. Typed. {CU Archives}.

1350 Taylor, Carl C.
1939. "Seeking security in rural life." Presentation at the Regional Conference of the Farm Security Administration on December 4, at Amarillo, TX. Typed. DC: USDA, BAE, [DFPRW]. {NAL}.

1351 Taylor, Carl C.
1939. "Basic rural life problems in the South." Presentation at the Annual Meeting of the Tennessee Extension Service on October 19, at Memphis, TN. Typed.DC: USDA, BAE, [DFPRW]. {NAL}.

1352 Taylor, Carl C.
1939. "Culture in agriculture." Presentation at the Farm Security Administration Annual Regional Meeting on October 3, at Mitchell, IN. Typed. DC: USDA, BAE, [DFPRW]. {NAL}.

1353 Taylor, Carl C.
1939. "The evolution of our major rural social problems." Presentation at the Farm Security Administration Annual Regional Meeting on October 3, at Mitchell, IN. Typed. DC: USDA, BAE, [DFPRW]. {NAL}.

1354 Taylor, Carl C.
1939. "Regional specialization, technological improvements in agriculture, and competition between commercial farmers and family-sized units, as related to rural poverty." Presentation at Conference of Regional Rural Rehabilitation Officials of Farm Security Administration, Wardman

1354 (continued).
Park Hotel, on September 18, at DC. Typed. DC: USDA, BAE, [DFPRW]. {NAL}.

1355 Taylor, Carl C.
1939. "Social adjustments to a changing agriculture." Presentation at the American Association for the Advancement of Science on June 23, at Milwaukee, WI. Typed. DC: USDA, BAE, [DFPRL]. {NAL}.

1356 Taylor, Carl C.
1939. "The effects of population mobility upon regional and national development in the United States." Presentation at the National Conference of Social Work on June 19, at Buffalo, NY. Mimeo. DC: USDA, BAE, [DFPRL]. {NAL}.

1357 Taylor, Carl C.
1939. "Psychological adjustments and institutional change." Presentation at the Farm Security Administration Discussion Group School on May 10, at Ames, IA. Typed. DC: USDA, BAE, [DFPRL]. {NAL}.

1358 Taylor, Carl C.
1939. "Psychological adjustment and historical change." Presentation at the Farm Security Administration Discussion Group School on May 11, at Ames, IA. Typed. DC: USDA, BAE, [DFPRL]. {NAL}.

1359 Taylor, Carl C.
1939. "Some elements in security for the rural South." Presentation at the Southwestern Social Science Association on April 7, at Dallas, TX. Typed. DC: USDA, BAE, [DFPRL].

1360 Taylor, Carl C.
1939. "The place of social programs in the Extension Service." Presentation at the Annual Extension Conference, Cornell University, on March 30, at Ithaca, NY. Typed. DC: USDA, BAE, [DFPRL]. {NAL}.

1361 Taylor, Carl C.
1939. "The changing needs of agriculture: An outline." Outline of presentation to the American Federation of Government Employees on March 27, at DC. Typed. DC: USDA, BAE, [DFPRL]. {NAL}.

1362 Taylor, Carl C.
1940. "Planning for the people who live on the land." Outline of presentation atthe University of Arkansas on July 31, at Fayetteville, AR. Typed. DC: USDA, BAE, DFPRW. {CU Archives}.

1363 Taylor, Carl C.
1940. "Planning by the people on the land." Outline of presentation at the University of Arkansas on August 1, at Fayetteville, AR. Typed. DC: USDA, BAE, DFPRW. {CU Archives}.

1364 Taylor, Carl C.
1940. "Rural life and national welfare." Presentation at the American Association of School Administrators on February 27, at St. Louis, MO. Also presented at the National Catholic Rural Life Conference, St. Cloud, MN, September 30. Mimeo. DC: USDA, BAE, DFPRW. {CU Archives}.

1365 Taylor, Carl C.
1940. "National defense and family living." Introductory remarks, Annual Conference for Massachusetts Extension Workers on December 9, at Amherst, MA. Typed. DC: USDA, BAE, [DFPRW]. {NAL}.

1366 Taylor, Carl C.
1940. "What is the outlook for farm youth?" Radio address, WOR, on December 4, at DC. Typed. DC: USDA, [DFPRW]. {NAL}.

1367 Taylor, Carl C.
1940. "The relationship of the Farm Security Administration program to comercial and noncommercial farming: An outline." Presentation at the Indiana Annual State

1367 (continued).
Conference of FSA Employees on November 26, at Mitchell, IN. Typed. DC: USDA, BAE, [DFPRW]. {NAL}.

1368 Taylor, Carl C.
1940. "The development of folk society in rural America." Presentation at Conference of Social Work on November 14, at Lexington, KY. Typed. DC: USDA, BAE, [DFPRW]. {NAL}.

1369 Taylor, Carl C.
1940. "The people's part in land and water conservation." Presentation at the National Reclamation Association on September 25, at Great Falls, MT. Typed. DC: USDA, BAE, [DFPRW]. {NAL}.

1370 Taylor, Carl C.
1940. "Recent trends in research in rural sociology." Presentation at the Sociological Research Association on September 4, at Chicago, IL. Typed. DC: USDA, BAE, [DFPRW]. {NAL}.

1371 Taylor, Carl C.
1940. "Cooperation in rural sociological research on an interstate and regional basis." Presentation at Conference on Teaching and Research in Sociology on August 30, at Blue Ridge, NC. Mimeo. DC: USDA, BAE, [DFPRW]. {NAL}.

1372 Taylor, Carl C.
1940. "Democracy and group leadership." Presentation at Farmers Institute of Public Affairs on July 24, at Pryor, OK. Typed. DC: USDA, BAE, [DFPRW]. Also presented at the Farmers Institute of Public Affairs on July 7 at Okemah, OK. {NAL}.

1373 Taylor, Carl C.
1940. "The owner-operated, family-sized farm." Presentation at Farmers Institute of Public Affairs on July 23, at Pryor, OK. Typed. DC: USDA, BAE, [DFPRW]. {NAL}.

1374 Taylor, Carl C.

1374 (continued).
1940. "Rural youth and our civilization of tomorrow." Address on April 2 [audience and location unknown]. Typed. DC: USDA, BAE, [DFPRW]. {NAL}.

1375 Taylor, Carl C.
1940. "Can we build a decent rural civilization on the backs of sharecroppers?" Outline of presentation for National Sharecroppers' Week, Friends' Meeting House, on March 8, at DC. Typed. DC: USDA, BAE, [DFPRW]. {NAL}.

1376 Taylor, Carl C.
1940. "Rural life and national welfare." Presentation at American Association of School Administrators on February 27, at St. Louis, MO. Mimeo. DC: USDA, BAE, [DFPRW]. {NAL}.

1377 Taylor, Carl C.
1940. "Rural youth." Presentation at the American Youth Congress on February 10, at DC. Typed. DC: USDA, BAE, [DFPRW]. {NAL}.

1378 Taylor, Carl C.
1940. "Country planning." Presentation at the American Society of Landscape Architects, Mayflower Hotel, on January 29, at DC. Typed. DC: USDA, BAE, [DFPRW]. {NAL}.

1379 Taylor, Carl C.
1940. "Situations and problems of older rural youth." Presentation at the Association of Land-Grant Colleges and Universities on November 12, at Chicago, IL. Also undated mimeo. DC: USDA, BAE, [DFPRW]. {usda 17}.

1380 Taylor, Carl C.
1941. "The role of the rural sociologist in national defense." Presentation at Rural Sociological Society on December 29, at New York, NY. Typed. DC: USDA, BAE, [DFPRW]. {NAL}.

1381 Taylor, Carl C.
1941. "The implementation of democracy." Presentation as part of panel, Political Sociology Section of the American Sociological Society, on December 28, at New York, NY. Typed. DC: USDA, BAE, [DFPRW]. {NAL}.

1382 Taylor, Carl C.
1941. "The role of the bureau integrators." Presentation at a staff meeting in H. R. Tolley's [BAE] office on November 7, at DC. Typed. DC: USDA, BAE, [DFPRW]. {NAL}.

1383 Taylor, Carl C.
1941. "Land settlement and development." Presentation at American Railway Development Association, on October 29, at Chicago, IL. Typed. DC: USDA, BAE, [DFPRW]. {NAL}.

1384 Taylor, Carl C.
1941. "Human welfare and national strength: An outline." Outline of presentation for the Texas Welfare Association on May 1, at Dallas, TX. Typed. DC: USDA, BAE, [DFPRW]. {NAL}.

1385 Taylor, Carl C.
1941. "Present cultural patterns and national strength." Outline of presentation for the Texas Social Welfare Association on April 30, at Dallas, TX. Typed. DC: USDA, BAE, [DFPRW]. {NAL}.

1386 Taylor, Carl C.
1941. "Rural health and national defense: An outline." Outline of presentation for Iowa Farm and Home Week, Home Economics Session, on February 10, at Ames, IA. Typed. DC: USDA, BAE, [DFPRW]. {NAL}.

1387 Taylor, Carl C.
1941. "Democracy in the face of crisis." Presentation at Iowa Farm and Home Week, on February 10, at Ames, IA. Also broadcast over WOI radio, Ames, IA. Mimeo. DC: USDA, BAE, [DFPRW]. {NAL}.

C. 1942-1945

1388 Baker, O. E.
1942. "Some economic factors affecting rural Virginia and the future outlook." Presentation at the Annual Conference of Teachers of Vocational Agriculture of Virginia on July 14, at Massanetta Springs, VA. Undated mimeo. [DC]: USDA, BAE, [DFPRW]. {usda 24}.

1389 Ensminger, Douglas.
1945. "If I were a rural pastor." [outline]. Presentation at Emory University School for Town and Country Ministers on June 28, at Atlanta, GA. Undated mimeo. DC: USDA, Extension Service. {usda 41}.

1390 Folsom, Josiah C.
1944. "Social Security proposals for farm workers." Revision of a paper prepared for meeting of Baptist Ministerial Association on January 3, at DC. Dittoed. [DC: USDA, BAE, DFPRW]. {usda 36}.

1391 Goldschmidt, Walter.
[1944]. "Statement on the Arvin-Dinuba (Central Valley) study in California." Radio address on the Country Commentator Program on May 11 broadcast by Station KTEC, at Visalia, CA. Undated ditto. [Berkeley, CA: USDA, BAE, DFPRW]. {usda 36}.

1392 Johansen, John P.
1945. "On the significance of the rural church in the Great Plains." Presentation at meeting of the District Superintendents of the Norwegian Lutheran Church of America on January 17, at Fargo, ND. Undated mimeo. Lincoln, NE: USDA, BAE, [DFPRW]. {usda 39}.

1393 Niederfrank, E. J.
1944. "Understanding how the wheels go around in New England rural communities." Presentation at the New Hampshire Regional Conference of Social Agencies in June, at Northampton, MA, and in other Extension meetings. Mimeo. [Upper Darby, PA]: USDA, BAE, [DFPRW]. {usda 37}.

1394 Raper, Arthur F.
1944. "When farmers think of post-war prospects." Statement to the Farm Marketing Group of the American Marketing Association on December 14, at Sheraton Hotel, NYC. Dittoed. [DC: USDA, BAE, DFPRW]. {usda 37}.

1395 Raper, Arthur F., and Rensis Likert (USDA, BAE), and Wallace Kadderly (USDA, Radio Service).
1945. "Prospects for farming after the war." Radio address on January 2, at DC, recorded. Mimeo. DC: USDA, [BAE]. Timely Farm Topics No. 11b (Agriculture After the War No. 6). {usda 41}.

1396 Taylor, Carl C.
1943. "Population planning and policy." Presentation for Post-War Planning Conference on July 26-31 at Milwaukee, WI. Dittoed. {usda 28}.

1397 Taylor, Carl C.
1943. "Agricultural relations between the United States and Argentina in the Good Neighbor Policy." Presentation at annual meeting of the Association of Land-Grant Colleges and Universities on October 26, at Chicago, IL. Typed. DC: USDA, BAE, DFPRW. {CU Archives}.

1398 Taylor, Carl C.
1944. "Rural health." Transcript of a radio broadcast on CBS Country Journal on October 14, at DC. Typed. DC: USDA, BAE, DFPRW. {CU Archives}.

1399 Taylor, Carl C.
1944. "Human resources of the Appalachians." Presentation at annual meeting of the Conference of Southern Mountain Workers on March 8, at Asheville, NC. Typed. DC: USDA, BAE, DFPRW. {CU Archives}.

1400 Taylor, Carl C.
1945. "The cultural approach to extension." Outline of presentation for Latin American students of USDA Extension Service's Foreign Student Program on March 12, at DC. Also presented for Chinese students on September 14.

1400 (continued).
Typed. DC: USDA,BAE, DFPRW. {CU Archives}.

1401 Taylor, Carl C.
1945. "Postwar...." Outlines of four lectures: "Social institutions," "The church in the local community," " Problems related to the larger society," "Citizenship from local community to world society;" given at Virginia Summer School for Rural Ministers, sponsored by Virginia Polytechnic Institute, on July 10 and 13 at Blacksburg, VA Typed. DC: USDA, BAE, DFPRW. {CU Archives}.

1402 Taylor, Carl C.
1945. "Rural sociology work in Latin American countries by State Department and Office of Foreign Agricultural Relations." Outline of presentation for the Office of Foreign Agricultural Relations on September 5, at DC. Typed. DC: USDA, BAE, DFPRW. {CU Archives}.

1403 Taylor, Carl C., and Wallace L. Kadderly.
1944. "Security for farm people." Radio broadcast in the USDA's portion of National Farm and Home Hour over stations associated with the Blue Network on January 21, Undated mimeo. [DC: USDA, BAE, DFPRW]. {usda 36}.

D. 1946-1953
1404 Ducoff, Louis J.
1949. "Socioeconomic backgrounds of the migratory agricultural labor situation." Presented at the National Conference on the Church and Migratory Labor of the Home Missions Council of North America on September 27, at Chicago, IL. Undated mimeo. [DC]: USDA, BAE, [DFPRL]. {usda 52}.

1405 Ducoff, Louis J.
1950. "Outlook for farm manpower and farm wages." Statement at the 28th Annual Agricultural Outlook Conference on November 2, at DC. Undated mimeo. [DC]: USDA, BAE, [DFPRL]. {usda 53}.

1406 Ducoff, Louis J.

1406 (continued).
1951. "The farm manpower situation and outlook." Statement at the 29th Annual Agricultural Outlook Conference on October 30, at DC. Undated mimeo. [DC]: USDA, BAE, [DFPRL]. {usda 54}.

1407 Ellickson, John C.
1946. "Trends in farm income and tenure and their relation to farm home improvement." Presentation at the 24th Annual Agricultural Outlook Conference on October 10, at DC. Undated mimeo. [DC]: USDA, BAE, [DFPRW]. {usda 45}.

1408 Hagood, Margaret Jarman.
1952. "Indexes of levels of living for counties and other geographic areas." Presentation at the 30th Annual Agricultural Outlook Conference on October 21, at DC. Undated mimeo. [DC]: USDA, BAE, [DFPRL]. {usda 55}.

1409 Johansen, John P.
1946. "Orientation of the churches toward life in the Great Plains." Presentation at the Mid-Winter Convocation of Luther Theological Seminary on January 31, at St. Paul, MN. Undated mimeo. [DC: USDA, BAE, DFPRW]. {usda 47}.

1410 Longmore, T. Wilson.
1949. "Community development." Presentation at the 27th Annual Agricultural Outlook Conference on November 1, at DC. Mimeo. [DC]: USDA, BAE, [DFPRL]. {usda 52}.

1411 Raper, Arthur F.
1948. "The church in a changing rural scene." Presentation at the Southeastern Convocation of Churches in spring 1948 at Atlanta, GA. Undated mimeo. Atlanta, GA: Southeastern Jurisdictional Council. {usda 51}.

1412 Taylor, Carl C.
1946. "Levels of living." Presentation at BAE Conference on August 16, at Gulfport, MS. Dittoed. [DC]: USDA, BAE, [DFPRW]. {usda 45}.

1413 Taylor, Carl C.
1946. "New facts about rural life." Notes for presentation for the National Convocation on the Church in Town and Country on November 12, at Des Moines, IA. Dittoed. DC: USDA, BAE, DFPRW. {CU Archives}.

1414 Taylor, Carl C.
1946. "Rural housing problems and how we can meet them." Outline of presentation for Farm and Home Week Program, Oklahoma State University on August 1, at Stillwater, OK. Typed. DC: USDA, BAE, DFPRW. {CU Archives}.

1415 Taylor, Carl C.
1947. "Why cooperatives succeed or fail." Presentation at Rural Electrification Administration Conference on June 24, at DC. Mimeo. DC: USDA, BAE, DFPRW. {CU Archives}.

1416 Taylor, Carl C.
1947. "How big are farm incomes." Radio address with O. C. Stine broadcast on "The American Farmer" over 187 stations affiliated with ABC on November 22, at DC. Mimeo. DC: USDA, BAE, DFPRW. {CU Archives}.

1417 Taylor, Carl C.
1947. "Professional social work and public welfare come late to rural areas." Speech given October 9 (to American Public Welfare Association?). {CU Archives}.

1418 Taylor, Carl C.
1948. "The significance of sociology in dealing with real problems in rural life." Outline of presentation at American University seminar on March 11, at DC. Mimeo. DC: USDA, BAE, DFPRL. {CU Archives}.

1419 Taylor, Carl C.
1948. "How to organize a county to do what the people want to do." Outline of presentation at County Farm Bureau Leaders' banquet on March 12, at Martinsburg, WV. Mimeo. DC: USDA, BAE, DFPRL. {CU Archives}.

1420 Taylor, Carl C.
1948. "Social science as science." Presentation for Sigma Xi on March 22, at Manhattan, KS. Dittoed. DC: USDA, BAE, DFPRL. {CU Archives}.

1421 Taylor, Carl C.
1948. "The family farm and its implications for rural life." Presentation at a seminar at Teachers College, Columbia University on April 15. Typed. DC: USDA, BAE, DFPRL. {CU Archives}.

1422 Taylor, Carl C.
1948. "Social implications of farm cooperatives." Presentation at Farm Credit Association Workshop on December 13, at DC. Typed. DC: USDA, BAE, DFPRL. {CU Archives}.

1423 Taylor, Carl C.
1948. "The status of rural sociological research in the Department of Agriculture." Presentation at annual meeting of Rural Sociological Society on December 29, at Chicago, IL. Typed. DC: USDA, BAE, DFPRL. {CU Archives}.

1424 Taylor, Carl C.
1948. "The interviewing techniques of Kinsey study." Presentation at annual meeting of the American Sociological Society on December 27-30, at Chicago, IL. Typed. DC: USDA, BAE, DFPRL. {CU Archives}.

1425 Taylor, Carl C.
1949. "Implications of intergroup tensions for democracy." Presentation at the Institute on Intergroup Relations in Rural Life, The National Conference of Christians and Jews on December 1, at Des Moines, IA. Typed. DC: USDA, BAE, DFPRL. {CU Archives}.

1426 Taylor, Carl C.
1949. "The land and the people." Outline of presentation for the Extension Conference on November 14, at Lincoln, NE. Typed. DC: USDA, BAE, DFPRL. {CU Archives}.

1427 Taylor, Carl C.
1949. "Social-economic effects of industrialization." Presentation for the Lecture-Seminar Series of the Foreign Service Institute, State Department, on November 7, at DC. Typed. DC: USDA, BAE, DFPRL. {CU Archives}.

1428 Taylor, Carl C.
1949. "Today's challenge to adult education." Outline of presentation at State Conference of Adult Education, University of Virginia, on July 29, at Charlottesville, VA. Typed. DC: USDA, BAE, DFPRL. {CU Archives}.

1429 Taylor, Carl C.
1949. "Community organization and action." Outline of presentation at the annual meeting of the St. Louis County Club and Farm Bureau on December 2, at Duluth, MN. Typed. DC: USDA, BAE, DFPRL. {CU Archives}.

1430 Taylor, Carl C.
1949. "The relation of censuses to rural social research." Talk before faculty and graduate students, University of Guatemala, in spring 1949. Typed. DC: USDA, BAE, DFPRL. {CU Archives}.

1431 Taylor, Carl C.
1949. "Farm adjustment and Social Security programs." Outline of presentation at meeting of the Social Security Administration on April 21, at DC. Typed. DC: USDA, BAE, DFPRL. {CU Archives}.

1432 Taylor, Carl C.
1949. "Social security for farmers and farm workers--history and social background." Presentation at Extension Institute and Seminar, USDA, on April 21, at DC. Typed. DC: USDA, BAE, DFPRL. {CU Archives}.

1433 Taylor, Carl C.
1949. "Significant trends in rural life." Outline of presentation at Midwest Conference on Rural Life and Education on March 31, at Lincoln, NB. Typed. DC: USDA, BAE, DFPRL. {CU Archives}.

1434 Taylor, Carl C.
1949. "The available contribution of sociology to business and public administration." Presentation at the Washington Chapter of the Association of American Executives on January 25, at DC. Typed. DC: USDA, BAE, DFPRL. {CU Archives}.

1435 Taylor, Carl C.
1949. "What contribution does sociology have to make to a knowledge of public relations." Outline of presentation at Washington Chapter of the Association of American Executives on March 28, at DC. Typed. DC: USDA, BAE, DFPRL. {CU Archives}.

1436 Taylor, Carl C.
1950. "Summary of panel discussion on possible contributions of sociologists and anthropologists to Point IV programs." Annual meeting of the American Sociological Society on September 8, at Denver, CO. Typed. DC: USDA, BAE, DFPRL. {CU Archives}.

1437 Taylor, Carl C.
1950. "Insurance for Virginia home life, or what do we want to bring into homes in the future?" Outline of presentation for the Institute of Rural Affairs, Virginia Polytechnic University on July 21, at Blacksburg, VA. Typed. DC: USDA, BAE, DFPRL. {CU Archives}.

1438 Taylor, Carl C.
1950. "U.S. agriculture and rural life." Outline of presentation to 40 Germans at the USDA on July 17, at DC. Typed. DC: USDA, BAE, DFPRL. {CU Archives}.

1439 Taylor, Carl C.
1950. "The cultural approach." Outline of presentation at the Institute for Missionaries on Agricultural and Rural Development on July 13, at DC. Typed. DC: USDA, BAE, DFPRL. {CU Archives}.

1440 Taylor, Carl C.
1950. "What is happening to your community?" Presenta-

1440 (continued).
tion at National 4-H Club Conference on June 16, at DC. Typed. DC: USDA, BAE, DFPRL. {CU Archives}.

1441 Taylor, Carl C.
1950. "The changing world challenges the community, state and family." Outline of presentation for the Family Life Conference, Virginia Polytechnic Institute at Roanoke, VA. Typed. DC: USDA, BAE, DFPRL. {CU Archives}.

1442 Taylor, Carl C.
1950. "Significant trends in rural life--major social changes and their impact on rural life." Outline of presentation at Farm and Home Week, Ohio State University, on March 23, at Columbus, OH. Typed. DC: USDA, BAE, DFPRL. {CU Archives}.

1443 Taylor, Carl C.
1950. "Relationship of agriculture to other occupations." Outline of presentation to foreign service personnel of the USDA at DC. Typed. DC: USDA, BAE, DFPRL. {CU Archives}.

1444 Taylor, Carl C.
1951. "Social research." Outline of presentation at a social science seminar, Pennsylvania State University, on May 7. Typed. {CU Archives}.

1445 Taylor, Carl C.
1951. "The value of sociological training for government work." Outline of presentation at the Trinity College Sociology Club on February 2, at DC. Typed. DC: USDA, BAE, DFPRL. {CU Archives}.

1446 Taylor, Carl C.
1951. "The role of the social scientist in Puerto Rico's progress." Notes for a presentation to the social science faculty of the University of Puerto Rico on February 2, at San Juan, P.R. Typed. DC: USDA, BAE, DFPRL. {CU Archives}.

1447 Taylor, Carl C.
1951. "What is rural sociology?" Notes for presentation at the College of Agriculture, University of Puerto Rico, on January 18, at San Juan, P.R. Typed. DC: USDA, BAE, DFPRL. {CU Archives}.

1448 Taylor, Carl C.
1951. "Social stratification in rural areas." Presentation at the National Council for Social Studies on November 15, at Detroit, MI. Typed. DC: USDA, BAE, DFPRL. {CU Archives}.

1449 Taylor, Carl C.
1951. "Beyond quantitative analysis." Presentation at Annual Meeting of the Rural Sociological Society on September 2, at Madison, WI. Typed. DC: USDA, BAE, DFPRL. {CU Archives}.

1450 Taylor, Carl C.
1951. "Safeguarding the essentials of modern community organizations and relationships." Presentation at the National Methodist Town and Country Conference on July 21, at Sioux City, IA. Typed. DC: USDA, BAE, DFPRL. {CU Archives}.

1451 Taylor, Carl C.
1951. "Serving the rural community." Outline of presentation for the National Congress of Parents and Teachers on May 22, at Miami, FL. Typed. DC: USDA, BAE, DFPRL. {CU Archives}.

1452 Taylor, Carl C.
1952. "Farmers in an urbanized society." Presentation at the National Council of Life and Labor on April 22, at DC. Typed. DC: USDA, BAE, DFPRL. {CU Archives}.

1453 Taylor, Carl C.
1952. "The human factor." Outline of presentation to the Pan American Union, Department of Cultural Affairs on February 19, at DC. Typed. DC: USDA, BAE, DFPRL. {CU Archives}.

1454 Taylor, Carl C.
1952. "The influence of changes on Southern agriculture in the last fifty years, and the outlook for farm operators." Presentation at Tuskegee Institute in January, 1952 at Tuskegee, AL. Typed. DC: USDA, BAE, DFPRL. {CU Archives}.

1455 Taylor, Carl C.
[1948?]. "What is a good rural community?." Undated ditto. [DC: USDA, BAE, DFPRL]. {usda 51}.

1456 White, Helen R.
1952. "Population trends." Presentation at the 30th Annual Agricultural Outlook Conference on October 22, at DC. Undated mimeo. [DC]: USDA, BAE, [DFPRL]. {usda 55}.

VII. Publications Issued by the Division or Cooperatively on Periodic or Occasional Basis

1457 "Directory of teachers giving courses in rural sociology and rural life." Mimeo. DC: USDA, BAE, [DFPRL]. Issued annually 1930-36 as of October 1. Title change: "Personnel in rural sociology: Teachers, research workers, extension workers." Issued annually 1937-1940 except for 1938 as of October 1. Title change: "Personnel in rural sociology: Teachers, research workers, extension workers. Part I--By states; Part II--Alphabetical index." Issued October 1, 1941 and June, 1949.

1458 "Employment, wages and earnings of agricultural workers living in Farm Security Administration migratory labor camps in California and Arizona." No. 1-3, Feb. 5-[May], 1940. Title change: "Employment situation of agricultural workers living in FSA migratory labor camps [Arizona--California]. Current situation report. For official use only." No. 4-6, June 5-Aug. 21, 1940. Title change: "Employment situation of agricultural workers living in FSA farm labor camps [Arizona, California, and Northwest]: Current situation report. For official use only." No. 7-12, Sept. 10, 1940-Jan. 24, 1941. Mimeo.

1458 (continued).
Berkeley, CA: USDA, BAE, [DFPRW], and Farm Security Administration.

1459 *Farm Population and Rural Life Activities: A Review of Current Research and Other Related Projects of the Division of Farm Population and Rural Life and Institutions and Agencies Cooperating.* Vol. 1, No. 1-Vol. 16, No. 1, March 1, 1927-Jan. 1, 1942. DC: USDA, BAE, [DFPRL].

1460 "Farm population estimates." Mimeo. DC: USDA, BAE [DFPRL]. Issued annually 1923-40, 1943-45, and 1948-49 as of January 1.

Farm Population Estimates: Special issues.

1461 "Farm population estimates: United States and major geographic divisions, 1910-1942." November 1942.

1462 "Farm population: Annual estimates by states, 1930-1940." April 1943.

1463 "Farm population: Annual estimates by states, 1920-1940." February 1944.

1464 "Farm population estimates: United States and major geographic divisions, 1910-1946." June 1946.

1465 "Farm population estimates: United States and major geographic divisions, 1940-1947; States, 1940-1945." August 1947.

Series Census-BAE: Cooperative releases on farm population estimates and related statistics initiated in 1945 by the U.S. Department of Commerce, Bureau of the Census and the USDA, BAE, [DFPRW].

1466 No. 1. *Estimates of Farm Population and Farm Households: April, 1944, and April, 1940.* January 14, 1945.

1467 No. 2. *Farm Population Changes in 1944.* April 9, 1945.

Periodicals

1468 No. 3. *Farm Operators in the United States: April, 1944, and April, 1940.* May 7, 1945.

1469 No. 4. *Net Movement Away from Farms in the United States, by Age and Sex: 1940 to 1944.* June 19, 1945.

1470 No. 5. *Recent Changes in Farm Population.* July 2, 1945.

1471 No. 6. *Off-Farm Work of Farm Operators and Members of Their Households: 1943.* October 15, 1945.

1472 No. 7. *Farm Population Changes: April, 1940, to January, 1946.* May 2, 1946.

1473 No. 8. *Recent Farm Population Changes: April, 1946.* October 17, 1946.

1474 No. 9. *Farm Dwellings and Farm Population: January, 1945.* August 12, 1947.

1475 No. 10. *Farm Population: January, 1947.* August 18, 1947

1476 No. 11. *Farm Population Changes: 1940 to 1947.* June 4, 1948.

1477 No. 12. *Estimates of the Farm Population of the United States: 1940 to 1948.* June 8, 1949.

1478 No. 13. *Estimated Farm Population of the United States: January, 1949.* June 29, 1949.

1479 No. 14. *Estimates of the Farm Population of the United States: 1940 to 1949.* January 13, 1950.

1480 No. 15. *State Economic Areas of the United States.* August 3, 1950.

1481 No. 16A. *Estimates of the Farm Population: 1910 to 1950.* July 18, 1951.

1482 No. 16. *Revised Estimates of the Farm Population of the United States: 1910 to 1950 (supersedes 16A).* March 9, 1953.

1483 No. 17. *Estimates of the Farm Population of the United States: April 1950 and April 1951.* October 26, 1951.

1484 No. 18. *Estimates of the Farm Population of the United States: April 1950 to April 1952.* March 9, 1953.

1485 No. 19. *Economic Subregions of the United States* (by Donald J. Bogue and Calvin L. Beale). June 1953.

1486 "Persons, members of parties in need of manual employment entering Arizona and California by motor vehicle." No. 1-7, May 1, 1940-Oct. 21, 1941. Mimeo. Berkeley, CA: USDA, BAE, [DFPRW], and Farm Security Administration.

1487. "Publications relating to farm population and rural life." Mimeo. DC: USDA, BAE, [DFPRL]. Issued May 1, 1928 (with a supplement issued May 16, 1929); April 1, 1930; July 1, 1931; December 1, 1932; June 1, 1933. Title change: "Publications relating to farm population and rural life issued at the various state colleges of agriculture." Issued March 15, 1935; January, 1936.

Addenda

II. Books

B. 1935-1941

1488 Baker, O. E., Ralph Borsodi, and M. L. Wilson.
1939. *Agriculture in Modern Life.* New York: Harper and Brothers.

D. 1946-1953

1489 Miner, Horace.
1949. *Culture and Agriculture: An Anthropological Study of a Corn Belt County.* Ann Arbor, MI: University of Michigan Press. Occasional Contributions from the Museum of Anthropology of the University of Michigan, No. 14.

1490 Sanders, Irwin T.
1950. *Making Good Communities Better: A Handbook for Civic-Minded Men and Women.* With Selected Guideposts by Seventeen Authorities [including DFPRL staff members Douglas Ensminger, Margaret J. Hagood, Arthur Raper, and Pauline S. Taylor]. Lexington, KY: University of Kentucky Press. Revised 1953.

IV. Research publications

B. 1935-1941

1491 Ashby, Richard.
1941. "Town farming in the Great Plains." *Rural Sociology* 6(4): 341-343.

1492 Baker, O. E.
1936. "The agricultural prospect." Pp. 177-236 in A. E. Parkins and J. R. Whitaker (eds.), *Our Natural Resources and Their Conservation*. New York: John Wiley and Sons.

Keywords: Population trends; agricultural production; migration; social change/ trends. Germany.

C. 1942-1945

1493 Taeuber, Conrad.
1943. "Reviewing the facts on farm manpower." *Extension Service Review* 14(1): 6.

Keywords: Farm labor; labor force; World War II-impacts on rural areas.

D. 1946-1953

1494 Ensminger, Douglas.
1950. [see cite 1490].

Keywords: Community clubs/ organizations; community development.

1495 Hagood, Margaret J.
1950. [see cite 1490].

Keywords: Community clubs/ organizations; community development.

1496 Montgomery, Mary.
1946. "Central Valley project--highlights of its history." *Land Policy Review* 9(1): 18-21.

Keywords: Planning-Central Valley, California; reclamation projects; public policy. CA.

1497 Raper, Arthur.
1950. [see cite 1490].

Addenda 281

1497 (continued).
Keywords: Community clubs/ organizations; community development.

1498 Taylor, Pauline S.
1950. [see cite 1490].

Keywords: Community clubs/ organizations; community development.

V. Restricted use reports and manuscripts

B. 1935-1941

1499 Loomis, Charles P.
1940. "A farmhand's diary." Typed(?). [DC; USDA, BAE, DFPRW]. Note: In 1979 this manuscript, which had been placed in the Ernest Correll Collection in the Archives of the Mennonite Church, Goshen, IN, was published in the *Mennonite Quarterly* 53(3): 235-256 (Keywords: Sociology of agriculture. Amish. PA.)

C. 1942-1945

1500 Frame, Nat T.
1944. "Cultural reconnaissance of Hamilton County, Iowa." Preliminary report. Attached are "Current and anticipated rural migration problems: Postwar planning-Hamilton County, Iowa," December 1944; "Hamilton County, Iowa-Current problems and postwar prospects," May 1945; and "Current and anticipated rural migration problems, Hamilton County, Iowa," revised June 1945. Typed. Milwaukee, WI: [USDA, BAE, DFPRW]. (NAL).

1501 McKain, Walter C., Jr.
1944. "When the Japanese return to California." For administrative use. Dittoed. [Berkeley, CA]: USDA, BAE, [DFPRW]. (NAL).

1502 McKain, Walter C., Jr.

1502 (continued).
1945. "Imperial Valley holds an 'anti-Jap' meeting." For administrative use. Typed. [Berkeley, CA]: USDA, BAE, [DFPRW]. (NAL).

1503 Montgomery, James E.
1943. "Rural Life trends-Dallas County, Alabama. Report No. 6." For administrative use only. Mimeo. [Atlanta, GA]: USDA, BAE, [DFPRW]. (NAL).

1504 Montgomery, James E.
1945. "Cultural reconnaissance survey of Taylor County, Florida (summary)." For administrative use. Attached are "Current and anticipated rural migration problems" and "A summary of current problems and postwar prospects." Mimeo. [Atlanta, GA]: USDA, BAE, [DFPRW]. (NAL).

1505 Montgomery, James E.
1945. "Reconnaissance survey of Union County, South Carolina (summary)." For administrative use. Attached are "Current and anticipated rural migration problems" and "A summary of current problems and post-war problems." Mimeo. [Atlanta, GA]: USDA, BAE, [DFPRW]. (NAL).

1506 Montgomery, James E., and Edward B. Williams.
1945. "Reconnaissance survey of Dallas County, Alabama." For administrative use. Attached are "Current and anticipated rural migration problems" and "A summary of current problems and post-war prospects-Dallas County, Alabama." Mimeo. [Atlanta, GA]: USDA, BAE, [DFPRW]. (NAL).

1507 Roberts, Roy L.
1945. "Reconnaissance survey of Harnett County, North Carolina." For administrative use. Attached are "Current and anticipated rural migration problems" and "A summary of current problems and post-war prospects." [DC]: USDA, BAE, [DFPRW]. (NAL).

Keyword Index

I. Substantive Areas

Adoption-diffusion, 0588

Age roles, 0916

Aging, 0288, 0845, 0851, 0964, 0965

Agricultural Adjustment Administration, 0556, 0763

Agricultural Agencies, 0363, 0701, 0704, 0712, 0765, 0810, 0829, 0830, 0835, 0838, 0839, 0892, 0919, 0922, 0934, 0935, 1000

Agricultural ladder, 0268, 0472, 1028

Agricultural production, 0227, 0318, 0324, 0582, 0583, 0603, 0643, 0649, 0659, 0696, 0744, 0781, 0802, 0809, 0949, 1492

Agricultural technology, 0858, 0872, 0903, 0931, 0985

American Farm Bureau Federation, 1029

Attitudes/opinions, 0106, 0107, 0111, 0114, 0138, 0140, 0164, 0205, 0212, 0213, 0216, 0219, 0226, 0227, 0228, 0235, 0277, 0279, 0292, 0303, 0329, 0357, 0422, 0432, 0450, 0464, 0472, 0522, 0570, 0621, 0712, 0727, 0736, 0739, 0786, 0826, 0836, 0957, 0982, 0992, 1011, 1036

Children, 0095, 0207, 0692, 0878, 0929

Church, 0099, 0162, 0242, 0307, 0340, 0348, 0632, 0884, 0988, 1026

283

Collective bargaining-farm workers, 0807

Colonization, 0787

Community, 0065, 0072, 0078, 0079, 0111, 0125, 0147, 0149, 0242, 0252, 0253, 0254, 0255, 0265, 0275, 0292, 0294, 0302, 0329, 0331, 0333, 0340, 0345, 0347, 0381, 0386, 0387, 0402, 0413, 0417, 0418, 0427, 0428, 0429, 0430, 0439, 0440, 0459, 0461, 0463, 0471, 0475, 0547, 0548, 0549, 0550, 0563, 0565, 0567, 0574, 0575, 0586, 0590, 0594, 0612, 0624, 0666, 0677, 0683, 0698, 0708, 0710, 0722, 0727, 0731, 0733, 0734, 0749, 0795, 0823, 0837, 1032

Community buildings and centers, 0065, 0236, 0237, 0238, 0239, 0240, 0241, 0242, 0249, 0252, 0369, 0474

Community clubs/ organizations, 0067, 0073, 0074, 0078, 0140, 0190, 0204, 0229, 0245, 0279, 0285, 0297, 0298, 0299, 0474, 0829, 0830, 0835, 0838, 0839, 0852, 0892, 0918, 0919, 0922, 0934, 0935, 0953, 1000, 1494, 1495, 1497, 1498

Community development, 0060, 0065, 0072, 0093, 0111, 0118, 0125, 0199, 0204, 0229, 0239, 0240, 0241, 0242, 0243, 0248, 0249, 0250, 0363, 0423, 0437, 0660, 0665, 0877, 1494, 1495, 1497, 1498

Community processes, 0067, 0068, 0072, 0096

Community and cooperative services (RR-FSA), 0820, 0821, 0822

Cooperatives, 0212, 0214, 0215, 0219, 0220, 0226, 0228, 0303, 0591, 0593, 0667, 0812, 1029

Culture of agriculture, 0399, 0573, 0669, 0697, 0737, 0738, 0782, 0831, 0994, 0995

Cultural anthropology, 0396, 0690, 0695, 0788, 1025

Depression, 0432, 0955

Index 285

Division of Farm Population and Rural Life, 0084, 0094, 0425, 0440, 0449, 0511, 0516, 0529, 0717, 1019

Drought, 0336, 0345, 0346, 0414, 0423, 0492, 0493

Education, 0121, 0207, 0220, 0426, 0469, 0709, 0754, 0756, 0795, 0950, 0994, 1004

Evaluation, 0059, 0066, 0143, 0213, 0217, 0227, 0231, 0336, 0373, 0393, 0498, 0506, 0531, 0588, 0591, 0592, 0593, 0621, 0633, 0661, 0663, 0667, 0675, 0587, 0700, 0701, 0703, 0705, 0724, 0728, 0729, 0763, 0764, 0767, 0768, 0769, 0770, 0771, 0787, 0819, 0820, 0821, 0822, 0890, 0919, 0939, 0940, 0944, 0957, 1017, 1020, 1036

Experimental health programs (USDA), 0564, 0670, 0686, 0687, 0700, 0711, 0723, 0724, 0767, 0768, 0816, 0957, 1036

Experimental Rural Rehabilitation Program, 0769, 0770, 0771, 0940

Extension, 0132, 0227, 0552, 0613, 0614, 0616, 0691, 0697, 0699, 0763, 0788, 0789, 0831, 0850, 0873, 0874, 0918

Family life cycle, 0196, 0421, 0431

Family relocation, 0544

Family selection for settlement projects, 0384, 0391, 0576

Farm family, 0063, 0071, 0099, 0148, 0153, 0156, 0160, 0165, 0170, 0195, 0196, 0208, 0261, 0262, 0263, 0269, 0270, 0271, 0287, 0300, 0326, 0404, 0421, 0447, 0584, 0906, 0918, 0946, 0952, 0994, 0999, 1043

Farm organizations, 0138, 0218, 0228, 0279, 0285, 0918, 1004, 1029

Farm labor, 0328, 0349, 0350, 0351, 0352, 0353, 0355, 0359, 0360, 0366, 0370, 0371, 0732, 0373, 0380, 0382, 0383, 0412, 0519, 0530, 0532, 0533, 0534, 0535, 0536, 0537, 0538, 0539,

Farm labor (continued), 0540, 0541, 0542, 0571, 0577, 0589, 0596, 0600, 0602, 0603, 0606, 0609, 0620, 0622, 0626, 0645, 0653, 0664, 0713, 0716, 0719, 0735, 0737, 0744, 0745, 0772, 0773, 0800, 0801, 0802, 0807, 0845, 0847, 0848, 0849, 0854, 0855, 0857, 0858, 0859, 0860, 0861, 0862, 0864, 0865, 0866, 0867, 0868, 0870, 0871, 0882, 0891, 0893, 0907, 0931, 0943, 0967, 0969, 0970, 0971, 0972, 0973, 0975, 0976, 0978, 0979, 0982, 0986, 0997, 0998, 1009, 1010, 1030, 1035, 1039, 1040, 1041, 1045, 1493

Farm operator turnover, 0718, 0959

Farm population, 0102, 0105, 0106, 0107, 0108, 0109, 0115, 0120, 0123, 0126, 0127, 0128, 0134, 0135, 0136, 0223, 0289, 0310, 0322, 0339, 0367, 0410, 0415, 0443, 0448, 0476, 0477, 0479, 0480, 0482, 0484, 0487, 0489, 0523, 0572, 0601, 0648, 0726, 0790, 0832, 0833, 0836, 0894, 0898, 0901, 0903, 0907, 0966, 0995, 1031

Farm population estimates, 0129, 0131

Farm population trends, 0108, 0115, 0116, 0120, 0126, 0128, 0134, 0135, 0136, 0310, 0374, 0406, 0407, 0448, 0476, 0477, 0479, 0480, 0482, 0484, 0487, 0488, 0489, 0572, 0579, 0580, 0648, 0671, 0672, 0726, 0836, 0840, 0893, 0989, 0901, 0903, 0930

Farm Security Administration, 0356, 0392, 0394, 0498, 0531, 0556, 0564, 0658, 0659, 0670, 0686, 0687, 0700, 0711, 0723, 0724, 0738, 0763, 0767, 0768, 0769, 0770, 0771, 0807, 0811, 0816, 0937, 0939, 0940, 0941, 0944

Farm size, 0061, 0124, 0327, 0528, 0556, 0598, 0603, 0631, 0744, 0840, 0977, 0986

Farm size-economic class, 0843, 0900, 1031, 1043

Farm systems, 0167, 0328, 0353, 0420, 0595, 0669, 0732, 0748, 0751, 0757, 0796

Farm tenant purchase program, 0393

Index 287

Farm wage ceilings and stabilization, 0882, 0913, 0968

Farm wage rates, 0349, 0585, 0597, 0598, 0599, 0605, 0607, 0608, 0627, 0644, 0646, 0647, 0656, 0720, 0721, 0740, 0801, 0802, 0806, 0849, 0854, 0859, 0862, 0864, 0865,0866, 0867, 0868, 0967, 0969, 0970, 0971, 0972, 0979, 0997, 0998,1009, 1010, 1039, 1040, 1041

Farm women, 0114, 0277, 0592, 0713, 0737

Farm-nonfarm population comparisons, 0116

Farmers Home Administration, 0950

Fertility, 0313, 0379, 0494, 0496, 0497, 0900, 0911, 1043

Fire protection services, 0250

4-H Clubs, 0139, 0143, 0285, 1042

Gender roles, 0746, 0907, 0916

Graphic analysis, 0123, 0127, 0137, 0289, 0314, 0315, 0316, 0318, 0319, 0324, 0333, 0355, 0582, 0583, 0749, 0752, 0993

Health, 0208, 0956

Health and medical care, 0208, 0210, 0244, 0687, 0700, 0814, 0846, 0885, 0886, 0888, 0889, 0920, 0921, 0923, 0924, 0925, 0926, 0936, 0942, 0945, 0946, 0947, 0948, 0957, 1036

Hospitals, 0199, 0243, 0244, 0368, 0890

Housing, 0264, 0271, 0356, 0759, 0809, 0966, 1031

Income, 0063, 0195, 0361, 0383, 0584, 0585, 0603, 0750, 0870, 0909, 0943, 0952, 0987, 1001, 1031

Income-low, 0112, 0170, 0188, 0412, 0519, 0521, 0659, 0672, 0681, 0682, 0793, 0909

Industries, 0963

Informal groups, 0427, 0430

Information sources, 0928

Information sources-mass media, 0261, 0426

Irrigation, 0433, 0810, 0837, 0840, 0959, 0977

Juvenile delinquency, 0980

Labor force, 0585, 0600, 0601, 0671, 0672, 0702, 0716, 0730, 0800, 0801, 0827, 0855, 0861, 0870, 0891, 0893, 0963, 1493

Labor requirements for agriculture, 0587, 0713

Land purchase programs, 0335, 0462, 0621, 0729

Land tenure, 0061, 0062, 0064, 0077, 0127, 0153, 0218, 0263, 0264, 0265, 0267, 0280, 0288, 0371, 0380, 0383, 0403, 0412, 0426, 0472, 0473, 0518, 0519, 0556, 0655, 0744, 0760, 0761, 0779, 0781, 0824, 0977, 0984, 0985, 0990, 0991, 0992, 0994, 1028

Land use, 0314, 0556

Land-use planning, 0329, 0344, 0359, 0395, 0507, 0509, 0524, 0527, 0543, 0636, 0818

Landlords, 0061, 0064, 0266

Leadership, 0078, 0211, 0279, 0329, 0554, 0555, 0562, 0797, 0818, 0884, 0918, 0994

Leadership-neighborhood, 0557, 0560, 0568, 0673, 0674, 0676, 0685

Level of living, 0070, 0077, 0097, 0145, 0148, 0154, 0155, 0156, 0157, 0159, 0161, 0164, 0165, 0166, 0167, 0169, 0170,

Index 289

Level of living (continued), 0171, 0172, 0173, 0174, 0175, 0176, 0177, 0178, 0179, 0180, 0181, 0182, 0183, 0185, 0186, 0187, 0188, 0189, 0223, 0256, 0257, 0269, 0270, 0271, 0286, 0292, 0293, 0300, 0332, 0339, 0342, 0356, 0392, 0412, 0426, 0444, 0447, 0472, 0518, 0519, 0595, 0618, 0654, 0655, 0732, 0748, 0751, 0752, 0757, 0758, 0761, 0798, 0841, 0879, 0880, 0881, 0884, 0895, 0905, 0906, 0933, 0951, 0952, 0958, 0986, 0987, 0990, 0999, 1000, 1006, 1013

Levels of living indicators, 0640, 0880, 0883, 0896, 0961, 0962

Libraries, 0066, 0199, 0206, 0247, 0248, 0887, 0927, 0928, 1005

Land division/ settlement patterns, 0629, 1033

Local government, 0216, 0217, 0221, 0222, 0224, 0225, 0231, 0295, 0395, 0445

Locality groups, 0197, 0200, 0234, 0275, 0302, 0381, 0386, 0387, 0417, 0440, 0455, 0459, 0461, 0463, 0563, 0566, 0785, 0797, 0798, 0811, 0829, 0830, 0835, 0838, 0839, 0852, 0875, 0884, 0892, 0918, 0919, 0922, 0934, 0935

Marketing, 0212, 0213, 0214, 0215, 0219, 0226, 0228, 0303, 0341

Mechanization, 0375, 0482, 0484, 0643, 0761, 0949, 0977, 0979, 0982, 0983, 0986, 0990

Methodology, 0090, 0290, 0291, 0357, 0396, 0411, 0418, 0431, 0481, 0517, 0530, 0657, 0718, 0843, 0899

Methodology-health research, 0945, 0946, 1007, 1008

Methodology labor force analysis, 0604, 0863, 0869, 0908

Methodology-levels of living indicators/ scales, 0163, 0454, 0637, 0639, 0641, 0897

Methodology-local leader identification, 0555, 0917

Methodology-locality group identification/ classification, 0341, 0381, 0417, 0459, 0460, 0461, 0471, 0527, 0553, 0563, 0623

Methodology-population analysis, 0378, 0525, 0581, 0743, 0775, 0844, 0856, 0910, 1044

Methodology-regional analysis, 0638, 0642, 0804, 0805

Methodology-social participation scales, 0914

Methodology-sociometric, 0437, 0439, 0698

Migrant farm workers, 0354, 0372, 0794, 0807, 0853, 0855, 0856, 0860, 0878, 0929, 0973

Migration, 0072, 0102, 0105, 0106, 0107, 0108, 0115, 0116, 0120, 0126, 0131, 0134, 0135, 0136, 0137, 0144, 0149, 0223, 0278, 0308, 0309, 0313, 0322, 0323, 0332, 0361, 0362, 0364, 0379, 0385, 0388, 0389, 0405, 0410, 0412, 0415, 0423, 0448, 0452, 0453, 0466, 0472, 0476, 0477, 0478, 0479, 0480, 0483, 0485, 0487, 0488, 0491, 0492, 0493, 0495, 0520, 0545, 0570, 0579, 0580, 0655, 0658, 0669, 0671, 0677, 0678, 0688, 0706, 0730, 0772, 0775, 0794, 0836, 0844, 0851, 0856, 0891, 0894, 0911, 0930, 0943, 0960, 1492

Mortality, 0911

Neighborhood, 0197, 0200, 0234, 0275, 0276, 0333, 0381, 0386, 0387, 0440, 0459, 0461, 0463, 0554, 0558, 0563

Neighborhood discussion/ action groups (RR-FSA), 0561, 0680, 0681, 0682, 0762

Occupations, 0388, 0755, 0794, 1031

Part-time farming, 0117, 0578, 0803

Planning, 0236, 0237, 0239, 0240, 0241, 0246, 0347, 0425, 0474, 0526, 0546, 0586, 0595, 0660, 0732, 0748, 0751, 0757, 0796, 0799

Index 291

Planning-Central Valley, California, 0974, 1034, 1496

Planning-Columbia River Basin, 0618, 0809, 0810, 0879, 1013, 1015, 1032, 1033

Planning-community services, 0243, 0250, 0833, 0834, 0887, 0928

Plantations, 0328, 0366, 0380, 0654, 0982, 0983

Population, 0069, 0080, 0081, 0127, 0144, 0232, 0308, 0313, 0320, 0325, 0355, 0367, 0376, 0409, 0415, 0416, 0419, 0443, 0493, 0500, 0524, 0548, 0581, 0654, 0684, 0742, 0761, 0960, 1038

Population composition, 0069, 0080, 0081, 0082, 0083, 0144, 0211, 0223, 0257, 0263, 0319, 0325, 0339, 0364, 0415, 0435, 0474, 0478, 0489, 0500, 0508, 0579, 0654, 0655, 0671, 0684, 0750, 0817, 0836, 0841, 0844, 0845, 0849, 0855, 0856, 0860, 0864, 0865, 0866, 0871, 0910, 0960, 0967, 0969, 0970, 0971, 0972, 0973, 0997, 0998, 1009, 1010, 1030, 1031, 1039, 1040, 1043

Population projections, 0902, 0910, 0911, 0912, 1044

Population trends, 0069, 0088, 0232, 0305, 0307, 0313, 0317,0319, 0323, 0325, 0405, 0415, 0474, 0483, 0486, 0490, 0493, 0494,0497, 0500, 0512, 0523, 0545, 0650, 0677, 0741, 0795, 0828, 0911,0943, 0990, 1042, 1492

Post-war II planning, 0614, 0716, 0725, 0755, 0812, 0813, 0814,0815, 0827, 0938, 0981

Prisoners of war, 0849, 0972, 1009, 1010

Public policy, 0323, 0370, 0420, 0465, 0503, 0508, 0523, 0556, 0577, 0606, 0651, 0778, 0780, 0784, 0786, 0799, 0807, 0809, 0810, 0815, 0878, 0879, 0929, 0939, 0941, 0974, 0980, 0988, 1013, 1032, 1033, 1496

Race, 0144, 0472, 0698

Race relations, 0692

Reclamation projects, 0391, 0433, 0810, 0974, 1034, 1496

Recreation, 0122, 0240, 0245, 0344, 0462

Religion, 0201, 0253, 0254, 0255, 0385, 0668, 0994

Replacement rates, 0652, 0774, 1002

Research, 0085, 0090, 0133, 0150, 0168, 0440, 0470, 0715, 0717, 0753, 0806, 0808, 0899, 0904, 0955, 1017, 1021, 1025, 1038

Resettlement, 0335, 0392, 0394, 0419, 0424, 0427, 0429, 0435, 0437, 0438, 0439, 0452, 0466, 0506, 0520, 0654, 0725, 0799, 1003, 1012

Retirement, 0288, 0825, 0851, 0964, 0965, 1011

Rural, 0088, 0232, 0415, 0742

Rural development-less developed countries, 0690, 0691, 0695, 0850, 0874, 1025

Rural family, 0207, 0321, 0504, 0548, 0884

Rural industries, 0059, 0117, 0230, 0251, 0337

Rural life, 0059, 0067, 0086, 0087, 0089, 0091, 0092, 0097, 0098, 0099, 0100, 0101, 0103, 0111, 0114, 0119, 0122, 0125, 0130, 0169, 0205, 0235, 0262, 0264, 0277, 0282, 0283, 0284, 0301, 0306, 0311, 0312, 0330, 0365, 0373, 0390, 0397, 0399, 0401, 0413, 0458, 0499, 0502, 0512, 0522, 0546, 0550, 0566, 0575, 0635, 0666, 0685, 0693, 0694, 0710, 0722, 0776, 0781, 0783, 0823, 0831, 0836, 0875, 0985, 0989, 0990, 0993, 0994, 0996, 1023, 1024, 1026, 1027, 1037

Rural nonfarm population, 0134, 0443

Rural rehabilitation, 0394, 0400, 0469, 0498, 0531, 0703, 0704,

Index 293

Rural rehabilitation (continued), 0738, 0793, 0937, 0939, 0941, 0944

Rural-urban population comparisons, 0095, 0880, 0951, 0958, 0961, 0962

Schools, 0121, 0199, 0207, 0340, 0446, 0547, 0636, 0689, 0707, 0736, 0884

Social agencies, 0296, 0298, 0438, 0548, 0829, 0830, 0835, 0839, 0852, 0892, 0919, 0922, 0935, 0995, 1032

Social and economic areas (rural-urban relationships), 0075, 0076, 0079, 0146, 0151, 0152, 0198, 0202, 0209, 0233, 0258, 0259, 0260, 0273, 0274, 0281, 0295

Social change/ trends, 0100, 0101, 0121, 0200, 0201, 0202, 0209, 0215, 0219, 0230, 0265, 0305, 0308, 0309, 0314, 0316, 0318, 0320, 0321, 0323, 0331, 0365, 0383, 0385, 0397, 0398, 0399, 0408, 0422, 0444, 0573, 0654, 0677, 0736, 0737, 0739, 0754, 0761, 0776, 0790, 0828, 0837, 0841, 0842, 0847, 0848, 0853, 0872, 0876, 0880, 0881, 0895, 0896, 0905, 0906, 0907, 0931, 0933, 0941, 0944, 0954, 0955, 0968, 0981, 0982, 0983, 0985, 0986, 0989, 0990, 0991, 0992, 0993, 0994, 0995, 0996, 1022, 1028, 1030, 1491, 1492

Social class, 0210, 0632

Social insurance, 0350, 0352, 0824, 0826, 0845, 0964, 0965

Social organization, 0060, 0067, 0076, 0079, 0118, 0125, 0152, 0197, 0198, 0199, 0200, 0201, 0202, 0203, 0233, 0253, 0254, 0255, 0259, 0265, 0273, 0274, 0276, 0281, 0282, 0283, 0284, 0294, 0302, 0340, 0419, 0455, 0471, 0547, 0586, 0594, 0612, 0613, 0632, 0636, 0668, 0763, 0765, 0828, 0829, 0830, 0831, 0838, 0850, 0852, 0875, 0876, 0884, 0892, 0918, 0919, 0922, 0934, 0935, 0986, 0994, 1000, 1006, 1037

Social participation, 0063, 0068, 0073, 0074, 0111, 0125, 0139, 0190, 0195, 0218, 0223, 0285, 0329, 0395, 0427, 0429, 0430, 0510, 0750, 0835, 0838, 0839, 0915, 0916, 0918, 0935

Social psychology, 0068, 0138, 0220

Social security, 0619, 0651, 0715, 0778, 0780, 0784, 0808, 01011

Social status, 0473

Social-cultural groups, 0144, 0201, 0668, 0669

Socioeconomic status-aggregate/ area, 0112, 0280, 0289, 0373,0807

Socioeconomic status-individual/ family, 0148, 0166, 0327, 0343, 0405, 0684, 0750

Sociology of agriculture, 0104, 0167, 0253, 0254, 0255, 0353, 0398, 0420, 0631, 0672, 0858, 1491, 1497

Sociology-rural sociology, 0132, 0150, 0501, 0504, 0505, 0514, 0747, 0753, 0777, 0788, 0789, 0899, 0904, 0955, 0989, 1014, 1016, 1017, 1018, 1020, 1021, 1025

Soil conservation, 0423, 0464, 0520, 1022, 1023, 1024

Soil Conservation Service, 0950

Standard of living, 0110, 0113, 0153, 0158, 0160, 0162, 0163, 0166, 0169, 0184, 0191, 0192, 0193, 0194, 0195, 0196, 0272, 0287, 0326, 0338, 0404, 0433, 0434, 0435, 0436, 0472, 0518, 0752, 0879, 1006, 1013

Structure of agriculture, 0061, 0062, 0064, 0263, 0264, 0266, 0267, 0268, 0271, 0272, 0305, 0316, 0320, 0371, 0382, 0519, 0528, 0569, 0631, 0807, 0815, 0585, 0872, 0984, 0988, 0995, 1045

Subsistence homesteads, 0428, 0591, 0592, 0593, 0661, 0662, 0663, 0667, 0675, 0705, 0728, 0819

Success in rural life, 0071, 0141, 0142

Index 295

Theory, 0513

Towns, 0076, 0151, 0152, 0198, 0199, 0202, 0281, 0295

Trade centers, 0152, 0209, 0260, 0281, 0302, 0841, 0955, 1032

Uses of rural sociology research, 0109, 0132, 0425, 0465, 0513, 0515, 0516, 0517, 0676, 0760, 0777, 0792, 0873, 0912, 0932, 1015, 1016

Values, 0334

Veterans, 0709, 0755, 0756, 0791, 0815, 0827, 0861, 0898, 0907, 0936, 0943, 0954, 0981, 1001

Villages, 0068, 0079, 0080, 0081, 0082, 0083, 0152, 0233, 0241, 0246, 0281, 0404, 0841, 0842

Voluntary associations, 0203, 0285

Wealth, 0545

Women, 0510, 0684, 0738, 0918, 0953, 0994, 1031, 1043

Women in agriculture, 0845, 0849, 0855, 0860, 0864, 0865, 0871, 0967, 0970, 0971, 0972, 0973, 0994, 0997, 0998, 1009, 1010, 1030, 1039, 1040

World War II, 0562, 0649, 0656, 0659, 0685, 0696, 0702, 0709, 0737, 0739, 0753, 0755, 0775, 0777, 0940, 0955, 0968

World War II-impacts on rural areas, 0548, 0549, 0565, 0574, 0590, 0600, 0601, 0624, 0650, 0664, 0671, 0672, 0678, 0683, 0688, 0689, 0706, 0708, 0719, 0727, 0730, 0731, 0734, 0764, 0766, 0795, 0800, 0801, 0827, 0831, 0833, 0859, 0867, 0882, 0894, 0896, 0938, 0954, 0987, 0999, 1001, 1493

World War II-mobilization of local areas, 0551, 0553, 0554, 0555, 0558, 0559, 0571, 0577, 0588, 0611, 0617, 0630, 0633, 0628, 0634, 0714, 0763, 0764, 0765

Youth, 0063, 0073, 0074, 0139, 0164, 0235, 0278, 0304, 0307, 0308, 0358, 0363, 0377, 0441, 0442, 0456, 0457, 0467, 0468, 0569, 0570, 0610, 0615, 0625, 0665, 0678, 0679, 0706, 0746, 0794

II. Ethnic-Cultural Groups

Amish, 0417, 0666, 0668, 1497

Blacks, 0069, 0081, 0082, 0083, 0078, 0080, 0127, 0139, 0164, 0182, 0234, 0280, 0302, 0328, 0333, 0338, 0353, 0357, 0366, 0379, 0380, 0381, 0383, 0387, 0412, 0415, 0435, 0459, 0463, 0471, 0472, 0473, 0474, 0483, 0486, 0495, 0496, 0519, 0532, 0538, 0539, 0549, 0550, 0579, 0586, 0597, 0605, 0607, 0608, 0648, 0654, 0655, 0669, 0670, 0677, 0680, 0683, 0687, 0701, 0712, 0723, 0738, 0744, 0755, 0759, 0763, 0764, 0765, 0774, 0807, 0816, 0820, 0823, 0827, 0844, 0849, 0853, 0855, 0860, 0864, 0865, 0866, 0871, 0882, 0884, 0885, 0886, 0888, 0889, 0890, 0944, 0971, 0972, 0973, 0976, 0979, 0980, 0982, 0985, 0986, 0989, 0990, 0998, 1009, 1010, 1021, 1031, 1036, 1039, 1040, 1041, 1043

Dutch, 0340, 0424

Filipino, 0969, 0971, 0972, 0973

German, 0402, 0668, 0698

German Swiss, 0401

Indian-mexican, 0424, 0433

Indians, 0849, 0864

Jamaican Nationals, 0849, 1009, 1010

Mennonites, 0668

Mexican Nationals, 0720, 0740, 0864, 0969, 0971, 0972, 0976, 0979

Index 297

Mexicans, 0532, 0535, 0684, 0720, 0855, 0864, 0960, 0969, 0971, 0972, 0973

Mormon, 0253, 0254, 0255, 0676

Orientals, 0542, 0855

Spanish American, 0413, 0430, 0660, 0676, 0686, 0688, 0692, 0700, 0702, 0703, 0704, 0740, 0749

III. Geographical Location

Alabama (AL), 0172, 0177, 0183, 0185, 0219, 0357, 0387, 0402, 0471, 0474, 0667

Appalachia, 0339, 0434, 0443, 0744, 0783, 0793, 0828, 0884, 1001, 1002

Argentina, 0779, 0781, 0782, 0785, 0787

Arkansas (AR), 0142, 0328, 0412, 0675, 0680, 0683, 0763, 0766, 0796, 0816, 0820, 1030, 1036

Arizona (AZ), 0362, 0452, 0740, 0794

California (CA), 0360, 0361, 0388, 0391, 0433, 0452, 0542, 0617, 0630, 0632, 0633, 0634, 0675, 0718, 0719, 0720, 0721, 0740, 0794, 0802, 0851, 0960, 0967, 0968, 0969, 0970, 0971, 0972, 0973, 0974, 1003, 1012, 1034, 1496

Colorado (CO), 0071, 0416, 0469, 0535, 0543, 0559, 0568, 0757

Columbia Basin, 0879, 1015, 1032, 1033

Connecticut (CT), 0178, 0816, 0847, 0848, 0857, 0963, 0964, 0965, 1000

Europe, 0403

Florida (FL), 0607, 0882

Georgia (GA), 0227, 0333, 0547, 0548, 0549, 0586, 0595, 0701, 0738, 0823, 0828, 0884, 1030

Germany, 0390, 0419, 0420, 0478, 0494, 0497, 1492

Great Britain, 0644

Great Plains, 0330, 0336, 0423, 0477, 0479, 0493, 0651, 0741, 0834, 1491

Idaho (ID), 0452, 0590, 0629

Illinois (IL), 0296, 0297, 0340, 0533, 0678, 0679, 0876

Indiana (IN), 0304, 0358, 0467, 0468, 0706, 0746, 0935

Iowa (IA), 0144, 0175, 0287, 0292, 0293, 0331, 0536, 0574, 0722, 0727, 0728, 0930, 0931, 0932, 0933, 0934, 1037

Japan, 0991, 0992, 0994

Kansas (KS), 0070, 0145, 0157, 0159, 0176, 0345, 0356, 0417, 0537, 0557, 0560, 0575, 0741, 0838, 1031

Kentucky (KY), 0070, 0145, 0157, 0159, 0174, 0182, 0184, 0231, 0251, 0256, 0257, 0329, 0538, 0572, 0671, 0672, 0818, 0821, 0857, 0891, 1001

Latin America, 0690, 0693, 0694, 0695, 0696, 0697, 0699

Louisiana (LA), 0146, 0 147, 0366, 0380, 0459, 0539, 0605, 0654, 0655, 0764, 0765, 0796, 1030

Maine (ME), 0342, 0462, 0730, 0915, 0916, 0917, 0918

Maryland (MD), 0212, 0215, 0341, 0464, 0594, 0887, 0892, 0927, 0928

Massachusetts (MA), 0181, 0457, 0731

Michigan (MI), 0151, 0436, 0569

Index

Minnesota (MN), 0187, 0260, 0303, 0357, 0436, 0540, 0624, 0751, 0819, 0829

Middle Atlantic, 0080

Midwest, 0082, 0160

Mississippi (MS), 0227, 0381, 0496, 0723, 0724, 0729, 0796, 0799, 0885, 0886, 0888, 0889, 0890, 0982, 0983

Missouri (MO),0068, 0069, 0070, 0145, 0148, 0154, 0157, 0159, 0234, 0544, 0551, 0831, 0936, 0966

Montana (MT), 0060, 0065, 0067, 0211, 0830

Nebraska (NE), 0261, 0262, 0263, 0264, 0265, 0266, 0267, 0268, 0269, 0270, 0271, 0272, 0356, 0490, 0555, 0556, 0564, 0567, 0708, 0733, 0758, 0835, 0837, 0840, 0841, 0842

New Hampshire (NH), 0186, 0710

New Jersey (NJ), 0224, 0353, 0363, 0445, 0446, 0447, 0591

New Mexico (NM), 0413, 0430, 0433, 0660, 0673, 0676, 0686, 0688, 0692, 0700, 0702, 0703, 0704, 0749, 0757, 1030

New York (NY), 0063, 0079, 0149, 0152, 0153, 0179, 0232, 0233, 0259, 0273, 0274, 0275, 0276, 0281, 0294, 0295, 0364, 0588, 0621, 0750, 0795, 0846, 0849, 0915, 0916, 0920, 0921, 0922, 0923, 0924, 0925, 0926, 0942, 0945, 0946, 0947, 0948, 1009, 1010

North Carolina (NC), 0077, 0219, 0227, 0280, 0302, 0386, 0421, 0622, 0648, 0713, 1001, 1008

North Central, 0188, 1038

North Dakota (ND), 0061, 0062, 0064, 0171, 0298, 0299, 0300, 0356, 0377, 0394, 0565, 0570, 0589, 0636, 0836, 0839, 1013

Northeast, 0160, 0745, 0981

Northern Great Plains, 0553, 0563, 0566, 0649, 0650, 0652, 0832, 0833, 0954

Ohio (OH), 0070, 0075, 0076, 0145, 0157, 0159, 0173, 0189, 0210, 0226, 0228, 0285, 0286, 0441, 0442, 0456, 0625

Oklahoma (OK), 0258, 0357, 0461, 0570, 0682, 0762, 0766

Oregon (OR), 0376, 0391, 0433, 0452, 0629, 0810, 0822, 0959, 1013

Pacific Coast, 0453, 0716

Pacific Northwest, 0943

Pennsylvania (PA), 0073, 0074, 0541, 0588, 0664, 0666, 0668, 0919, 1497

Peru, 0691, 0698

Rhode Island (RI), 0635, 0714

Russia, 0420

South, 0081, 0160, 0227, 0483, 0500, 0508, 0550, 0669, 0744, 0759, 0827, 0985, 0989, 0990, 1021, 1035

South Carolina (SC), 0180, 0227, 0383, 0450, 0595, 0712

South Dakota (SD), 0205, 0206, 0207, 0208, 0209, 0326, 0327, 0356, 0404, 0405, 0455, 0707, 0732

Southeast, 0677

Southern Great Plains, 0410

Southwest, 0761, 0793, 1035

Tennessee (TN), 0059, 0174, 0182, 0184, 0401, 0463, 0534, 0593, 0725, 0824, 0825, 0826, 1001

Index 301

Texas (TX), 0161, 0174, 0182, 0184, 0374, 0392, 0531, 0532, 0681, 0687, 0711, 0726, 0728, 0734, 0766, 0852, 0857, 0957, 0975, 0976, 0977, 0978, 0979

Utah (UT), 0253, 0254, 0255, 0676

Vermont (VT), 0454

Virginia (VA), 0078, 0138, 0139, 0140, 0141, 0212, 0215, 0338, 0348, 0909, 1001

Washington (WA), 0278, 0279, 0282, 0283, 0284, 0301, 0406, 0407, 0452, 0466, 0545, 0592, 0629, 0883, 0884, 0940, 0949, 1013

Wisconsin (WI), 0190, 0191, 0192, 0193, 0194, 0195, 0196, 0197, 0198, 0199, 0200, 0201, 0202, 0203, 0288, 0436, 0801, 0911, 1011

West, 0083

West Virginia (WV), 0072, 0143, 0343, 1001